To

GOD I AM

DR. SAMUEL RAYAPATI

Xulon
PRESS

www.xulonpress.com

DEDICATED TO OUR DEAR SON
DAVID WINSTON RAYAPATI.

INTRODUCTION

"I and Father are one", Jesus Christ declared. "Father I commit my soul into your hands", Jesus declared. In unity with the Father, he transcended his separation and suffering. The solution to human suffering is in unity with Father in Heaven. It is redemptive power to surrender to God's will. God, I am (Aham Brahmasmi). We are all God's images, but veiled by sin. We restore our true divine nature through self realization and are able to say, "I and Father are one." In unity, the inner man is no more human, but a co creator with God.

David asked me write a book, combining Hindu mysticism and Christian theology. He read books written by Dr. Deepak Chopra, etc. and impressed with the way the human consciousness was analyzed. David died in road accident in Feb.2004. Our grieving soul needed more grace of God to live through the grief. This book, God, I am, mostly reflects our healing process from the loss of dear son. God, I am, simply an expression of an empowerment.

Jesus' presence was in around David at the time of the crisis. A student nurse was driving behind David.

She tried to reach the ambulance. A male student nurse was talking to David to keep him alert until the ambulance arrives. Dr. and Mrs. Carter stopped by and tried to help. The 'Ambulance arrived late and it took another thirty minutes to pull out David out of his crushed seat', Dr. commented later. As we grow in the grace of God, the memory of David has become part of our lives. God wants us to love him more than our children to be in kingdom of heaven. Now we love David more in spirit as we worship God in spirit. The human love is replaced with divine love. Bringing God into our flesh and blood more, brings in more grace into our lives. Our daily life is more rejoicing. We transcend our grief and we love our enemies. We have patience and positive energy at work and love and peace at home. The relationships are anchored well in the solid rock of Christ consciousness.

We are cloudy to decide whether we love or hate homosexuals or accept marriage among homosexuals? Good Lord reveals the truth in the reality of our transcendental experience. In the reality of unity with God, the multiple facets of a problem come together for Good. That is the real divine miracle.

I create positive thoughts in Christ consciousness. My thoughts have no expectations. I trust myself. I am a new creation in Christ. The energy from the electricity can be both destructive and constructive. The divine power is love and positive always. I am a loving pure soul. I play different roles in daily life. A divine soul communicates with other divine soul in peace and love. Any communication between two egos results in anger and hatred. You play your role with love and vibrate positive energy. Do not play other's role because they are not in your control.

Chapter-1

HUMAN CONSCIOUSNESS

Self and self: God and man

The self [small "s"] is our subconscious mind that makes us believe that we are separate from every other thing. It emanates from divine light, breaks off from the Godhead, and is trapped by the human body. We ignore the existence of this spark because of loss of memory. The "Self" is the essence that remains when the little self-dies that we call God or Holy Ghost. The Self is discovered when the dormant spirit awakens and its glory is revealed vividly when the self is stripped away. It is Brahman of Vedanta. What remains is God when you remove the self in the provision of grace. The Self is not found in transient things. The root of human suffering is desire and the self-concepts cannot liberate us from the suffering. The knowledge of self-alone liberates us from the suffering. What you seek is what you will become and seek self within who you really are. Seek the awareness of self. The intuitive faith alone reveals self and makes self your eternal object of devotion. One who knows himself is enlightened. We dissolve back into Godhead when the memory returns [Gnostics]. One who seeks knowledge accumulates it each day and one who seeks wisdom forgets all that he learns. "That which remains when there is no more grasping is the Self" [Taoism, the ancient religion in China]. To define God is to limit him. It is our limitation, not the reality of God that leads to our concrete thinking and speaking about God [Rabbi Kushner who authored 'nine essential things we need to know in life]. The self-realization is to realize self, which is already inside of you. Then you realize that you are God's children and you are already living in God's kingdom [gospel of Thomas]. You see God in all beings and you love that indwelling God in all beings rather than all things in your life. God is one meant God is all. We meditate on self and go beyond sorrow and joy. You become one with God that all things exist in God. Find Self within yourself first and you will find Lord everywhere in all beings [Upanishads]. The saint may dress in rags but his heart holds the greatest of riches. If you identify with the world, you receive the world. "We have nothing to achieve or to become", Ramana Maharishi, the 20th century sage in south India observed.

In self-realization, the natural mind seeks an answer to some that can be recognized by the supernatural mind. We are born as one with God in his own image but we lost memory of it. The mind is both the problem and solution. The spiritual world is beyond mental thinking and stop thinking so that the spiritual mind can take over the self. It is becoming master of your mind but not a slave of it. That which fuels the fire consumes itself. He who says that he knows; knows not. He who truly knows; says nothing at all. The good of the world is created in unity of all things. Bending like a tree in the wind, one becomes whole [Taoism]. Let go of the intellectual mind and concentrate your mind on God. You will stop thinking and attain quietness of mind [Bhagavat Gita]. Take refuge in Self and receive ultimate bliss. Be eager to attain the attainable . Recognize what is simple and keep the essential. Master that can be mastered and realize that can be realized. Then the fruit of your spirit shall multiply.

Definition of human consciousness. "The light dwells in us and lights everyman", Jn.1:9.

The human consciousness is awareness that without which I have neither life nor existence in a given embodiment. The Self is an individualized God. In deep sleep, we have neither thought nor mind but we wake up and find an unbroken experience. Self holds all experiences in continuity like the thread holding all the beads in a necklace. God is behind the multiplicity of this universe as gold is behind the jewelry of different name and form. Atman is Brahman like the space in a jar is part of the cosmic space. The self-consciousness, which is an active unconsciousness, deals with the duality of this world and the universal or divine consciousness, is an inactive consciousness that we revere as Brahman [Father in Heaven]. Atman is Brahman, but they are like the two birds sitting on the same tree; one eats both the bitter and the sweet fruits and the other is merely a free witness. The subjective mind deals with the spirit and the objective mind deals with the world. Brahman is, indestructible, all pervading, self-determined, unknowable, the oldest, stable, firm and immutable. The weapon cannot cleave, the fire cannot burn, water cannot wet and wind cannot dry him. The fire consumes all except the fire itself and the space. "When you walk through the fire you shall not be burned nor the flame scorch you", Isaiah 43:2. God placed this pure principle in the human mind. It is called by different names in different places and ages. It is not confined to any religion nor excluded from any. In whomsoever this takes root and grows, they become brethren in the best sense of their expression, irrespective of race and place.

"Those who are after flesh do mind the things of flesh", Rom.8:5.

Adam has one unified mind. The unified mind alone sees God. You see God through faith. Learn to see what is right in front you then you will be able to see which is invisible. The pure soul alone is able to see visions and ego mind cannot see any visions. The Self is God, which dwells in every being, but those with wisdom and right perception, having the ability to hold the mind steady will recognize this. When the senses obey the mind, God will be revealed [katha Up]. The mind controlled by attention alone sees self as the Self. Transcend the senses and purify the intention . It is bliss consciousness that a sage rejoices in all the time. The cosmos does not make any distinction between this or that, but the human mind does. Focus your mind on the present moment because neither the past nor the future exists. Our lives are the products of mind. What we are today is the result of what we thought yesterday.

Today's thought influences our tomorrow. The intuitive mind reflects emptiness and impermanence of this world as a mirror. "Tao [spirit] can only be understood in the present moment." The inspiration comes through the mind and illuminates the whole body. The mind in harmony shines forth everywhere that you make harmonious within you. The saint is like a lamp that does not flicker in the wind. His mind shuts off all senses. You will never be exhausted if you close the door and shut out the senses. The harmony will follow through unity of mind and spirit. It is a state of a new-born child with purity of inner vision. "Dwell in me as I dwell in you" [Gita].The joy follows always like a shadow of a person who acts from the purity of his mind. Transform your being at the deepest level of consciousness through replacing the discriminating mind with God consciousness.

"I am the vine, you are the branches; we abide
in each other", Jn.15:4.

The mind of silence alone creates harmony within yourself. When the subject becomes still, objects will cease to be. Think of self in the serenity of your heart and see God within yourself as you see yourself in the mirror. Those who seek him will find him. His body is the existence of the whole universe. The free mind alone travels beyond death. The wisdom penetrates into inner essence rather than the outer appearance. Find the inner peace in the stillness of your heart, which is free of fear and evil. God reveals his full glory to his children who take him into their hearts. Rest in self and desires pass away. The mind which is still alone drives away ego and brings in God into our flesh and blood. Some say, they know God and others say, they understood. But God is beyond human mind and he is visible through faith alone. The mind, which is free from thought, is at peace always. Know the child and you will know the mother. The world has many wondrous sights, but the true inner peace comes from staying at home. In unity with Father in heaven, you are the co creator and nothing is hidden from you. You created the mountain and if you say to the mountain, move it will move. God reveals himself to his children as the spokes of a turning wheel. You will reach farthest shore beyond all darkness through meditation on him.

"They that are after the flesh do mind the things of the flesh", Rom.8:5.

The ego mind is created when spirit identifies with the self or mind . The cosmic activity [karma] is the product of interaction between God and the world. The desire is the root of suffering which covers the ego like smoke covers the fire. The veiling power of ego disables self to discriminate good from bad; but the glory of self is well revealed when the veiling power of ego is annihilated by the saving grace of God. [Self-realization]. The insensitive ego causes pain to self and others. It is a coward and dull, though it pretends to be brave and smart. It never learns from mistakes, but the wisdom does and forgives as well. Instant retaliation is ego's ideal. The sage dies and sees no death, but the death of ego. The carnal mind cannot see the see-er and the seen at the same time like the telescope, which also cannot see the see-er, and the seen at the same time. The material world is the creation of the ego where we fulfill our destiny. The resentment, which is masked resistance, is the product of ego. The love in love marriage is the creation of ego and so there will be conflicts in love marriage too. The wife may bring either conflict or love.

"As man sows, so shall he reap", Job 4:8.

The karma is cosmic activity. An action is preceded by conscious or subconscious thought. The mental impressions [samskars] are those actions, which were done and forgotten, but stored, in the subconscious mind. The memory is the process of recalling those mental impressions to conscious mind. The sum total of mental impressions constitutes one's character. The mental impressions are acquired from family and environment as well from past life from Vedic point of view. One karma leads to another karma. Good deeds cause happiness and bad deeds cause unhappiness. It is the law of causation applicable to our mental and spiritual planes. The karma is unpredictable because the goodness does not produce happiness nor the bad deeds produce unhappiness all of the time. The law of justice and compensation well served in the next world is not a convincing explanation because in the theory of cause and effect of karma; the cause cannot follow the effect. The reason we seek the cause in the next world, is that the causation of karma assumes in the continuity of soul into next life. Hinduism thus explains the mystery behind the human suffering. God is not the cause of the human suffering. The foreknowledge and distinct memory of exceptional children makes us think that the experiences of the soul from the previous life cannot be annihilated. The karma has preexistence and the transcended soul is above karma because of its spiritual empowerment. All beings are in continuous cosmic action. God is behind the cosmic activity. He is the consciousness of all men.

The karma responds immediately most of the time. Those karmas that are not expressed immediately are stored up and all those stored up karmas, which are not expressed in this life, will be stored up again. The karma is neither fatalistic nor an imprisonment. You are not predestined by karma. We can do, undo, or even change the karma. The men impose on themselves and do their deeds according to their material modes of mind which are goodness, passion and dullness. A man who has no control over his present action is in the mode of dullness and his action is influenced by karmic effect of his past life. A man of awareness in the present moment has selective choice of his action. His soul is empowered to accept the consequences of his actions. The mode of dullness refuses to accept the consequences of his actions. The present thought is your destiny of tomorrow. It is sin not to relieve your neighbor's pain when you can and one who is relieved of his pain is rewarded by his good deeds in a previous life. The action associated with a desire is not redemptive. The good deeds with intent to gain salvation are evil. One who wants to reach Heaven alone shall never reach there. The urge to control others or the urge to be right always are indeed weaknesses though disguised as strengths. The karma demands good deeds. The karmas in the sage are turned into burned seeds like the fuel is reduced into ashes by the fire. The creation changes as the water become vapor and the potato become soft on boiling. God is the common cause of this creation but he is untouched by the plurality of the creation. The mango flavor is hidden in the seed and the same rain creates multiple potentialities in the plant kingdom.

Buddhism conceives that the material sheaths of the body, mind and intellect condition the human consciousness. The body and mind psycho-physicality is conditioned by the consciousness. The body and mind condition the six senses. The receptive function is conditioned by the six senses. The receptive faculty conditions the desire or feeling. The fulfillment of desire is conditioned by the feeling. The coveting is conditioned by the craving. The becoming is conditioned by the coveting or grasping. The birth is conditioned by the death. The aging and death is conditioned by the birth which is sorrow. The sorrow is removed when ignorance is removed. The nirvana is the ceasing of becoming; it is a state of peace. The intellect is the discriminative principle of our will. The will [Sankalpa] is conviction, and the conviction is faith. God appears through faith. We are more creative in God because he created us in his own image. The creative mind of Michelangelo who was a great painter and sculptor of Rome in medieval period once said, 'it is better to set higher goals and fail rather than set lower goals and succeed'. We rather aim high and realize our full potential in spirit. In God the mind is still and we forgive others and forgive ourselves. The soul admires inner essence unlike the ego that admires outer appearances. The soul admires the innate glory of a flower unlike the ego that admires the external color alone. The wisdom speaks that there is neither success nor failure. For wisdom money is nothing, the health is something and the character is everything. For 'still mind', faith is a friend, health is a gain and contentment is the greatest wealth. The evolving soul, conceives a woman as sensual at body level consciousness. The same woman becomes motherly at mind level consciousness. She becomes an object of divinity at intellect level consciousness.

"God created man in his own image", Gen.1:27.

A thought is an universal vibration that is produced by the brain as a response to the body's need. Emotion is the body's reaction to the mind. The fluctuations in thought cause fluctuations in emotion. Anger and fear are negative emotions, and love and service are positive emotions. A panic attack is an emotional excess caused by misinformation from the mind. A seemingly quiet person suddenly bursts out because of the built up subconscious emotions. Fear is a sense of continuous threat. Anger destroys the discretion power of the intellect. The mind in itself is a problem, and so it cannot solve any problem either individual or other. However, it responds readily to divine grace in crisis. Our ceaseless thinkers do better if they think less and experience more stillness of mind. The still mind has space between perception and conception: the space is truth. The object next to light becomes light similarly, the object next to fire becomes fire. We become God's children the moment He enters into our flesh and blood. The divine power flows into every cell of our body. Then I am no more a fragment suspended in creation from birth to death but a co creator. All God's children are equal in his sight: there is neither student nor teacher since we all come from one source.

Phantom future and buried past.

Fear and anxiety haunts us always because our mind is twined with the past identity and the future anticipation. The sun's rays seek their identity with the sun, but we do not seek our identity with the Son of God. The memory of the past glory and the hope in the future are good feelings, but they are illusive in the end. The painful memories from the past create misery in the present. The pain becomes part of you if you identify with it. Human nature dwells in the illusive past or seeks salvation in the phantom future, ignoring the present provision. We neglect to build our house on the solid rock of Christ in the present. Neither the buried past nor the phantom future can redeem you from sorrow. Fear is a sense of continuous threat and anxiety. Anxiety is created when you are here and want to be there. The future wants you somewhere other than where you are now. One who wants the future wants something he does not have and one who rejects the present reality rejects what he has now. Attention to future blinds us to the present provision. Patience is a virtue, but it takes us into the future. The promise of proletarian dictatorship for a bright future through present violence means is incompatible with the love and the peace of God. It is phantom future to escape the imperfect present. The conformity in cults destroys the freedom and the integrity of the spirit.

Freedom from pain and anxiety is in the redemptive power of resurrection of Jesus Christ. "Aham Brahmasmi, a Sanskrit translation to God, I am", becomes reality when the relativity between the observer and the observed is eliminated. The human innate nature is to love. Wisdom witnesses and isolates pain. Awareness of pain inspires your soul to seek the redemptive power of Christ's resurrection. The moment of inspiration is the moment of salvation. You are free from pain the moment you know that you are in pain. You cease to be unconscious the moment you know that you are unconscious. The self-realization transforms the unconscious nature into conscious behavior and dissolves the past guilt and future anticipations. Hope is alive even in the great sinner because the spirit behind his darkness is still alive. The sinner dies and the pain disappears in the resurrection power of Christ. The flame of Christ consciousness consumes all pain. Divine grace flows freely into transfigured body, mind and soul and the grace that anchors within never leaves. It is becoming one with Father in Heaven.

The enlightened mind, which has transcended thought and emotion, is one with Father. The conscious virgins had oil [consciousness] and the burning lamps [spirit]. The inspired intellect captures the arrival of the bridegroom. The unconscious virgins missed the feast [salvation].

"That was the true light which lighted every man that cometh into the world", Jn.1:9.

'To be born in sound body is the reward of the virtues of past lives' [Vedic]. The life's fulfillment is in the physical body though it is the illusory creation of the mind. It is God's temple. Man is the ultimate between God and the world and God reveals his glory through men alone. Salvation brings God into our flesh and blood. The inner man grows stronger and the outer man grows weaker. Grace emanates from you to others like the sun's rays emanate from the sun. We cannot change others or ourselves, but God alone brings change within us and within others. We resist change because of the fear of losing the familiar unhappiness and identity. What is within reflects to outside and the inner cleaning removes the outer pollution. You are replenished with the divine energy each time you forgive and so "Judge not and you shall not be judged: condemn not and you shall not be condemned: forgive and you shall be for-given', Luke 6: 37. Going to church to worship God without the spirit of forgiveness is futile. Attention is the focused power of consciousness where the body, mind and soul rejoice in cosmic life in their undifferen-tiated state prior to their fragmentation into multiplicity. We are to die every moment to the past in order to live every moment in the present salvation. God chose to deal with the evil in the restraint of his power, which is our redemptive power.

"You are alive in Christ when you die to this world", Collossians 2:3.

A Christian dies first to this world before he dies. Human relationships are in harmony forever in Christ's love alone. The belief system is mutually acceptable in Christ's love. The thoughts and functions of the mind ['samskars']are in harmony in both the spouses in Christ. Human love cannot sustain the relationship. St. Paul advised husbands to love their wives and the wives to obey their husbands. Obedience is love, too. Mutual love lessens friction in between. The husband and wife's relationship is compared to the relationship of Christ and church. Human relationships are hate and love situations and we live in between perfection and imperfection. The spirit is in touch with God and the mind is in touch with the world. The will of a pure soul vibrates positive energy and influence positively the other soul. Every soul in Christ has expectations. The pure soul understands the other soul in its true form and influences positively other soul. The soul that is anchored in Christ's love cannot be influenced. At work, the relationships goes smooth all day when Lord sits on the altar of your heart. The ego mind retaliates and does not accept responsibility. It does not forgive but blames others always. The discussion is wisdom and the argument is ignorance. Evil prevails in argument and dissolves in agreement. The argument mirrors each other's pain. You become unconscious when you react to an unconscious behavior. Be anchored to your soul through prayer and meditation of scriptures. The inspiration descends and dissolves disharmony in the relationship spontaneously. If you are not content with what you have now, you may not be contented with the riches you may have in future. The inspiration descends the moment you recognize your unconscious behavior. You are in spirit the moment you are aware that you are not in spirit. Every moment is the moment of salvation. Annihilate the unconscious behavior in the loving embrace of divine grace. The conscious mind receives senses calmly, as the ocean receives the turbulent rivers calmly. Peace within and around you absorbs other's turmoil. We surrender all that we may become the masters of all. Surrender is not a defeat, but accepting the divinity as the Lord of your soul. In surrender, the sound intellect unfolds your spirit and the spirituality becomes a living reality. Your surrender is your victory that no force on earth can defeat you. The surrender removes the wall of separation. The inner renunciation removes the outer isolation. Embrace the grace of God without resistance that may guide us in the fog of our lives.

"Blessed are the pure in heart", [Chitta Suddhi] Mt.5:8.

"Blessed are the poor in spirit", Lk.6:20. God lives in a high and holy place and looks down from Heaven to earth. "He raises the poor from the dust and lifts the needy from the ash heap", Ps.3:5. "He has anointed me to preach the good news to the poor", Lk.4:17. The world exploits the poor and the humble receives no recognition. The mourners receive no consolation. The persecuted with pain of death and scorn are cast bodily out of the world. God alone provides to the hungry and the thirsty. The meek and merciful open their hearts to their neighbor. The peacemakers overcome the might by reconciliation. Peacemaking is not weakness. Their courage confronts the might.

The pure soul is in active communion with God all the time. The sunlight behind the clouds is still undisturbed. The saint deals with this world without losing touch with God. He seeks action in consciousness, which is the power behind the thinking without thinking. He shares his food with others but the fool cooks food for himself. One who does not return his blessings to God is a thief. The saint does not grieve for the dead because he knows that the soul is undying. His desire less actions are worship unto the Lord. Lord accepts the daily inevitable actions [sarir karma] and the actions for a noble cause [karati]. The exercise of human freedom is conditioned but not cancelled by the necessities of the nature. The saint has burned his desire as well his anger in the sacrificial fire of Christ consciousness. The anger arises when the desired object is not obtained. It creates confusion and memory loss. The intellect [buddhi] loses its discretion power. The religion itself is one source of desire in the name of ending it. The desire bound action is bondage. The sinner's worship to reach heaven alone is unspiritual and he never reaches heaven either. "When he swears by the temple, he is swearing by it and by God who lives in it", Mt.23:21. The articles in the church are viewed as holy. Idol worship violates the principle that God is an abstract principle. "We worship him in spirit and truth", Jn.2:24. The virtue gained through idol worship is not redemptive, but it inspires the soul to align with God [Gita]. The idols are a human creation since the true nature of God is inconclusive. The illiterate cannot comprehend the invisible essence of God. Idol worship is the true seeking of the truth for them and the rituals they perform are their unspoken convictions. The essence of any worship depends on the gift, the giver and the receiver. The attention determines the intention of the worship. God is one behind the many idols but he is not one of them. "As men approach me so do I accept them", [Gita]. His grace is sufficient even to those who worship finite forms. The difference between salvation by grace and salvation through idol worship is not much of a difference in the sight of God, who knows the intensity of our hearts. "God is one and we can seek him in a temple, in a mosque and in a church and praise him in any tongue", swami Vivekananda observed. Idol worship is better than no worship. The worshipper is aspiring for healing and we help him to climb. Our critical view toward the idolaters is self-righteous. The attention to treasure is one kind of idol worship because your heart is where your treasure is.

During our missionary service in Nigeria, we visited a small village close to Cameroon border. A humble old woman was sitting on the floor in front of her hut with a small leaf in front. We stared at each other blankly since we could not communicate. A Catholic missionary from Europe was ministering in this village. I cannot comprehend as to how much the old woman could understand the gospel message, but surely God reaches every one with his salvation plan. A story says that a devotee was worshipping one hundred idols because he did not know the one true God. Advised by a guru, he broke all the idols and kept the one that did not break, which happened to be a stone. The milk and banana offered to the stone God was swallowed by a mouse. The devotee worshipped the mouse. Then, he worshipped the cat, which swallowed the mouse, and later he worshipped his own wife who chased away the cat because it drank the milk kept for her husband. One day she apologized to her husband for she had missed a small stone in the rice that troubled his teeth. The devotee ultimately realized that the power was within himself. We seek God everywhere except within ourselves. Inspiration comes to those who have the capacity to respond. God created us equal, but we express him unequally. Some are great sinners and others try to live better. Keep the muddy water until the fresh water arrives [from the Orient].

Levels of consciousness: [koshas]

Consciousness [cit] and Being, [sat] have no sheaths because they transcend manifestation. Consciousness unfolds its expressions from the lowest to the highest. Nature's capacity to do so is the organic process of cosmic evolution. The physical body consciousness is centered on action, desire and alienation. We predate because we have alienation tendency in us. We interact well with this temporal world in physical body consciousness. We should nourish our body well because it shelters the divinity. Prayer and devotion evolves physical consciousness into higher planes of consciousness. The levels of consciousness in an individual are interdependent and shared in reference to the creation. A change in one level of consciousness effects a corresponding change in all other levels of consciousness. In physical consciousness, interdependence and mutual cooperation exists among various biological units. It is more obvious at cellular level. The sense of alienation in body consciousness is an illusion. We do live with common food habits, cultural norms and traditions. The ultimate ideal is to be one with the creation.

The life's breath consciousness [pranamaya] predominantly expresses wholeness and unity with creation. We share air not only with other individuals, but also with animals and plants. We breathe oxygen in and exhale carbon dioxide out. The man is simply a part of web of life of this creation. We can evolve into wholeness and be more loving to other beings. Breathing exercises purify the thoughts, unify us with God, and enrich oxygenation in the heart and lungs, helping to prevent diseases. Smoking, which harms the lungs and heart, is human irresponsibility. In breathing, the whole universe is connected.

The mental body consciousness [manomaya] is an invisible body of thoughts and memories, which are floating in the air. The thoughts are shared because they descend from cosmic origin. The mind consciousness is in free play with the cosmos. The shared ideals witness the wholeness. The self-realization generates the thoughts of wholeness. Man is what he thinks. The mind is complex and multidimensional and has the choice to create positive energy in unity or negative energy in disunity with the creation. It can associate with ego and experience temporal pleasure and pain or transcend the duality and be one with eternity. In mental body consciousness, we witness separation tendencies through conflicting political and religious ideologies. It creates fear and prejudice and builds artificial boundaries. The ego is the force behind the alienation tendency and success in this world.

Consciousness of ego and intellect [vijnanamaya] is for separation from creation. Our social security and identity comes from the ego. World admires the ego drive; it is conditioned by body, mind and intellect [manas]. It is the root of sad destinies of life. Repressed emotions and loneliness create alienation in the ego world. The intellect is our discriminative principle. The divine intellect expresses love and service and the ego intellect expresses hatred and prejudice. It is the consciousness in evolution and the self-realization occurs in this level of consciousness. One who embraces wholeness loves his neighbor as himself and one who loves his neighbor indeed loves himself.

"Be renewed in the spirit of your mind and put
on the new man", Eph.4:23.

Bliss consciousness is wholeness and vibration of
the spirit where the separation is delusion. It is the state
of deep awareness and his own experiences as a reason
to be here. It is the consciousness of subtle objects. The
sage is bliss of himself. He has dissolved his physical
body and needs only least ego to live in embodiment.
He can see into his afterlife, where there is no body
and mind. He exists everywhere and nowhere at the
same time. He is above delusion even in his subconscious state. The five levels of consciousness, which
we live in converge to express life as a whole. One who
knows God verily is God. The destruction of nature
is our destruction and disrespect to nature is a sign of
alienation. Man can evolve into bliss consciousness
from any level of consciousness and express unity with
God. Unity with God is real and alienation from God
is delusion.

"Who shall change our vile body, that it may
be fashioned like unto his glorious body",
Philippians 3:21.

As Hindu sages viewed, we have human body in
two levels. One is the body of glory and the other one
is not the body of glory. The body of glory is the body
of bliss consciousness. It is resurrected body in spirit.
The physical body [stula sarir] is aware of gross objects.
We are in physical bodies in life. The aggregate cosmic
reflection of the body consciousness is the universal
consciousness called 'Virat' in Vedas. The mental body

[sukshma sarir] is the dream consciousness, which experiences internal objects with no help from the senses. The aggregate cosmic reflection of mental body is the cosmic mind called hiranyagarbha. The causal or the resurrected body [karan sarir] is the consciousness in deep sleep, which is devoid of all awareness. It is Brahman [Father in Heaven] who is the pre existence principle. Siva is the existence principle. The aggregate cosmic reflection of causal body is Siva. Turiya [fourth] is the transcendental consciousness, which is one with Father in Heaven. He is conscious of neither internal, external, or in between objects. The physical, mental and causal bodies correspond to our body, mind and spirit respectively. The breath [pran] mediates between the physical and mental bodies. The intellect mediates between the mental and causal bodies. The bliss state mediates between the causal body and the Being [turiya]. The physical and the mental bodies need spiritual growth, but the causal body, which is the resurrected body, is one with the Father in Heaven. The Hindu trinity of Godhead, Brahma, Vishnu and Siva correlate well Father, Son and Holy Spirit of Christian Faith.

> "On the Lord's Day I was in spirit and I heard behind me a loud voice. When I turned I saw seven golden stands and among the lamps stands was someone like a son of man", Rev.1:10.

The saints experience visions. The projection turns invisible impulses into physical reality. God has projected multiple thoughts condensed invisible electrons into visible particles and created this universe of multiplicity. God consciousness is the creative womb.

The angels are spirit particles who exist in every level of consciousness. They are visitors in the physical dimension and the guardian angels in the ego dimension. They are subtle bodies in dream consciousness and causal bodies in bliss consciousness. The visions vary as the projections vary. The projection is a dynamic process, which is more empowered in the unity of subject, object and projection itself. In projection, we refuse to accept our negative emotions and simply project them onto others. We hang the subjective state on an object outside of ourselves. The projection of cosmic consciousness condenses the electrons and creates the subtle images in the dream world. The dream world experience leads us into a deeper and closer relationship with God. The electrons are mystic energy particles and their inherent vibrations produce enormous energy. They are paired but exist far apart. A change in one electron is instantly observed in another, which is far away. Einstein called this as "spooky action at a distance." The projection is real in this world as well as that the Toyota brand projected in market circles as more valued. The recognition precedes the value. The sage devalues what the world values. The world values the saint, but devalues his message. Religions and races project against each other. The world exploits the weak seer. Empower yourself in the unity of the seer, the seen, and the projection and be victorious in all the worlds.

"He who descended is also is the one who ascended far above all the heavens", Eph.8:10.

We descended from God and surely, we ascend to him. Heaven is not a state of being dead or alive, but it is a state of eternal stillness. The soul in Heaven is well revealed in truth and not aware of either gross or subtle objects. The creation emanates from this eternal stillness. The universe oscillates in and out of this stillness. There is stability behind the constant change in the creation. The city of heaven with golden streets as described by Apostle John, reflects heavenly glory and serenity. The structural heaven is beyond human comprehension. In creative suicide, the chromosomes from each parent cell split in half and the two halves merge to form a single embryonic cell. The cell divides and divides until a newborn is created with flesh and blood. We live and die every second and this phenomenon is known as "conscious dying." Millions of dead cells in the body are replaced by new cells every second. Likewise, our body requires a continuous oxidative process to live. It is "living through burning."

"In the beginning God created the heaven and the earth", Gen.1:1.

Adam and Eve are the primordial man and woman. God created us in his infinite dream consciousness. Our dream consciousness is finite. The self-realization of man is the milestone in the evolution of consciousness. The evolutionist and the creationist are at odds to comprehend the incomprehensible mystery of God. The brain shelters the human consciousness and the cosmos shelters the cosmic consciousness. The brain and the consciousness ultimately become energy and merge with the cosmic energy. The creative consciousness reincarnates. The cosmic mind creates beings and the brain creates thoughts. The brain filters huge amount of information before it retains a few essentials. The atoms constitute the matter and the DNA molecule might connect us to the consciousness at energy level. Creation is known for predictability behind the unpredictability. The creative human mind is able to deal with the unpredictability of the creation. The cosmic activity [karma] as well our thoughts are unpredictable. We have no control over them nor can we accept their control. However the unpredictability opens new doors and new possibilities. The open mind adapts new experiences well and we experience what we believe in. The dynamic beliefs become behaviors. The new beliefs bring in new thoughts and behaviors. Accept the new belief on its own terms without compromising with the old. One single thought or act requires the whole universe to respond. "No man puts a piece of new cloth unto an old garment, for that which is put in to fill it up taketh from the garment and the rent is made worse", Mt.9:16.

"Father, into thy hands I commend my spirit", Lk.23:46.

Jesus cried on the cross because he felt "separation" from Father. It is the cry of "hell", which is the lowest ebb of human consciousness where there is no hope. It is living in alienation from God and the self. Jesus submitted to the Father's will and the alienation disappeared spontaneously. The intention to truth unfolds eternity spontaneously. Our innate nature is to become one with the Father. The 'hell' is the lowest ebb of human consciousness where thre is no hope. The "lake of fire "which the Bible describes, refers historically to the "lake of fire", where the trash of the city of Jerusalem was burnt day and night outside the city gates during Lord's time. Every end point is also a beginning point. What we are afraid of losing is unreal and death is unreal because the soul is eternal. Death dissolves the consciousness of all objects.

Creation evolves continuously and prayer takes us into a universal experience. St. John's vision of seven lamps is consistent with the sevenfold spirit level. The soul disembodies and enters into the astral world for evolution. The astral soul is the replica of earthly soul. The astral evolution of the soul depends on the degree of its attention. The soul in evolution loses all senses gradually, sound being the last. It is sound that appears first in mother's womb. The sinner's soul evolves in the astral world and is reborn on earth for further evolution. The soul is reborn each time with more enlightenment. The pure soul becomes a part of cosmic consciousness. The finer cosmic vibrations create higher spiritual experiences. An experience is energy and expressed by the brain as an emotion or a thought. The discriminative power of the intellect [will] accepts or rejects the experience. The healing miracles occur in unity of God [cosmic], bliss [prayer] and body consciousness [sickness]. These are the subjective experiences of our ancient Indian sages.

"On the Lord's Day I was in the spirit and I heard behind me a loud voice like a trumpet", Rev.1:10.

The bliss consciousness vibrates at higher frequencies and travels freely across the heavens. The saint sees angels and the sinner sees demons in their dream world. We see what our consciousness is tuned for. We miss other tunes behind the musical rhythm. One frequency cannot negate the existence of another. The sage hears when the "Word" vibrates. The solids vibrate coarsely and the subtle consciousness vibrates finer. The lower astral plane has a higher frequency than the highest physical plane. The dream world is the lower astral world where we encounter visions and voices. The sages caution that the mental body in the dream world should maintain connection with the physical existence on earth. If not, death may ensue if the connection is severed. Man has a choice to expand, contract, progress, or regress his mind. He may express or repress his mind, or be selfish or selfless. He can seek individualism or conformity, or even deny or accept God. God graciously gave us the choice to choose. It is our empowerment and self-respect.

Life and death are the two creative leaps of the nature. The dying person has astral contact because of primordial vibrations as such he could see the departed souls of his loved ones. His disembodied soul moves into an astral body and sleeps there for a while as if he slept in mother's womb. The soul in sudden death spends restless time in astral body. It also spends more time in the lower astral world in order to exhaust the unexhausted karma because of sudden death. Our son David died around 6 p.m. on February 13 of 2004 on his way to Eufaula to see me. I reached Phoebe Putney hospital in Albany at midnight. I wept on David's body and went to sleep in an upstairs guest room. I saw David in my dream coming out of the elevator, which I had used couple of hours ago. He was trying to find me with a puzzled look on his face. He was well dressed as usual and had an executive brief case in his hand. David loved his life and this creation. David was a creative and positive thinker. He lived in Atlanta as website developer and visited his mother in Vidalia for his birthday. He planned to leave his mother with me in Eufaula and leave to Atlanta on the same evening. David was not in his apartment in Atlanta, but in the mortuary of Phoebe Putney hospital in Albany. He was fully conscious and vibrant four hours ago and now, he is no more. His eyes closed and heart stopped beating. My heart broke. David started his travel from Vidalia at 4 p.m. by his Mercedes car, which he really enjoyed. The day was rainy and cloudy. He missed a right turn near Albany, Ga. An eighteen-wheeler truck hit him directly when he was turning back from an "S" curve. The truck slid to left lane and caused a head on collision. The soul travels to higher astral planes on further evolution. The individual in sudden death sees all his life experiences in front of him as a flash. Karma unwinds like a thread around the spindle. Each moment of karmic activity is displayed during the transition of the soul from the physical to astral status. This unwinding occurs slowly in regular deaths. Our prayers to the departed dear ones may hinder their entry into astral world. We are born unasked. We come in one way and exit in another way. These are the intuitive subjective imaginations of ancient Hindu sages.

"But seek ye first the kingdom of God and his righteousness; and all these things shall be added unto you", Mt.6:33.

God is wisdom (Pragnanam Brahman). The philosophy attunes reason toward the spiritual quest. Reason organizes, but cannot cognize the truth. We know not the source of wind nor the end of ego. The universe exists for self. Self-experience is beyond mental perceptions. Inspiration descends in silence and submission. Hope is still alive, even in the greatest sinner. The healing is the intrinsic nature of living body and so does the living soul. God is abundance and you are that abundance in the kingdom of God. God's kingdom is above prejudice. The stream of love flows freely when the dam of prejudice is broken. The conscience is the intuitive reasoning. Persuasion is an assumed opinion. Good information creates good perception and good conception. The response to perception is unique in every individual. It depends on the mental impressions [samskars] of the individual. The mule knows the weight of the box, but not the worth of the gold in the box. The sorrow is not God sent because it hurts him, too. Your action is your destiny. The action is done simultaneously, the moment you created the thought. You have done adultery, the moment you created a carnal thought. Suffering is a good teacher if you listen to it. Failure is transformed into success in divine guidance and what you achieve in the realm of divinity is always a success. The surface water is clear only when the mud settles at the bottom and the pure consciousness surfaces when the restless mind calms down.

"Faith is the substance of the things hoped for,
the evidence of the things not seen", Heb.11:1.

We live through faith that is able to move even the mountains, Rom.1:7. Intuitive faith, which sprouts in the stillness of consciousness, is able to perceive the truth directly. The intuitive faith transforms conviction into direct perception and the salvation attained through intuitive faith is unaltered. The intuitive feeling arises from aggregate of consciousness [chitta/Sanskrit] and sense consciousness arises from the mind [manas]. Self is an individualized God and we receive him through intuitive faith. The faith behind the healing miracles connects us to God directly. The little faith blocks us from perceiving the truth. Faith expands human consciousness. A cup cannot receive the ocean. An expanded consciousness through intuitive faith alone can receive God. God rewards those who pray from self. "Pray to Father who is in secret shall reward thee openly", Mt.6:6. The belief is to trust somebody, which may turn into disbelief. It is an idea that is upheld in one's heart. Faith is a positive belief, which possesses rationale and experiential justification. Blind belief is a superstition with negative energy. The will and the imagination are two creative powers in the creation from which belief arises. The assumptions adapted emotionally create negative beliefs and fanatic tendencies. Let us submit to God's love rather than to his rule.

"Let the children come to me and do not stop
them, kingdom of heaven belongs to such as
these", Matt.19:14.

Children are Godly and and their speech is spontaneous. We become God's children through self-realization. The mind and body are spiritualized and resurrected into Christ consciousness in self-realization. Christ consciousness baptizes the human soul in unity of God. The resurrection is to relive and the resurrected eye alone sees the resurrected Lord. The living dead are buried in the soil of sin. "Let the dead bury the dead", Mt.8:22. We resurrect from the consciousness of fear and sickness. Sickness is delusion of mind and healing comes from divine power through faith. Salvation is not by acquisition, but by free will. Guide the seeker to self-realize, but do not indoctrinate.

"If your eye be single, your whole body shall be full of light", Mt.6:22.

Jesus saw spirit in matter, but we believe in solid reality of matter. Our spiritual quest should be like the young frog, which determined to swim and survive from drowning in the milk pot. Whereas the mother frog gave up, drowned and died in the milk pot. However, the young one continued to swim and churned the milk and stood fearlessly on the solid butter that the churned milk produced. The body is solid divine consciousness. The astral body sustains the physical body like the light and the bulb. The disembodied soul is the astral body, which needs evolution. The causal body is beyond all vibrations and does in actuality what a man can do in imagination.

"If your hand offends you, cut it off", Mk.9:43.

We cut off the sin instantly as we cut off a branch. Do not blur the demarcation line between the sin and virtue. Let, the born again self be your will power. Listen to the Lord in the silence of your heart. You generate pure thoughts from your pure soul. Your actions are divine and you create divine destiny for yourself and others. What I am now is the result of what I was, and what I will be, will be the result of what I am now. Our actions determine our destiny. Good vengeance is doing the opposite of what your enemy did. The bees seek honey and the flies seek filth. "Son of man manifested to destroy the works of evil", 1ˢᵗ Jn.3:8. The evil is the ceaseless becoming of nature. "He that overcomes will I make a pillar in the temple of God", Rev.3:12. 'Therefore, we ought to the more earnest to the things which we have heard, lest at any time we should let them slip', Heb.2:1. The Word is the vibratory realm of the creation. He transcends into bliss consciousness and becomes one with the Father. He woos, but never coerces. He persuades, but never compels. We are drawn, but not driven away.

Chapter-2

HEAVEN AND HELL

'To live is Christ but to die is gain', Ph.1:21. In death, the existence ceases and the experience of reality ends suddenly. The disembodied soul continues to live after the physical body goes back to the earth. The dead body eventually becomes energy and merges with the cosmic pool of energy. We speak of death only from this side of the grave. Death is unreal and a delusion to the apostle Paul. He viewed death as the transition of soul from a physical consciousness into a heavenly consciousness. It is like a long pause between two breaths, or vapor condensing into water and vice versa.

"When you eat of it, you will surely die", Gen.2:17.

Satan is the conceptualized embodiment of sin. The caged bird refuses to fly into the freedom of the skies, because it loves its familiar comfort and security of the cage. We fear death because it is a journey into the unknown. We need salvation today rather than tomorrow because the death may ensue any time.

Cross the river of death by the boat of divine grace. You cannot escape death if you neglect such a great salvation. Those who are prepared to die are really prepared to live. The born again soul is one with the Father even in life. The raised dead [resurrected] are like angels, Mk.11:13. The dead bodies coming out of graves physically is beyond human conceptualization. Such a belief is a positive feeling but misleading as well.

"By the breath of God frost is given: and the breadth of the waters is straightened", Job 37:10.

We all owe our breath to divine authority. Death and birth are the two creative leaps of human consciousness. One who excludes death excludes life, too. Death belongs to the body and the mind and soul are eternal. The vibrations of physical consciousness cease and the cosmic vibrations start in death. The function of the senses and the clock's time cease. Earthly memories cease and the consciousness becomes void. The heaven dawns in death. The dying person is in touch with both the worlds because of primordial vibrations. The soul floats into the skies, looking down at his corpse on the death bed. The soul may see angels and the departed dear ones in the cosmic world if the vibrations match. The subtle consciousness only can enter into subtle worlds. A saint's soul is able to communicate with heavenly souls at will. St. John saw the heavenly visions in his trance, which he described in his prophetic book of Revelation. Jesus said to Nicodemus, "You cannot enter into kingdom of heaven unless you are born again." "It is sown a natural body; it is raised a spiritual body. There is a natural body and a spiritual body",

1st Corinth.15:44. The natural body cannot inherit the kingdom of God. Heaven is beyond the creation. The soul disembodies the dead body as if one removes his old shirt and re-embodies in a new body as if one wears a new shirt. It migrates from one body to another like a caterpillar, which withdraws its body from one blade of grass to another [intuitive subjective imagination of Vedic saints]. The soul in Heaven knows the mystery behind this creation.

"His kingdom is an everlasting kingdom", Dan.4:3. The dream, astral and the bliss [Heaven] consciousness are in the ladder of spiritual evolution. The physical body [stula sarir] is conditioned by time and space and visits the dream world as mental body. The astral body [sukshma sarir] inhabits the astral world where there is neither space nor sense perception. The soul in the astral world is in between perfection and imperfection. It needs evolution and rebirth. The perfected astral soul needs no rebirth. The Mormons believe in kramamukti. The resurrected body [causal body] is one with the Father in Heaven. The causal body takes a creative leap in the astral world and directly merges with the Father in Heaven. The resurrected souls visit us in our need, as Moses and Elijah did on the mount of transfiguration. Our physical bodies are sown in weakness, but the resurrected bodies are personified in power. The resurrected soul possesses unbound awareness and freedom in all the worlds. The sinner's soul has no freedom in any world and his soul may remain on earth as a ghost until his passions are dissolved. The karmic load inhibits or enhances the evolution of the soul. Karma follows us into all the worlds and gives us what we deserve. Sin [papa] accumulates faster than we exhaust it. The soul for re-embodiment, possesses body, mind, and intellect from past lives. These are the subjective and intuitive imaginations of the ancient Indian sages.

HEAVEN

"Thus says the Lord. The heaven is my throne and the earth is my foot stool: where is the house that ye built unto me? and where is the place of my rest?", Isa.66:1.

Heaven is where God is and he is as high as heavens above. He is at hand within our hearts too. 'This same Jesus which is taken up from you into heaven, shall so come in like manner as you have seen him go into heaven', Acts.1:11. "Yet once more I shake not the earth only, but also heaven", Heb.12:26. "Your will be done on earth as it is in heaven", Matt.6:10. "If heaven is in the skies the birds enter before we enter and if heaven is in the sea the fish are closer to heaven." Gospel of Thomas. All existence, both visible and invisible, is created in consciousness and all dissolve into consciousness in the end. Heaven is bliss consciousness [satchitananda]. Heaven is what we create through our deeds. "Blessed are they which are persecuted for righteousness sake: for theirs is the kingdom of heaven", Matt.5:10.

"The word became flesh and dwelt among us", Jn.1:14. Faith brings God into our flesh and blood. "The light shines, but the darkness pays no attention to it", Jn.1:5. We discover the light within us as we uncover the gold from the dirt. The sage is in Heaven on Earth. "Many will come from east and west and sit with Abraham", Matt.8:11. Heaven is an universal principle. "The truth that encompasses all the experiences has to be realized within ourselves", Vedanta concludes.

"Jesus said to his disciples, it is given unto you to know the mysteries of the kingdom of heaven'. 'Therefore, I speak to ordinary people in parables because they seeing see not; and hearing they hear not, neither do they understand'", Matt.13:11, 13. 'And I saw a new heaven and a new earth for the first heaven and the first earth were passed away; and there was no more sea', John observed in his trance: Jn.21:1.

Human conceptions are both well defined and ill defined. The structural Heaven where the saints live eternally and the structural lake of fire where the sinner suffers eternally is consensually inconceivable to the human mind. The evolution is the destiny of the universe. What we choose today shall ripple through a thousand tomorrows. Ignorance breeds doubt and doubt opens the mind into the unknown. Know what you are today and you will know what you will be tomorrow. We believe in physical existence more than in the invisible; but we also believe in our birth though we have not seen it. Wisdom knows that the water is the substratum behind the ice and the vapor. God exists in love and service. Human love is transformed into divine love in heaven. A person is what he thinks. Bad thoughts lead to bad actions and our deeds decide our destiny [karma phala.] Every experience is a level of energy and we express them as memory and thought. Inspiration opens the door for transformation, which is the moment of freedom.

"Let the air be filled with the birds", Gen.1:2.

Bible scholars recognized three levels of Heaven. The atmospheric level is the domain of the clouds, which may correlate with the physical body consciousness. The air is filled with the birds in this domain of Heaven. The next level is filled with the sun and the stars, which may correlate with dream and astral consciousness. "Let the light appear in the sky", Gen.1:14. Apostle Paul had a third Heaven experience that correlates with deep sleep or cosmic consciousness. "I know the man who was snatched away to paradise [I do not know whether it was actual or a vision; only God knows]" 2nd Corinth 12:4. 'Many rooms in my Father's mansion' as Jesus affirmed in gospels, could be suggestive of a multilevel consciousness. "And I turned to see the voice that spoke with me. And being turned, 'I saw seven golden candle sticks.' 'And in the midst of the seven candle sticks one like unto the Son of man, clothed with a garment down to the foot and a gold band around his chest'", Rev.1:12-13. This seven golden candlesticks could refer to sevenfold spirit. "Behold the heaven and the heaven of heavens is the Lord's thy God, the earth also with all that there in is", Deut.10:14. Apostle Paul views heaven as, 'what no one ever saw or heard, what no one ever thought could happen, is the very thing God prepared for those who love him', 1st Corinth.2:9.

Self is an individualized God. The universe is within self. Man projects his worlds on his finite dream space and God projects universes on his infinite space screen. The brain shelters the consciousness, but it is not the birthplace of it. My thoughts are not mine, but they are shared. The whole universe responds to a single thought. We think through the creative self-consciousness. The brain and the mind are like hardware and software. The astral body is the energy field created by the consciousness. The consciousness connects us to infinite cosmic consciousness now and after death. The consciousness is equal in all and all achieve equally with equal opportunity. The mind controls the events of this world and the cosmic mind controls the events beyond the time and space. The creative principle of cosmic mind even codes and decodes our future incarnations. The psychic reading is shared phenomena of consciousness.

'And one of them smote the servant of the high priest and cut off his right ear. And Jesus answered and said, suffer ye thus far. And he touched his ear, and healed him', Lk.22:51-52.

The consciousness is creative. Jesus projected his thought of healing and the severed ear healed. The universe is within the atom and the spaces within atoms are filled with intense information and energy, which later unfold as thoughts and memories through brain. The brain shelters the intelligence meant that the intelligence is embedded in matter and this intelligence may pass on to atoms when brain decomposes into atoms. The intelligence and the memory are thus connected to the cosmic mind. Some sages know about their past life because they might access into the stored information of cosmic mind. "Your Father knows what things ye have need of, before ye ask him", Matt.6:8. 'Thou knowest my down sitting and mine uprising; thou understands my thought afar off', Ps.139:2. The MRI brain scans of schizophrenics differ before and after the treatment, which implies that the brain landscape changes as the world of thoughts change. A person revived from crisis exhibits normal brain function. The consciousness is intact in unconscious patients under anesthesia. The person whom we think dead, is not dead. The mind is behind the real brain activity. The compass moves to the magnetic signals and similarly; the brain might respond to signals from cosmic mind. Know your true nature to know your destination in life.

"There was abyss between Hell and Heaven", Lk.16:22.

"The angels threw Satan into abyss...locked and sealed it so that he could not deceive the nations anymore", Rev.20:3. "The devil was thrown into lake of fire where the beast and the false prophet had already been thrown. Then the death and the world of death were thrown into the lake of fire [this is the second death]", Rev.20:14.

"And he cried and said Father Abraham, have mercy on me and send Lazarus, that he may dip the tip of his finger in water and cool my tongue; for I am tormented in this flame", Lk.16:24. The abyss is an imaginary demarcation between sin and righteousness rather than a physical border [Dr. Jeremiah]. The soul in Hell is in eternal pain. The rich man died and his soul went to Hell but Lazarus' soul was carried to Abraham's bosom [Heaven]. Hell is a state of separation from God and self. It is the lowest ebb of human consciousness where there is no hope [Vedanta]. It is the misery in this life and more misery in the next life. "And about the ninth hour Jesus cried with a loud voice saying, 'My God, my God, why hast thou forsaken me?'", Matt.27:46. It is the cry of separation from the Father. The separation ended when he said, "Father into thy hands, I commend my spirit: and having said thus, he gave up the ghost", Lk.23:46.

The heavenly peace descends in union with the Father in Heaven. God judges our inner state of consciousness based on what we have done, see Rev.12:13. The response to your actions is spontaneous that we experience Hell or Heaven even on earth. The judgment is now rather than tomorrow. 'I charge thee therefore before God, and the Lord Jesus Christ who shall judge the quick and the dead at his appearing and his kingdom', llTim.4:1. We fear God who has power to throw us in the hell, Lk.12:4. "Henceforth there is laid for me a crown of righteousness which the Lord, the righteous judge shall give at that day: and not to me only, but unto all them also that love his appearing", llTim.4:8. Lord Jesus Christ can appear now and give you the crown of righteousness now rather than tomorrow. The expressions of physical pain and suffering in the hell are symbolic merely. The experience of hell or heaven are abstract active principles connected to consciousness. Everything in realm of God is not physical since God is spirit. "The saints who died in Christ will rise first and we alive at the time join them in the clouds to meet the Lord in the air", 1st Thess.4:16.

The 'rapture' is viewed as a metaphysical event even from the first century. The dead saints were buried and their decayed bodies can only resurrect in spirit. The belief in the unbelievable is superstition. This writer is a Christian believer with born again experience. I belive that the 'rapture' is an invisible spiritual event and my faith in Jesus is unshaken. Believing in the unbelievable is negative energy. Christ has been raised from the dead and he is able to resurrect us from the dead, too. Apostle Paul connects Christ's resurrection to the gospel message. "So then, as the one sin condemned all people, in the same way the one righteous act sets all people free and gives them life", Acts.5:18. "For since we have become one with him in dying as he did, in the same way we shall be one with him by being raised to life as he was", Acts.6:5. Physical death is inevitable to all. In Jesus' presence, the inner man resurrects and our mortal body is transformed into heavenly body, see 2nd Corinth.5:4. By nature, we live and then die, but the believer in Christ dies to live. The physical body consciousness contrasts with the resurrected or bliss consciousness and the "Resurrected soul leaves the body to be with Christ", Phillip.1:23. Death should not be feared for this reason. "Now I know in part but then I shall know just as I also am known", 1st Corinth.13:12. "To redeem them that were under the law, that we might receive the adoption of sons", Gal.4:5. Our adoption as sons and daughters leads to resurrection of our bodies, Rom.8:23. "I am crucified with Christ: Christ lives in me", Gal.2:20. Jesus returning and raising the dead physically is beyond human comprehension. "For as the lightening cometh out of the east and shines even unto the west, so shall also the coming of the son of man', Matt.24:27. The cosmic Christ fills the whole cosmos that every eye will see him. "To reveal his son in me, that I might preach him among the heathen; immediately I conferred not with flesh and blood', Gal.1:16.

"The creation is subjected to frustration not by its choice but by the will of God", Rom. 8:19. "The whole creation groans within ourselves waiting for the redemption of our body", Rom.8:23. 'O death where is thy sting? O grave where is thy victory?' 1st Corinth15:55. 'The last enemy that shall be destroyed is death', 15:26.

The 'death' is our enemy both physical and spiritual. We have physical body which dies inevitably and the spiritual body dies because of sin. 'The sting of spiritual death is sin and the strength of sin is the law. But thanks be to God which gives us the victory through our Lord Jesus Christ', 1st Corinth.15:56-57. 'There are also celestial bodies and terrestrial: but the glory of the celestial is one and the glory of the terrestrial is another', 1st Corinth15:40. Heaven is the human intrinsic hunger that is waiting to be fulfilled. 'In a moment in the twinkling of an eye, at the last trumpet: for the trumpet shall sound and the dead shall be raised incorruptible, and we shall be changed', 1st Corinth.15:52. The divine inspiration descends and transforms the sinner's soul instantly. 'And the angel answered and said unto the women, Fear not ye: for I know that ye seek Jesus, which was crucified', Matt 28:5. In God we have no fear and the angel of Lord encompasses those that fear him. "God's invisible qualities and divine nature have been clearly seen... so that men are without excuse", Rom. 1:20. We leave behind our self-accusatory inhibitions and embrace the redemptive grace of God, who is the author of both the beginning and the end. "God will have an eternal house in heaven", 2nd Corinth.5:1. "He answers our prayer from Heaven", Jn.14:14. The glimpse of bliss experienced in prayer [dyana yoga] becomes an external experience in Heaven. The dead who die in the Lord will rest from their labor for their deeds follow them. "We will receive what we deserve according to everything we have done, good or bad, in our bodily life", 2nd Corinth.5:10. The soul has expectations and the pure soul is expected to do good deeds.

'This is how it will be when the dead are raised to life. When the body is buried it is mortal; when raised it will be immortal. When buried it is ugly and weak; when raised it will be beautiful and strong. When buried it is physical body; when raised it will be a spiritual body. There is of course a physical body, so there has to be a spiritual body', 1st Corinth.15:42-44. "For just as all people die because of their union with Adam, in the same way all will be raised to life because of their union with Christ', 1st Corith.15:23. 'The first man, Adam, was created a living being; but the last Adam is the life giving spirit', 1st Corinth.15:45.

Apostle Paul is struggling here to convince the then believers that the resurrected body is spiritual or celestial body. The traditional belief in our orthodox church of today that in rapture the physical bodies of dead saints shall be raised from their graves. It is inconceivable as to how the physical bodies shall meet Jesus in mid sky who declared 'God is spirit and we shall worship him in spirit and truth'. 'That Jesus was buried and that he was raised to life three days later, as written in the Scriptures; that he appeared to Peter and then to all disciples', 1st Corinth 15:4-5. Apostle Paul concludes saying: 'Last of all he appeared also to me-even though I am like someone whose birth was abnormal', 1st Corinth.15:8. It implies that Paul has seen the resurrected Lord in spirit. A resurrected soul alone sees the resurrected Christ. After his resurrection, Jesus told Mary not to touch him, Jn.20:17., but later, Jesus let doubting Thomas touch his body, Jn.20:27.

Jesus ate bread and fish with his disciples, Jn.21:13. The post resurrection body of Jesus was identifiable, [as Scriptures described], but the physical resurrection was controversial even in the first century. The saints in Heaven retain their identity at some level somehow [David Jeremiah]. It is mystic and intuitive imagination of a saint though an intuitive faith could create an image. The seed and the plant is one continuity [Billy Graham]. Prophet Isaiah in his transcendental experience saw heaven as a place of peace and serenity." Wolves and sheep live together in peace, and leopards will lie down with young goats. Calves and lion cubs will feed together, and little children will take care of them', Isa.11:6. Heaven in essence is bliss consciousness but not a state of being. 'The king will say to the people on his right, 'Come, you that are blessed by my father! Come and possess the kingdom which has been prepared for you ever since the creation of the world', Matt.25:34.

Our intrinsic heart's desire is to attain something perfect based on eternity, Eccl.3:11. The saint receives his "crown of rejoicing" and the good shepherd receives the crown of glory, 1st Peter 5:4.

Each level of consciousness has a reward in Heaven. The rewards and the crowns are the subtle experiences of the saints. The twenty-four elders cast their crowns before the throne saying, "Thou art worthy, o Lord to receive glory and honor and power: for thou hast created all things, and for thy pleasure they are and were created', Rev.4:11. The tree of life in Heaven is symbolic of eternal life. "And on either side of the river, was there the tree of life, which bare twelve manner of fruits and yielded her fruit every month: and the leaves of the tree were for the healing of the nations', Rev.22:2. The stream of blood which flew from Jesus Christ is redemptive for all. "There is a river, the streams where of shall make glad the city of God. The holy place of the tabernacles of The Most High", Ps.46:4. "And I saw the Holy City, the new Jerusalem, coming down out of the heaven from God, prepared and ready, like a bride dressed to meet her husband", Rev.21:2. This is the expression of holy church on Earth. "Jesus said, 'Let the children come to me and do not stop them, because the kingdom of Heaven belongs to such as these. He placed his hands on them and then went away', Matt.19:14-15. The children are precious in the sight of God and so they do in our sight. The precious childhood exists though you have no definite memory of it. Children are innocent and they deserve Heaven as part of God. They speak plain truth spontaneously. At dinner table we had brief discussion one about God and his glory. Armaan six year old grandson said, looking at his mom, 'the food you are eating is itself God'. God's love and protection are behind every parent's love and protection. "Father in heaven does not want any of these little ones to be lost", Mt.18:14. The demented and miscarriages are also saved by God. King David's child is in Heaven, 2nd Sam.12:23. The babies in the womb have sin too, which is washed by the blood of Jesus. "In his great mercy we are born again into a living hope by the resurrection of Jesus Christ from the dead", Pet.1:3. The Heavens declare the glory of God. The heavens and the Earth now exist being kept for the day when Godless people will be judged and destroyed, 2nd Pet.3:7.

The merciful Lord may not annihilate the unsaved souls. The evolution of the soul in the heavens is

controversial among Christians. The Mormon group
of Christians do believe in salvation in Heaven. Hindu
belief is that no soul is lost. The soul goes through
numerous cycles of birth and rebirth until it becomes
one with Father in Heaven who is perfect. "Now we
see a poor reflection then we shall see face to face.
Now we know in part then we shall know fully even as
we are fully known", 1st Corinth.13:12. Armageddon
is one kind of world war, which may include nuclear
exchange. "The hills melted like wax at the presence
of the Lord of the whole earth', Ps.97:5.

Chapter-3

KINGDOM OF GOD

The Kingdom of God began as the hope of Israel. They lived in that hope during their exile and post exile period. "Lord brought you of Egypt to be a people of his own possession", Duet. 4:20. Yahweh chose Israel to represent his righteousness. Israel's depth of character is derived from its deep conviction in the covenant. Yahweh demands that his covenant be fulfilled, but Israel failed often. The focus of Israel during the exile and the post exile period was on redemption and the coming kingdom of God. The post exile period was a time of great revival and confusion for Jewish people. The apocalyptic and messianic expectations entered into Judaism during the time of prophet, Daniel. He served in Babylonian courts where the Persian religious beliefs were well rooted. The new idea of resurrection was rejected by Sadducees. Essenes believed in apocalyptic ideation and rejected animal sacrifices as a means of redemption. Jesus was a spiritual associate and a cousin of John the Baptist, who was a member of Essenes. Jesus' message and deeds were akin to Essenes' thinking.

"Repent ye: for the kingdom of heaven is at hand", Matt.3:2,

Jesus called for repentance, which transforms the heart from within. Jesus declared with authority. Nicodemus was told that, 'no one can enter the kingdom of God without being born of water and the Spirit', Jn.3:5. 'I am telling you the truth: no one can see the kingdom of God without being born again', Jn.3:3. The repentance Jesus called for belongs to the eschatological plane of spirit. The call is to inherit the kingdom of God, but not to escape from the fiery judgment of God, as the Baptist announced. The sinners heard his message and repented for their sins. The demon possessed were freed from their fetters and the lepers were healed. The dead were raised and the blind saw. Their world ended. The disciples denied this world and their world also ended. Jesus ultimately ended this world on the Cross. Those who did not repent were doomed to destruction. "The world ends" does not mean that this material world ends here and now. The indwelling kingdom of God is realized through faith and revealed through inner transformation. Its glory is expressed vividly when the world ends within us.

"Everyone who here this must also say, 'come!'. Come whoever is thirsty; accept the water of life as a gift, whosoever wants it", Rev.22:17.

The smallest mustard seed grows into a big tree and shelters many birds. The greatest of all can be hidden in the smallest of all. The most glorious can exist in the least significant. The seed that falls in good soil yields hundred fold. We do not know how the seed sprouts. The seed is bound to sprout and God's word does not return empty. The seed is symbolic of divinity and the sewer is the active principle. God reveals himself well in silence and concealment. The wheat and weeds grow together and any attempt to remove the weeds shall uproot the wheat. The seed falling in the ground speaks of the fate of God's word. The wisdom listens to divine voice always and be a tree of life in the kingdom of heaven.

It is the fate of the hearer in time and eternity. The end comes from the beginning and the fruit comes from the seed. The sowing ends in harvesting. Those who stand in the light of coming kingdom of God are granted their own present.

"Even now the axe is laid to the root of the tree", Mt.3:10.

The judgment is not a future event. It cannot be a future white throne judgment either. It is as short as that between laying axe to the root and striking a blow. The cause and effect of cosmic activity [karma] responds spontaneously. Righteousness is revealed at the present moment of judgment. The future is also found in the present moment. God alone predicts the coming kingdom of God, which is a supernatural event. "People who sat in the darkness have seen great light", Mt.4:6. The hope in the future creates despair and tension in the present. "Blessed be the kingdom of David that is coming", Mk. 11:10. It was not to restore the kingdom of David in its empiric majesty nor was the kingdom of Messiah. The Messiah was expected to destroy the enemies of Israel and redeem the nation from oppression. Jesus had no part in the messianic moment of zealots. His person is the expression of the coming Kingdom of Heaven. Once Jesus lamented that we were shrewd enough to observe the cosmic signs and predict the seasons, but dull enough to ignore the divine presence at hand. Sin dulls the intellect. Respond to the divine call in the present moment and do not be lost to yourself and God's future in the very attempt to possess it.

"Blessed are the poor for yours is the kingdom of God", Lk. 6:20.

God looked down on earth and raised the poor from the dust. God stands by his promise in his own freedom. "Blessed are the poor" cancels the conception of "chosen people." "Happy are those who know they are spiritually poor; the kingdom of heaven belongs to them!', Matt:5:3. The Kingdom of God transcended the tradition and the restriction. "Do not be afraid, little flock, for your father is pleased to give the kingdom', Lk.12:32. The Heaven is an universal principle. People from all nations from East and West come and sit with God.The last becomes first and the first becomes last in the Kingdom of God. God anointed Jesus to proclaim, "Who will rescue me from this body that is taking me to death?. Thanks be to God, who does this through our Lord Jesus Christ', Rom.7:24-25. The mourner who found no consolation and the meek who had no recognition were satisfied in God's provision. The merciful open their hearts and the peacemakers overcome the mighty through reconciliation. God waits no longer for those who wait for him. The sinner and Samaritan both received God's favor. "Turn away from your sins, because the kingdom of heavenn is near!', Jesus thundered', Matt.4:17. Jesus explained that great sinners like adulterers can enter into kingdom of God through Grace but those of hypocrisy and ritualism can never enter into kingdom of God. "Be happy and glad, for a great reward is kept for you in the heaven', Matt.5:12; which breaks now like the sun rays upon the darkness of the oppressed. The mourning is over and the time for wedding feast has arrived.

The Kingdom of God is the apocalyptic ideation for Jews. But for Jesus it is eschatological reality. The Kingdom of God is not a future event. It is no more for the lost sheep of Israel alone. "Jesus answered, It is not right to take the bread of children and throw it to the dogs, Matt.15:26. It is now obsolete in the provision of grace. "Go not into the way of the gentiles and into the city of the Samaritans enter ye not. But rather go into the lost sheep of the of Israel", Matt.10:5-6; was abandoned. 'Now go to the main streets and invite to the feast as many people as you find: so the servants went out into the streets and gathered all the people they could find, good and bad alike; and the wedding hall was filled with people', Matt.22:9. Later, the one without wedding clothes was thrown out. And Jesus concluded, 'many are invited, but few are chosen', Matt.22:14.

"When you go without food, wash your face and comb your hair, so that others cannot know that you are fasting-only your father who is unseen, will know. And your Father, who sees what you do in private, will reward you", Matt.6:17-18.

The young rich ruler kept all commandments, but he fell short of attaining the Kingdom of God. Repentance is the key to open the Kingdom of Heaven. It eliminates the distinction between the sinner and the self-righteous. It forgives and accepts the invitation to liberate from self. The Kingdom of Heaven dawns at the hour of salvation. Dispossess the kingdom to possess the Kingdom of God. It is a decision and an action, which begins with inspiration and ends in man's transformation. The grace convicts and the conviction realizes more grace. So little is the human effort in the way of preparation to receive grace; grace respects no person. Grace finds the lost, and the self-righteous are lost to grace. The prodigal son repented and returned to his father. The repentance humbles men before God. "Whoever makes himself great will be humbled and whosoever humbles himself will be great", Matt.23:12. Jesus was critical of the hypocritical and the traditional repentance. "But when you pray, go to your room, close the door, and pray to your Father who is unseen. And your Father, who sees what you do in private, will reward you", Matt.6:6. Repetitions begging with sad face are considered hypocritical for Jesus.

"For what is life? To me it is Christ. Death then will bring more", Ph.1:21.

"Whoever seeks to lose his life for Christ's sake will gain it." God's justice is neither predetermined, nor we can comprehend it fully. 'It is better for you to enter life with only one eye than to keep both eyes and be thrown into the fire of hell', Matt.18:9. We are asked to "Sacrifice the eye [in spirit] and have eternity with one eye rather than hell with two eyes." The man sells all his property to buy a field, which has treasure, and a merchant sells all he has to buy a pearl of much value. The worker who was hired last received the same reward. The prodigal son was lost, but now he is found. The king forgave his servant's debt, but he delivered the servant to the jailor when he found the servant was unkind to his debtor. 'What about those eighteen people in Siloam who were killed when the tower fell on them? Do you suppose this proves that they were worse than all the other people living in Jerusalem?.

"No indeed! And I tell you that if you do not turn from your sins, you will all die as they did", Matt.13:4-5. Jesus disagreed with the Jewish belief in guilt and fate concept. Great sinners receive much grace. The power of grace can annihilate the strength of karmic account from past life even. God bestows his kingdom on whom he wills. "Thy kingdom come", Matt.6:10. It happens spontaneously in the present moment like lightning flashing from one side to the other. "So will be the son of man be in this day: 'At that time two men will be working in a field: one will be taken away, the other will be left behind. Two women will be at a mill grinding meal: one will be taken away, the other will be left behind', Matt.24:40-41. This is eschatological phenomenon."Referring to the self-righteousness of Jews, Jesus said, "How terrible for you, teachers of the law and Pharisees! You hypocrites! You give to God one tenth even of the seasoning herbs... but you neglect to obey the really imortant teachings of the law. Blind guides!

You strain a fly out of your drink, but swallow a camel!' Matt.23:23-24. Hypocrisy is sin. "This year also", the gardener replied, Lk. 13:6. God's patience has a limit. Men are busy marrying and given in marriage. The saint who has subdued the self has all the time and patience to serve others.

The "Kingdom of God" descends upon us spontaneously when demons are cast out by divine power, Lk. 11:20.

It is as if Satan falls like lightning in the present moment of salvation. "The kingdom God is at hand", Jesus told his listeners. All implies that God's kingdom is a present event. "I shall not drink the vine again until the day when I drink new in the kingdom of God." Jesus speaks of the Kingdom of God" as a future event, but announces its arrival now in the present. "At that time two men will be working in a field: one will be taken away, the other will be left behind: two women will be at a mill grinding meal: one will be taken away, the other will be left behind', Matt.24:40-41. "Thy kingdom come", Matt.6:10. Similar sayings of Jesus pervade all the gospels. The present ideal and the future reality are clubbed together in the gulf between the present and the future. The dawn of God's kingdom reveals the future as salvation and judgment. The future is spoken of as unlocking and lighting up the present and reveals today as the day of decision. God's future is salvation to the man who apprehends the present as God's present and the hour of salvation. The future is the judgment for men who do not accept the "now" of God, but cling to his own present, past and future worlds. The moment we have denied is never returned by eternity. The present is the time of decision in the light of God's future. Those who reject God's present shall be judged in God's future. The future lays hold on the present hour of salvation, which the Father alone knows. Salvation includes conviction, confession and transformation. Jesus warned self righteous Jews: 'Blind guides!. You strain a fly out of your drink, but swallow a camel', Matt 23:24.

"Take heed to yourselves", Mk 13:33.

This is not an apocalyptic instruction, but it is an eschatological promise. Jesus' sayings about war and violence are believed to be from the late Jewish apocalyptic ideology, which has been set down as sayings of Jesus during the transmission of synoptic material, in a chronological order. The apocalyptic ideas, which entered into the early church continued until now. The apocalyptic believes that "The world ends", but he is at a loss to know which world ends. "Because the people of this world are much more shrewd in handling their affairs than the people who belong to the light', Lk.16:8. The men of this world are are self absorbed with the material things and spare no time to God. Where as the man of God has all the time to help his neighbor. The prudent servant prepared for his future in the present and the rich farmer built barns, though he was disgraced before God. Life is more than food and the body is more than clothing. "The foxes have holes, and birds have nests, but the son of man has no place to lie down and rest', Lk.8:20:", was Jesus' lamentation when the kingdom of God was not in complete fulfillment in the present moment. "I tell you this: not a single stone here will be left in its place:every one of them will be thrown down', Matt.24:2. Daniel prophesied about desolation and desecration of the temple by ungodly forces.

"Your righteousness should exceed those of scribes and Pharisees to enter into the kingdom of God", Matt.5:20. Jesus was critical about the way the law was interpreted and practiced. Jesus obeyed Moses' law and he fulfilled it in spirit. He came to fulfill the law. Jesus healed the leper and asked him to go and offer a sacrifice. Jesus was cautioned by the Jews about Herod's plot to kill him. Tradition overpowered the scripture. Jews believe in kosher that the food that go in may not defile the man spiritually but Jesus explained that what comes out of the mouth defiles man truly. 'The scripture says, it is kindness that I want, not animal sacrifices... for the Son of Man is the Lord of Sabbath', Matt.12:7-8. Jesus healed the paralyzed hand on the Sabbath. 'Which comes out of the mouth alone defiles Man', Matt.5:11. He opposed legal divorce because: "If a man divorces his wife for any cause other than her unfaithfulness, then he is guilty of making her commit adultery if she marries again; and the man who marries her commits adultery also', Matt.5:32. 'For this reason a man will leave his father and mother and unite with his wife, and the two will become one', Matt.19:5. Jesus established high moral standard. 'Anyone who looks at a women and wants to possess her is guilty of committing adultery with her in his heart', Matt.5:28. The moment you created a thought, the action is done. You have discredited the women in your heart. 'So if your right eye causes you to sin, take it out [in spirit of course] and throw it away', Matt.5:29. Moses granted divorce on the grounds of adultery. "Love your enemies and pray for those who persecute you, so that you may become the children of your Father in heaven', Matt.5:44-45. We love God in ascent of understanding: with all our mind and soul and Heart and strength.

The Kingdom of God is attained in its own terms. It creates incompatibility to patch an old garment with a new piece of cloth and put new wine in the old bottle. The Kingdom of God is God's will, which is realized in the present moment; it forbids lustful looks and vengeful retaliation. Say yes or no because any more comes from evil. God's law opposes an oath where one word is singled out above others as true. "Anyone who starts to plough and then keeps looking back is of no use for the kingdom of Heaven", Luke 9:62.

God's will is measurable in Jewish perception and the dualism of reward and punishment persists. Men's actions are bartered in transactions with God; the law is reduced to man's authority. God is concealed behind the law and the man has retreated behind his guilt. The law is too weak to connect us to God; the legal fence that surrounds us has as many gaps as posts. Jesus called for the separation of law and tradition from God. He eliminated the distinction between the self-righteous and the world through grace rather than the sacrifice. Be lost like a spoke in the cogwheel of this world and inherit the kingdom of God. There is no need to sacrifice anything to inherit and attain the Kingdom of God. We have one Master, who is Father in Heaven. No man can serve two masters. Doubt is primarily a traitor though it opens the mind, too.

"Love your enemy", Matt.5:44.

God is not exchanged for an idea. The relativity of man's actions depends on what he is and does. The law cannot stand between God and man, nor can the man take refuge behind his actions. The motif behind your thought decides your relationship with your God and with your neighbor. Loving your enemy is healing and excludes even rightful retaliation. Judaism failed to capture the human heart. Jesus appealed to our inner experience and rejected the outer proof. The hearer is in acknowledgement with the reality of God's will. The union of God's will and God's kingdom witnesses God's reign and judgment on this earth throughout our lives. We live in God's "present" and his future expectation. The duality on this earth is endured until divine grace descends on those who are called and heard. This world ends and God's world begins. This is the revelation of hidden eschatology. The born again [resurrected] soul lives in the Kingdom of God on earth, freed from the fire of apocalyptic imaginations. The believer is freed from this world and placed back in the same world as the salt of earth. Both the law and lawlessness of goodness ends. We do not swear by our head because we have no control over the thoughts or the color of our hair. Marxism is a secular eschatological doctrine of salvation, which is realized on this earth as the kingdom of man. Both the Kingdom of God and the kingdom of man are concerned about the future and both become real on earth.

'And the disciples call the blind man, saying unto him, 'be of good comfort, rise; he [Jesus] calls thee', Mk.10:49.

Cause and effect is the law of nature. The action [karma] receives it reaction spontaneously. When you comfort others, you are comforted too. What we wish that others should do to us, do so to them too. Goodness is always responded with goodness. And Jesus concluded, 'In your opinion which one of these three acted like a neighbor toward the man attacked by the robbers?. The teacher of the law answered' 'The one who was kind to him', Lk.10:36-37. In the parable of 'Good Samaritan', the man going to Jericho from Jerusalem was beaten by robbers leaving him half dead. A priest and a Levite saw the man suffering but walked on by on the other side one after the other. But the Samaritan stopped by and took care of the wounded man. The man who just passed by could be our true ncighbor, but he passes through the mind like a shadow. God holds men accountablc for what they already are rather than their ideal destiny. Not the desire born out of love, but selfless love is one with God's love. The Good Samaritan showed spontaneous love to the victim and it is God's love. Selfless love is whole whose reality is in God. It eliminates tension between God's will and human ability. Your love to your neighbor is the test of your love to God. God calls us into the person of our neighbor. The victim in the parable of the good Samaritan has no idea of who passed by and why they passed by. We are able to identifyour neighbor better when we ask within ourselves 'to whom I am a neighbor rather than who is my neighbor'? It gives you the direct experience of loving your neighbor as thyself. We are well skilled in self-love and so know well what we owe to our neighbor. God's will is to find no excuse to love your neighbor. Jews believe in guilt and destiny and Hinduism in karma and destiny. We fail to see our neighbor in front of us in the belief that 'this man suffers because of his karma'. Karma concept also concludes that it is sin if you do not help the needy when you can.

Recently, a young woman was asking for help while her two children were playing on the footpath, care free. My heart broke to see the children in the hot sun. I passed by with an instinct to provide some help, but legalistic thoughts arose in my mind as to whether the help would benefit the children or would the mother misuse that money. I falsely comforted myself by thinking that welfare activities fall on the public health department. My soul did not stop grieving, but I could not see them when I went to the same spot the next day. Last month I was in India, standing outside of the Secunderabad railway station waiting for a taxi. A woman passed by with a baby of days or weeks old. I let the woman pass by because I was afraid to open my wallet for fear of criminals snatching away my wallet or harming me in the process. Again, my soul was grieved. Inspiration never fails; spontaneity is divine. Obedience to God's will is not the dissolution of selfhood, but preparedness to his call. The freedom is the ability to be you.

'Your Father knows already what you need before you ask him', Matt.6:8.

Father in Heaven is omniscient. He knows the flap of a butterfly in my lawn at Vidalia. No sparrow falls without his knowledge. An ant bite only happens when God Siva approves, Hindus believe. God controls the cosmos in all aspects. The creation is what we see in front of us and it speaks of its creator. "The fig tree puts forth leaves and heralds the summer", Matt.21:30. It rains equally both on the just and the unjust. The lilies of the forest witness God's care, which makes a mockery of our daily tensions. The creation points beyond self. The pure soul loves all beings equally. The creation witnesses our love to our enemy. God's love is like the love of a yearning man for his unfaithful wife. Jesus' love, in its demand and promise, became a new being and a new activity. The growth and the harvest is his promise. "Forgive our debts as we have forgiven our debtors", Matt.6:14. If you forgive others the wrongs they have done to you, your Father in heaven will also forgive you. But if you do not forgive others, then your Father will not forgive the wrongs you have done. We approach him with empty hearts and reconcile with his purity. The life and action are indistinguishable. The victims still love and forgive their enemy seventy times seven for his sake. In our helplessness, God appears in front of us. Our love to this world stands in between the mortal and the immortal.

"Not even in Israel have I found such faith" Matt.8:10.

Jesus said when the Roman centurion asked, "Lord say only the word and my servant will be healed", Matt.8:8. Faith is the trust in God's power. It is the power where human weakness merges with divine strength. The miracle occurs beyond any human ability. Faith generates miracles, but miracles cannot generate faith. Healing is the sign of the dawning of the Kingdom of God. Faith does not need to wait for a miracle to occur.

Jesus did not change the stone into bread because, "Man lives not by bread alone", Matt.4:4. The miracle is not the evidence of God's power. The faith the size of the mustard seed receives the whole promise. Life's crises choke the faith more so in "little faith." The child's father pleaded, "I believe, help my disbelief", Mk.9:24. It is not destroying faith.

"Leave your offer before the alter and be reconciled to your brother and then come and offer your gift", Matt.5:24.

Worship without reconciliation with your brother or neighbor never reaches its destiny. We render to Caesar what is Caesar's and God what is God's. We recognize both God's rule and man's rule. God fathered both good and evil. The Father's goodness led to the conviction of the prodigal son. "Father I have sinned against heaven and before you", prodigal son said. Father kissed his lost son without observation. "It is not good to take the children's bread and throw to dogs", Mt.15:26. The woman replied, "Yet the dogs under the table eat the children's bread crumbs", Mt.15:27.

"His friend is expected to rise and give what he needs", Lk 1:8.

The seeker knocks on the door until salvation descends on him. The state of the spirit in a believer makes a difference before God. The pretentious and hypocritical prayer is surely declined. Heathen repetitions in prayer are expressions of assumptions and anxiety. God knows what you need before you ask. "Ask it will be given", Mt.7:7. The prayer is a challenge to unwavering trust and a proclamation of the nearness of God. The unanswered prayer leads to more earnest prayer. Man stands before God in his distress and prays, "Your will be done." The Lord's Prayer is for those who are yet to reach their goal.

"A servant receives no reward from his master", Lk.17:10.

Rather, we serve the inner master and become one with him. "You crowned them with glory and honor, and made them rulers over all things', Heb.2:7-8. Paul, the author of Hebrews contends: 'rulers over all things includes everything. We do not see however human beings ruling over all things now but in glory in Jesus Christ we will be co creators', Heb.2:8-9. 'You gave me two thousand coins... and here are two thousand that I have earned'. 'Well done, you good and faithful servant!', said his master. 'You have been faithful in managing small amounts, so I will put you in charge of large amounts, said the master to his servant', Matt.25:22-23. Each idle word we speak is relevant to life and death. What we think finished is eternally with God. Our thoughts and deeds are linked with the eternal decisions of God. Poor Lazarus went to Heaven after a stint of suffering on earth, but the rich man went to Hell. The foolish farmer expanded his barns, ignoring the reality of death and eternity. Man stands before God with the relevance of his earthly life and the eternal decisions of God. The reward is intrinsic to the expectation of the last judgment. The weakness of the creature before the creator finds definite expression in the relevance of the reward. God helps man's fulfillment. Good and evil are not necessarily the consequences of good and evil actions. Had we known what we missed in our daily life, we would not have failed. Those who fail to recognize Jesus in the poor and needy do not need to blame themselves at the hour of judgment. The reward or the punishment never determines the content of moral demand in itself. God rewards based on his divine justice, but not on the merit of the deed or the tradition. Justice by tradition opposes justice by grace. The brother of the prodigal son is lost to justice through grace that the father bestowed on his lost son. Workers hired at different times of the day received the same pay at the end of the day. The Father rewards us in secret, for our alms are secret. Our good deeds are like rags in the sight of God if they are not done in the provision of grace.

"Whoever puts hand on his plough and looks back is not fit to the kingdom of God", Lk.9:59.

The disciple is called beyond his choice and he does not look back. The disciples followed Jesus and stood for their master both in word and deed, but they had their times of "little faith." "Lord we are perishing, ' the disciples cried. 'Why are you afraid, you men of little faith?' Matt.6:30. Jesus replied. Little faith or no faith creates fear. The miracle follows the reproach, which creates calmness in the midst of storm. They fell asleep in the garden of Gethsemane, Peter disowned Jesus and Judas betrayed Him. Peter became the rock of the church because he received grace. The disciples were the nucleus of the coming Kingdom of God. The Kingdom of God is the post Easter resurrection experience. The past failures of the disciples are comparable to our distress and promise in the present. We do not indoctrinate nor impose our opinions on others. Leave alone the un inspired soul.

> "Anyone who says something against Son of Man can be forgiven; but whoever says something against Holy Spirit will not be forgiven; now or ever", Matt.12:32.

We preach the gospel to those who have capacity to receive it. It is inclusive when Jesus said, "One who is not against us is with us, Jesus concluded. The sons of Zebedee were not awarded to sit on either side of the Father because such an event occurs in the provision of grace alone. God's children alone inherit God's kingdom. The faithful receive their award in the hour of judgment, which is even the present moment. The disciples' distress and hope before death and after resurrection of Jesus is the story of believer's after Easter experience and before his return. Our acknowledgement of Jesus publicly is reciprocated by our public acknowledgement before the angels of God, Lk.12:8. Billy Graham, in his crusades invites new believers to come forward and accept Jesus publicly. "Whenever you refused to help one of these least important ones, you refused to help me", Matt.25:45. In other translation: "As you did it to one of these least of brethren you did it to Me." Our failure to recognize Jesus in the needy and poor is not an excuse of our neglect in the end time judgment.

"Leave the dead to bury the dead", Matt.8:22.

Jesus viewed this world as dead. It is one big corpse. He cleaned the temple and fulfilled the prophesy, that, "My house shall be called the home of prayer", Mk.11:17. Jesus said, "Into thy hands I commit my spirit", Lk.23:46. "He said, it is finished: and he bowed his head, and gave up the ghost", Lk.19:30. It was the destiny of Jesus Christ. "My God, my God why thou have forsaken me?" Matt.27:46, is not a cry of despair, but a cry of prayer. Jesus was in a solitary struggle in prayer in his complete humanity in the garden of Gethsemane. 'O my Father, if it be possible, let this cup pass from me: nevertheless not as I will, but as thou wilt', Matt.26:39. Jesus asked to remove this cup. He opposed abuse of God, but in turn he was abused and God himself as well. The people scorned him and said, "He saved others, but he cannot save himself", Matt.27:42. His power is limited because of his obedience to Father. "It was necessary that Christ should suffer these things and enter his glory", Lk.26:26.

"Christ is the Passover lamb", 1st Corinth.5:7.

Jesus died with a loud cry, "It is finished, Jn.19:30. God and men inflicted great suffering on him. The temple curtain was torn and the darkness spread all over the country in the hour of his death. It was the end of nature and a new nature started. "This man is surely the son of God", the centurion affirmed, Lk.23:47. Joseph of Arimathea buried him in his rock tomb, which made Jesus' death official. This was the dawn of the Kingdom of God. During the Passover time, the pilgrims were filled with eschatological hope. We remember his body that was surrendered unto death through bread and his blood that was shed for many through wine. It is the promise of the new oneness of disciples and Jesus in the Kingdom of God. His death was a redemptive, divine act.

"Tell no one what you have seen until the son of man should have risen from the dead", Mk.9:9.

The disciples glimpsed the coming glory of resurrection in that moment of transfiguration on the mount of Olives. Jesus did not want to reveal his messianic confession prematurely. He awakened the messianic expectation and spiritualized the traditional conception of the messiah. The power of resurrection awakened early church faith, which portrayed Jesus as the son of man. "He shall redeem their soul from deceit and violence: and precious shall their blood be in his sight", Ps.72:14. Messiah was the redeemer in the conviction of Israel. In Jesus' time, both the messianic prophecy and the messianic movement were linked in the faith of the people. Jesus' words and deeds had no relevance to messianic authority, but his followers saw messianic hope in him, especially when he cleansed the temple. The early church tradition shaped by faith saw a messiah in Jesus. The demons recognized his messianic power. Jesus accepted Peter's confession of him as messiah. His answer was "yes" when the Sanhedrin asked, "Are you the son of the blessed?", Matt.26:63.

"Whoever says evil things against the Holy Spirit will never be forgiven, because he has committed eternal sin", Mk.3:29-30.

Jesus said this because some people were saying, 'He has an evil spirit in him'. The Holy Spirit is indwelling God. The Kingdom of God is conceived as of today in the face of eternity. It is God's will in action. It is the Easter resurrection. The Holy Spirit reveals the mystery behind the resurrection and the transfiguration when we cease to enquire into historicity. The faith that was broken at the Cross was rebuilt on resurrection. "Blessed are you Simon for flesh and blood has not revealed this to you but my Father who is in Heaven", Matt 16:17.

"He descends in the clouds of heaven and is given everlasting kingdom and dominion", Dan.7:13.

The Christian legend speaks of Jesus as the son of man. The historical Jesus never used "son of man" for himself. The idea of the son of man received a new content in Jesus' person. The early church invested in Jesus the power of God to return and judge the world as the son of man. The early church identified Jesus as the son of man and introduced him into the church as its Lord and savior. Jesus saw himself in view of the contemporary apocalyptic hope as the heavenly judge of the world. He wanted this to be concealed until his resurrection. "And then hand him over to the gentiles, who will make fun of him, whip him and crucify him; but three days later he will be raised to life", Matt:20:19. He became lowly, who was delivered into the hands of man and entered into glory through suffering. The Messiah suffering for us is known to pre Christian Judaism. He wants us to give up the self and take the form of a servant even unto the death of cross. The resurrection is the revelation from above. He was aware of his death and future glory of resurrection as son of man. "I shall not drink again until the day when I drink it again anew in the kingdom of God", Matt.26:29. Jesus celebrated his last meal with his disciples in anticipation of approaching the Kingdom of God and his physical parting with them. It is an assurance of his presence both now and in future in an environment of awakened spirit. He was the victim of an extreme misunderstanding. "If Christ has not been raised your faith is futile and you are still in your sins, 1st Corinth.15:17.

"He is not here; he has been raised Just as he said", Matt.28:6.

The resurrection is a statement of eschatology, but cannot be an historical event. The post Easter events were the evidence of faith rather than the evidence of history. Christ was raised in the hearts of his disciples and they celebrated the resurrection of Jesus. Hope entered and the fear disappeared. That is the end of this world and the genesis of the Kingdom of heaven. The encounter with the risen Lord is the transcendence of this world. "That Christ died for our sins; that he was buried and that he was raised to life three days later as written in the scriptures', 1st Corinth.15:3-4. Jesus' resurrection, as viewed by Paul was the first fruits of those who have fallen. The early church viewed resurrection as the exaltation of Christ to the right hand of the Father. "The truth is directly experienced through faith", Acts 10:40. The crucified and the buried one were alive and those who survived were dead. "That he appeared to Peter and then to all twelve disciples', 1st Corinth.15:5. Mary and Mary of Magdalene saw him. The angel spoke to the women, 'you must not be afraid', Matt.28:5."He is not here; he has been raised just as he said", Matt.28:6. The risen Lord first encountered the disciples in Galilee. He walked on earth and subsequently ascended to heaven. The apostles gave empirical expression to the event of resurrection. The message of resurrection and the physical nature of the risen Christ have confusing versions. The physical resurrection was controversial, even in the early church. "By his great mercy, we have been born anew to a being through the resurrection of Jesus Christ from the dead", 1st Peter 1:3. The resurrected Christ reveals his mystery and person above the meaning of his suffering and death in the unity of the past and present. On the road to Emmaus he said, "Was it not necessary that Christ should suffer these things and enter into his glory?" Lk.24:26. He vanished soon after, but the words he spoke and the supper he ate had the pledge of his resurrection and promise.

"Jesus built his church on the rock of his resurrection and the powers of death shall not prevail against it", Mt.16:17.

Death cannot prevail against the transcended soul. The resurrection and the descending of the Holy Spirit at Pentecost are inseparable. "The spirit shall bring to you all that I have said", Jn.14:26. "The truth was revealed when the spirit descended on them", Jn.16:13. This is the time of end times when the world ended and the Kingdom of God has been established. The

Kingdom of God calls forth for righteousness, but not for apocalyptic catastrophe. The decision of the church to bind or lose on earth is linked to the ultimate future in Heaven. "The son of man has authority to forgive sins", Matt.9:6. You are the holy one of God, the disciples confessed. The church is God himself, but intertwined with the wicked world. Baptism is the symbolic of eschatological sacrament for forgiveness of sins and admission into the church. The confession of the early church was expressed through baptism, witness and martyrdom. The Sermon on the Mount mirrors our sins in front of us and turns our hearts toward the Savior. Loving your enemy and disowning all possessions contrasts and shakes the foundations of social fiber. Resist not evil is an action in consciousness, which leads men to rational existence.

"He who does not honor the son does not honor Father who sent him", Jn.5:23.

"My judgment would be true, because, I am not alone in this; Father who sent me is with me", Jn.8:16. We honor Jesus as the son of man and the Messiah. He descends on clouds from Heaven like lightning as the judge and the savior of the world. His cosmic presence is indwelling Holy Spirit in all of us. Jesus honored Father in heaven always. 'Our Father in heaven: May your Holy name honored', Matt.6:9. Jesus did not seek his own glory. God's call demands change of our hearts. Jesus spoke, "Whoever hears these of my words and obey's them is like a wise man who built his house on rock', Matt.7:24. "Remember me when you do this." The Lord's Supper is in expectation of his presence in

spirit. It is hope fixed in future. The early Christian confession of faith was expressed in devotion rather than
in theology. Men rejected him though he was wounded
for our transgressions. The end of the world expected by
Jesus has never materialized if that is the transformation
of mankind of all ages. Jesus spoke to individuals too.

Chapter-4

ONE GOD

God is one. It implies that God is in all and there is nothing that is not God. He is traditionally known as omniscient, omnipresent and omnipotent. "The only God to worship is the human soul in the human body", Swami Vivekananda, a sage of our time, affirmed. We were with Abner and Protima at Lexington, Kentucky last July. At the dinner table, there was a small discussion about God's existence in this world. Six-year-old grandson Armaan Raghav replied spontaneously to his mama, "Right now, the food you are eating is God himself." The Holy Spirit is as being in the presence of God. Attainment of bliss consciousness or salvation is the goal of all men. "The universal mind is an impersonal force in the universe. We know its ways through love, peace and sacrifice but in the end it is beyond our human mind." All religions point to one power source that what we call God, Brahman or Father in Heaven. He holds all things within himself, but nothing holds him. He is invisible and indivisible. He is formless eternal and all pervading. One who understands this truth becomes an immortal. He comes out of invisible elements and disappears into them again. All things both visible and invisible resolve into God through endless cycles. God is the source of knowledge and ignorance, enlightenment and darkness, happiness and sorrow, fear and fearlessness and life and death. One, who was breathless, breathed through his own nature. His breath is his spirit and he gave life to the seed of the universe. "Yet I do none of this but watch the drama unfold." He is the mind, the soul and the consciousness that dwells in all beings. He is the beginning, the middle and end of all lives. He is our moment and movement. He created this world and transcended it. "In the beginning when God created the universe, the earth was formless and desolate. The raging ocean that covered everything was engulfed in total darkness, and the spirit of God was moving over the water', Gen.1: 1-2. Once all was darkness and all remained unseen within the darkness-unknown and unknowable. Then the self existent Lord created the universe. 'Then God commanded, Let there be light'-and light appeared', Gen.1: 3. God is self existence. He is an active pre-existence principle. 'I am telling you the truth', Jesus replied. 'Before Abraham was born, 'I Am', Jn.8:58. He manifests from himself. Before he manifests himself, he existed within himself. Out of himself, he manifests all things. He has many names and many forms. He is neither form nor non-form. He has no qualities but he has all qualities. All that we see is what he revealed to us. He is beyond mind. He seeks himself and he alone understood his own image. He is an existence and giver of eternity. He is beyond all perfection. "I am, that I am', Yaweh told to Moses on the Mount of Sinai." The blessed One is changeless, pure light and the spirit flows from him like the water of life. The Father willed that all of creation return to him. He sees only himself, everywhere. He encompasses all with love, so that all things that come from him may become him. All beings in the universe exist within and in relationship to each other and all things in the end will return to their essential nature. He will return to himself in the end.

The philosopher is a renewed mind and a baptized spirit. The Philosophy [darshana] applied to social structure is religion. The study of the human mind and behavior is psychology. The human behavior in reference to moral standards in social life is ethics. The ancient Indian sages pursued the truth from within, While knowing which everything else will be known. The Sanatana [oldest] dharma is the love and service, which are intrinsic in every faith. The nature [swabhava] of man is love and service because he is created in the image of God, who is love and service, but not all men are divine because of sin.

Genesis of Vedic scriptures.

"He was bruised for our transgressionss", Isa.53:5. Legend says that Brahma uttered Om in his meditation, which became the seed of Vedic wisdom. God himself was the sacrifice in the sacrificial rite performed by gods and Vedic wisdom was born of that divine sacrifice. The Vedic philosophy is both mystic and spiritual. The mysticism is beyond logic. The truth is transcendental experience, which can be above reason, but should be within the human intellectual rationalization and comprehension. The new revelation has to conform to the present and the past revealed truth. God reveals his will through word and deed. The saints inspired by the Holy Spirit wrote the scriptures. The saints vary in their 'will' and imagination. The sages, with varying will and imagination interpreted scriptures numerous times through ages.

God manifests and communicates with us and we comprehend him in his true nature. God is abstract principle and faith alone takes us into unknown. God wants us to do his will, which is revealed through self-realization. The revelation is linked to inspiration and therefore the interpretation is subjected to controversy. Reveal meant unveil or disclose. The truth needs no evolution since it descended directly from God. The sage received the truth in his state of perfect evolution. The words of a truthful man follow the facts, but the facts follow the word of a sage. The Vedic religion started as worship of nature gods with the conviction that they are all many expressions of one God. God is one but many religions call him by many names. Each nature god was exalted to the level of one supreme God. "God has many names and he can be reached by many ways. Call him by any name and worship him in any way. Surely you will find him", Sage Rama Krishna observed.

In essence God is pre existence principle. He is Spirit without form but his offspring has form. He is the source of self, life and blood of this universe. In the beginning there was neither existence nor nonexistence. There is neither death nor deathlessness. There was no knowledge of distinction between the night and the day. There was gloom hidden in the gloom with

no distinction from its cause. There was deep fathom-
less abyss of water. God is light but existed with no
notion of life. The subtle elements what we call electrons could be covering the reality behind this universe.
The ancient Indian sages contended that the universe is
in many cycles. The new one [manifested] is born from
the previous [un manifest] one. God who dwells in his
own being creates and sustains this universe knows the
truth behind this creation.

God created the Heaven and the Earth, Gen.1:2.

"The Word was source of life", Jn.1:4.

The conviction of Judaism is that God has actually appeared in some fashion or done something. God
appeared in a vision or His voice had been heard. The
revelation claims that God has spoken, manifested and
communicated his will with the community. The revelation is understood through subjective experience and
it is linked to inspiration and subjected to varying interpretations. The experiences pass down through generation after generation and the community becomes the
part of the unfolding story of God's revelation. Moses
and Jesus were able to see God's will vividly in their
lives and responded in a definitive way because they
had direct communication with God. God's word
descended on them and empowered them. The subjective experience reveals God's will and our response to
it. God manifests in word and action. He desires partnership with us and demands a response. The inspiration descends on those who have capacity to respond.
Revelation is God's self-communication and is intended

for those who have ability to respond. The partnership begins when the inspiration is accepted and obeyed. New revelations flow in with a deeper understanding of God. God continues to reveal His Self and calls the faithful into deeper levels of understanding of Him. The revelation may receive varying interpretations through new generations based on their experiences. The revelation is an inspiration as a subtle psychological process as opposed to the belief of some that God dictated word by word to the prophets. God's word is literal for some and others consider historical context and intensions of the author. God's power is behind the inspiration and it is God revealing and God acting. The definition and refinement of it unfolds continuously. The skeptics dismiss this as an illusion. The book of Genesis tells us that God created out of nothing. He created both in word and in deed. God fashions man from the earth and the creation was good, He said. One should not think that the world is a prison. The creation testifies God's power and goodness. The revelation is His word and law as well. Jesus is the preexistent word of God. He is the creative power of God's word. "The word was made flesh", Jn.1:14. The self-communication of God for Christians is Jesus whose life, death and resurrection form the foundation of Christian faith.

The "fall of man" [falling away from the original intension of the creation] is due to human error according to Prophet Moses. The story of "original sin" explains the existence of evil in this world. The evil got into this world not because of God's mistake but because of man's sin. We believe in the power and beauty of the creation account. God is revealed as love and he is anxious to restore us from the "fall". He is the transcendent creator who stands above and outside human existence, but is willing to enter into relationship with mankind. He is remote, yet intimately involved as transcendence and immanence. God encompasses both the power and intimacy; as such, we need not choose power over intimacy. The story of creation is pre his-toric, but the prophets simply reflected their experiences and beliefs in their writings. They realized that God was good and his creation was orderly, but the world was a mess. Men chose their own will over God's will and disrupted the creation. God gave the gift of freedom and conditional joy that the first couple failed. Their dis-obedience changed things. Birth now occurred within the context of pain and sickness and death became a part of human existence. This moment of separation, or alienation, is called the "original sin." It is the religious explanation for the facts of life as the prophets and the congregation experienced them. Sin is explained in terms of direction. The people turned away from God and repentance and conversion imply a change of direc-tion. Repentance is an important concept in Judaism and Jesus called for repentance and conversion, which is precisely, turning away from sin.

Yahweh created, watched men make mess and then entered into that mess. He creatively fashioned out of it; a people, a law and a way. This is the divine provision for humanity. The continuing revelation is interpreted as pattern of call and response. God initiates the con-versation and relationship, but human freedom is intact because people may choose to reject or accept the invi-tation. Abraham was given a son in his old age, and the patriarch responded in faith. Abraham again stood the test of his faith by preparing to sacrifice Isaac. Faith and trust are an ongoing relationship. The covenant spells out the terms of God's relationship with his people. The nations of the world would be blessed through Abraham and his descendents. The promise was universal and particular. Moses also responded to God's call in faith. God made a covenant with whole people at Mount Sinai. The basis for tension arises when we love goodness because we are created in God's image and attracted to evil because of our sin nature. The fidelity is similar in all human history. In Jewish history, there is connection between their historical experience [self-understanding] and their perceptions about God. God's self-communication is revealed in an ongoing history of invitation and response. A religion has both an inside and outside view. Judaism is the only possible truth for a believer's inside view. The outside view gives the perspective of a religion as the truth among many.

God's presence. Nature is God's presence. Thunder is his judgment and the rain is his blessing. God is not in tragedy, but his presence is visible in love and sacrifice, which prevails during and after the tragedy. The source of tragedy is ultimately God. In Eliza's life, God spoke to him in a still voice that he should go back and serve the Lord in Israel. God was in that still voice that today, inspires souls to help others in need, but not in the wind nor fire that preceded. The myth is an event that may or may not happen, but always happens. The creation myth tells us something about this world we live in. God lives in relationships in the provision of grace. We accept all goodness of God so shall we accept any bad? Has what happened in our lives happened according to God's will? Accept what God willed in your life and do an act of love knowing that God knows that what he is doing. The Jewish nation's exile to Babylon is viewed as God's will because they strayed from His ways. Slavery in America is considered as God's will, based on the scripture, "He shall be a slave to his brothers", Gen. 2:5. God wanted the sheep to be sheared, if not, God could not have created the sheep, they remarked. We find God in quiet heroism and endurance, stretching to the limits to do what life called on him to do. God is in the willingness of love and sacrifice. We reject wrong even it is tempting and profitable. Ordinary people do extraordinary acts, surpassing themselves. It is the presence when men rise to life's challenges and find courage within themselves that they did not know they had until the day they needed them.

'I am with you always, even unto the end of the world', Matt.28:20.

God indwells within us always. We experience his absence in sorrow and pain. God sends neither the problem nor a solution, but he gives us strength to deal with the problem. His yoke is light. You may feel burdened, but not abandoned. God created this world and he indwells in his creation. But we do not experience his presence always. His visible presence is love and hope. Nature is harsh and unpredictable. The courage and determination of the affected during the floods and accidents speak to the power and presence of God. God is not in the tragedy, but he is in our response to tragedy. God is always with you meant, "I won't do it for you and I won't do it without you either". When you summon up courage and are ready to act, I will give you strength and soul that you did not know you were capable of.

The child has simple faith in what is said by it's parents. In an adolescent traumatic stage, the breaking of myths begins. We are beyond skepticism in the third stage. Many things may not be historical or literally true, but they could be valuable. He is memory of guilt [Rabbi Kushner]. We outgrow our adolescent skepticism and outgrow the concept that God lives in Heaven and grants or denies our prayers. We affirm the reality of God's power that replenishes our courage beyond our anticipation. God is surely with us when we reach inside of ourselves and try to find the capacity for forgiveness.

When we cry against God for our problems, it is rather not about God, but a cry of pain. The victim is better comforted by a hug rather than a detailed theological discourse. During the loss of a dear one, God gives us the strength to bear and deal with the pain. We cease to think the loss as a source of anguish. God becomes a source of love and enables us grieve for the loss. Parents do not approve a child's birth and we care for the child in the provision of grace. In the loss of a child, God's miracle is to pour his grace upon men and enable them to bear the pain. His grace pours upon the place of pain and wound. A child with a congenital problem is born not because God disfavored you. That the miracles happen at all is miracle enough. The endurance of fire fighters during the 911 tragedy demonstrates divine presence. They were called to do more than they ever believed they were capable of doing. Alzheimer's care needs more patience that the grace of God alone endures.

God created the universe and he entered into it. He encompasses the whole universe and remains whole. I am a God particle like a drop of water is a part of the ocean. He is identical with my deepest self, which cannot be ejected into an objective world. The evidence of his existence comes from direct spiritual experience. It is an illusion for skeptics. God is created in the consciousness of man. Invisible God creates visible forms. He is inaccessible, yet more intimate to the soul than the soul to itself. He is heavenly, and immanent, and personal and impersonal. He is undetermined as divinity and determined as cosmic activity. His name is not this, not this [na iti, na iti] through exclusion process. We cannot name God and it is a betrayal of God to name him. Everything is self itself. God is void and we worship him in spirit and truth. Revelation is God's self-communication. Jesus is the self-communion of God. The duality of the known and the unknown is eliminated through self-realization, which implies non-discussion. God is comprehended through wisdom, but not through discussion. Silence is better than argument. We cease "discussion" because God is no discussion. The sense oriented religious rituals [karma kanda] are not redemptive.

The Father in Heaven is the creator. He is pre-existence active principle [Brahman] who is unconcerned with the world of action. Jesus is God's self-disclosure and cosmic dynamicity. The Holy Spirit is our inner Self and God's power at work. The self in its transcendental, cosmic and individual aspects represents the Father, Son and Holy Ghost, which corresponds to the trinity of Vedanta: Brahma, Vishnu and Isvara. Brahma is the creation, Vishnu is love and stability and 'Siva' is the end and decay of the creation. 'Siva' is the reflection of cosmic activity and he is burdened to redeem mankind. Our wounds heal in the provision of grace that radiates from the foot of the Cross. Hinduism conceives 'Siva' as total human consciousness who is immanent God. Maya/Satan is the conceptualized sin which is the creative power of the sin to produce mutable nature. Maya is the cosmic delusion which alienates self from God. The alienation is the human strife that we endure every day.

'Gunas': [material modes of human behavior]. Kapila, ancient Hindu sage discovered three 'gunas'. Our nature is cloudy because we live in three material modes of behavior. They are like three twisted bands of a rope, which are named goodness, passion and dullness. They all identify with ego. Goodness rises up and dullness sinks down. Goodness sees divinity and passion sees multiplicity. Dull clings to the effect and ignores the cause. Goodness acts with no desire to the fruits, but passion acts to please the desire. Desire is bound to take rebirth to exhaust itself. The prayer for material fulfillment is passion. Dullness worships sin. Wisdom breeds goodness and passion breeds pleasure. Dullness breeds pleasure, which ultimately ends in bitterness.

Non-violence [ahimsa] is a transcendental experience and it is applicable to transcended souls. The universal application of ahimsa is not compatible in this world. The fanatic ideology placed under the flag of gods disrupts the integrity of spirit. The cultic environment stunts the evolution of the spirit. Anything imposed on others against their will, even in the name of God, is evil. The democracy is an integrated variety. The human race is one, but the individuals vary in their potential. Nature and duty are intertwined as such one realizes his full potential through his own being [swadharma]. One should live his religion according to the law of his being. Jesus spoke to ordinary people in parables that they can understand his teaching through their own being. Trust and surrender to your own self will The deed that takes us closer to God is the best worship. It makes no difference whether they are gold or iron chains, as long as you are chained.

"Let your light shine before men so that they will see the good things you do and praise your Father in Heaven", Matt.5:16.

The truth of consciousness is not opposed to the expression through the matter. The human nature is willed, but not imposed by God. God is responsible for both the ideal and the material medium. The immanent God creates the perceptible world. The concretization of the conceptual plane requires a fullness of existence, which is an objectification in the medium of potential matter. God's ideas are seeking existence and the world of existence is seeking perfection. Our personal God enters into a personal relationship and stirs our hearts to devotion. He is the immutability of Brahman and the mutability of becoming. He creates, contains and controls. The supra cosmic God supports the cosmic manifestation in space and time.

"Depth of the darkness is as great as the habitation of the light", [Manduka upanishad].

Good and evil are together in one another and neither of them has a beginning nor an end. Strife continues between them and God is actively involved in the strife. The distinction between good and bad are not arbitrary constructs and the tendencies to error are also not arbitrary possibilities. This fact does not reflect any weakness in God's power. God graciously gave us free will and he knows how we use it. God is Grace [Prasad] and we receive grace through faith alone. God loves all his creation and we love every one in grace of God. What God does not know is not a fact. He knows the indeterminate tendencies and he knows them when they are actualized. We resist those tendencies to error through his grace alone. We know the universal knower through self and the conviction takes us beyond self. We fear God because our elders told us to do so that we may not error. The fear is negative energy, rather we love God that we may receive his grace and not error. When Lord lives in us our life perspective is always positive and peaceful.

Brahman [Father in heaven] is above distinctness of subject and object. He has neither attributes nor qualities. He is our immanent will. He ensouls and presides over the individual souls in cosmic becoming. He controls the souls who work out their destinies along the lines determined by their own natures. He fills our being and fulfills our mind. All souls dissolve into him in the end. He is being and becoming and transcendental and immanent. He is changeless, but brings changes in this world. This manifested universe is created in his consciousness. The glory of consciousness is revealed in the evolution of cosmos. His un-manifested divinity is beyond mind. The soul is assimilated into divine substance in its transcendental state. Nature is spiritualized without destroying it in self-realization. Nature is divinized with no loss of individuality. It is crossed over from unreal to real through self-oblivion. It is a state being one with the Father in heaven. The branch, which abides in the vine, is one with vine. The consciousness, which is attached to the world, is in involution. It is the Kingdom of Heaven. It is Samadhi for Hindus and nirvana for Buddhists. The vision of spiritual reality is not a mental construction, but a disclosure of truth from beyond the mind. God's grace removes the veil of delusion and reveals divine glory. The ego becomes an empty form in the Kingdom of Heaven as such we rather disown ego and own the universe in God.

"Father and I are one, Jn.10:30. God is divided in unrealized soul. It is a partial manifestation of God. The world is real for sinners. God influences our choice of freedom, but he does not control our lives. Sin cannot be removed through good deeds or self-effort because they further bind us to cosmic process with an endless chain of cause and effect. The immanent divinity changes according to the changes in the individual. Wisdom and action are like light and darkness. The action falls away when the wisdom dawns. All action occurs in the world of becoming. The born again soul does action, less action. The transcended soul commends his spirit unto God. The saint sees God within himself, but the sinner sees no God, even if he seeks. The sinner lives not by spontaneity of spirit, but by greed. God is the cause and the universe is the effect. The seed of consciousness penetrated the womb of the nature and produced the universe. Evil and good are the creation of God and the man is the combination of good and bad. In the beginning, the creation was free from sin. "Original sin" entered and polluted the divinity. Faith is an inward sense of truth that points to an object over which a fuller light is shed. It is the force, which urges mankind for a better world both in here and in the next world. It is the power of mind to focus on the ideal believed. The believer's heart is the ultimate evidence of faith and his power of spirit testifies his faith. He is what his faith is.

The manifested existence [cosmic egg] is the product of interaction between God and nature. Karma is the interaction between God and the world. It is the creative force and the principle of movement behind this world. God himself is functioning in this world. God and men participate in the cosmic evolution. Divinity, polluted by sin, transforms into a process of becoming. God and the world are the expressions of one, but they represent the opposite poles of the reality. The cause of strife between God and men is incomprehensible. The temporal movement is connected to the depths of eternity. Eternity is the transformation of the time. Time and space are the constricts of the mind. Sin veils God and men fail to seek him; intuitive faith helps us to find God. The saving wisdom penetrates the truth. The truth, obtained through subjective experience, is beyond discussion. It is the knowledge by acquaintance, but not by description. The truth described is like a light to be seen. Salvation unites man and God into one whole, like father and son. The born again soul is being and the unrealized soul is nonbeing. Nature is bound to be transformed to the image of its creator. God is our conscious self; one who cannot believe in conscious self as the immanent divinity cannot see God.

"Where shall I go from thy spirit", Psalm 139.

The idea of idol worship is to find the formless through the form. It is better to worship any form when the true form is unknown [Vedanta]. Idol worship somehow awakens self and connects it to the soul. God is not one in many idols, but he is one behind the many idols. God sees the intensity of devotion and rewards proportionately. He is the immutable center for endless mobility. Pantheism refers that everything is God and pane theism refers that everything dwells in God. All beings exist in God, as air exists in space. God lives in us, but in reality, we live in him. He lives in us equally, but we live in him unequally. God appears to those who seek him diligently. His grace is sufficient for the sinners, too. God is seen behind love and we are saved by grace.

> "The Word was God. He was in the beginning with God. In him was life and the life was the light of men and the light shines in darkness and the darkness did not comprehend it", John 1:1-5.

The man has no existence without self -consciousness and the self is part of the cosmic self, which we revere as God. The creation is God transformed. God and self are distinct in relation to time and timelessness. The self-realization ends the distinction. The truth is the denial of the experience of the external objects in search of reality. The time, the space and the causation are essential to experience the world, which is obliterated the transcendental consciousness. The innate divine spirit inspires self to embrace salvation. Salvation is bestowed on those who are selected by divine grace. The heat is the sun's nature. It is human nature to seek unity with God. This world is a joy, but Heaven is an eternal Joy.

"God dwells in everybody", Exodus 25:8.

Human consciousness is in three states, which are waking, dream and sleep states. The fourth [turiya] is the divine consciousness, which contains all other three states. Consciousness in deep sleep is devoid of consciousness, thought, and transcends time and space. The conscious man bears pain and sorrow. The dream consciousness is mental body. We are born to transcend and dissolve into Heaven. The soul evolves continuously here on this earth and the world after. The ego hinders the evolution of soul. The transcended soul sees God all the time directly. The saint's expression of divine will in his interactions with the empiric world is the evidence that God dwells in all beings. "You are God" [tat tvam asi] and "I am God" [a ham Brahma] are the Vedic affirmations. The clay is the substratum behind the multiplicity of pots. All rivers flow into one ocean leaving behind their name and form. The nectar from many flowers merges into honey. The transcended souls merge with cosmic soul. The breath is the cosmic energy, which conforms to the shape of the body as water conforms to the shape of a vessel. The mind conforms to the shape of the physiological man. The ego and intelligence are the two inner most layers of the self. The outer sheaths being the body, mind and intellect. The Self is God and this reality needs no other proof except self-realization. The world and God are like body and soul; they are whole, but distinct. The universe was in potential form before it was manifested. "I am your servant from the view point of body, I am part of you from the view point of ego and I am thy

Self from the view point of Self", sage Ramakrishna Paramhamsa observed.

Sankaracharya, 7th.century [AD] saint in south India believed in non-duality, which precludes seeing other and hearing from other. The finite universe is the mis-interpretation of the infinite. The world exists like the son of a barren woman. The illusive multiplicity is tran-scended through self-realization. The world is relative when it is experienced in relative consciousness and it becomes unreal when the relative consciousness is obliterated by the divine consciousness. The world is an intermediate existence. God and the universe are twined like the snake and a rope. Adwaita is total identity of man with God in transcendental state.

Brahman is the supreme reality with attributes [11th century saint Ramanuja]. God consciousness created this universe, which was in potential form before the creation. The world, for this reason, is not an illusion. God created this universe out of his nature and so the world is not alien to him. God is both the instrumental and material cause of the world. The universe is his body, which lives in his cosmic soul like the human body lives in human soul. God controls the principle of soul and the soul controls the principle of body. God and soul are one not that they are identical, but God indwells deep within the soul. The source of soul is God. The immanence is not identity. The creation and the creator are distinct in time and eternity. The soul recognizes immanent divinity only when saving grace descends upon him/her. Grace descends on those who are elected. We worship him with all our body, mind and soul and say, "God is myself" [tat tvam asi]. The consciousness is a dependent principle since the ego disappears in transcendence of the soul. The world is God transformed. Self is superimposed by self like a snake lying over a rope, which results in a combination of real, and unreal; it is unity in difference. The man is part of one totality [visistadwaita]. The image, which is devoid of pain and fear that you see in your eye is God. Your image that you see in the water is not God because it changes as the body changes.

God and man are eternally separate [Dwaita concept of Madhvacharya]. God is identical with self, but they are different eternally, which is a self-contradictory view. God and the world are different, but God is superior. The born again soul is one with God. The human souls are God particles like sparks of fire. Jesus' cry on the cross is the state of conscious body separate from God. His unity with Father was restored when he said, "Father forgive them, they do not know what they are doing", Lk.23:34. "I am the vine and you are the branches", Jn.15:5. is an expression meaning the creation can become one with creator.

God is our Father [Yajur Veda]. The total consciousness of men is God, which excludes the discussion of the atheists. God consciousness is our inner principle and qualitative content of life. He is experienced as you and I in the higher planes of consciousness. He is not an intellectual abstraction, nor a mode of thinking. He appears in front of you in need. He is diffusely expressed like the sound in ether. He is the creator of the things yet to be. He reaches us from above in spirit and from within through mortal appearance. The idea of a personal God is the expression of oneness with God. The kingdom of God is within you, is an expression of being one with God. God is above love and hatred and only the fool thinks that God favors him. God damns none nor elects any. "He gave the power to become the sons of God to those who receive", Jn.1:12. Each man is a descendant from God. We have a choice to be free as a child of God or be enslaved as man. "One who sees all beings in Me is never separated from Me", [Gita]. Faith possesses a direct perception of God. Heaven is a state of immortality, but not a living individual. Nature is eternal in the sense that the rain is recurrent eternally. Karma follows us into all the worlds eternally though it can be exhausted and altered. Time is the duration of the existence and the dissolution of nature. The destructive power of the time creates fear among the mortals.

"Then you will be able to live as the Lord wants and will always do what pleases him. Your lives will produce all kinds of good deeds, and you will grow in knowledge of God', Col.1:10.

We strive to be perfect because our Father in heaven is perfect. We are required to forgive other's sins that Father in Heaven may forgive our sins. "One who is striving for spiritual perfection does not perish" [Gita]. Man is universally infinite in subjective form and he is a finite individual in objective form. He is more a divinity than the material. The objectification is the ejection of the subject into the world of objects. The transformed soul is compared to a humming bee after being filled with sweet nectar. The ego is the artificial construction obtained by abstraction. Sin is external, but is a human necessity. Desire is something yet to have and passion is the attachment to something in possession already. Good desire kindles the heart and reveals the sin. The saving wisdom cuts through the veiling power of sin and sees God directly. God stoops to reach the sinner as the sinner approaches him. God answers our prayers at the level we approach him and he rewards every level of faith. "So it is with faith: if it is alone and includes no actions, then it is dead", James, 2:17.

Jesus' word was always followed by deed. 'I, your Lord and teacher, have just washed your feet. You then wash one another's feet', Jn.13:14. In medical missions in Africa, we served the needy and sick. Owen and Celia from Indiana were busy in digging wells and provided clean water to drink. Dora and Marion Showalter from Modesto California kept all vehicles ready to run. Marion was kind to teach me driving. Jesus affirmed that he came here to serve but not to be served. His presence is vividly experienced in service. It is our worship to God. The hypocrite retains his desires in his mind and tries to restrain his senses. The social authority is opposite of self-integrity. The saint is at peace in the midst of turmoil. The strong wind drives away the boat on the waters and the strong senses scatter the mind away from God. Let inspiration set the boat to sail to experience the breeze. It is like boat in water, but not with water in the boat. As our purpose is, so our life is.

Chapter-5

SELF-REALIZATION

"For God loved the world so much that he gave his only son, so that everyone who believes in him, may not die but have eternal life", Jn.3:16. Salvation is to realize your own immanent divinity and attain transcendental consciousness. God is revealed when the veiling power of sin is removed. We are born with an instinct to know God. The love we seek is an expression of the divine urge in us. God is beyond the human mind and the evidence of his existence is in the human experience of self-realization. Inspiration descends on those who have the capacity to respond. Self-realization demands faith, faith guides you to repent for your sins. Repentance is the resolve and the power, which prevents you from sinning anymore as well as spontaneously washing away all your past sins. The fire of repentance burns the seeds of sin into ashes; the ego has died and the desire has been annihilated. Repentance is the cause and the conversion is the effect. The cycle of birth and death ends spontaneously. This is our destiny and we should not neglect such a great salvation like the beggar who sat on the old box day in and day out begging for years, not knowing that the box was filled with gold. The knower of God is God, no matter what religion he belongs to. The light remains the same but the color of the light beam changes according to the color of the light bulb. The coal is black but the burning coal is not black.

The sun is heat and light which is its law of being [dharma]. The soul is eternal; its preexistence cannot be denied for the reason that it cannot be explained convincingly. The subjective experience overrules the objectivity. The migration of soul continues from one body to another until the cycle of birth and death ends and the soul becomes one with God. The physical body is in continuous transition from childhood to old age and death is another transition [Vedic thought]. When you climb the staircase, you forget the steps below. The process of elimination is the nature of this world. Both the body and soul are from one source, which is the Being. Man is heavenly tree born of earth and still connected to his heavenly kindred. Wisdom illumines knowledge and reveals God. The cosmic tree in the Garden of Eden is symbolic of human intellect. The tree of this world grows and the branches stretch forth. We cut the tree with the sword of wisdom and seek refuge in God. Salvation is the state of being born again.

"Jesus raised up in union with Christ to rule with him in heavenly world", Eph.2:5.

The attainment of salvation is through listening [sravana] to gospel. The Holy Ghost convicts men to confess their sins. Reflection [manana] on the truth of God leads to intellectual conviction; the conviction is faith [shraddha] and the faith releases divine grace. "Jesus turned around and saw her, and said, 'Courage my daughter. Your faith has made you well', Matt.9:22. Faith is healing. Grace descends through faith alone. Grace is subtle, divine energy that empowers the new believer in his struggle against sin. The transcended soul grows in the knowledge of God through continuous prayer and meditation. 'Repent: for the kingdom of God is at hand', Matt.4:17. The sinner repents and sobs for forgiveness. Grace descends through repentance, but not through self-effort because the self-effort is ego in itself. The great sinner has hope for salvation because the divine light in him is still un-extinguished. "Christ dwells in our hearts by faith", Eph.3:17. Faith is the aspiration of the soul to gain saving wisdom. The will is faith and the self-will is ego, which is unsteady like the wind. Faith fades away when God is realized. Man becomes God through salvation. "God, I am", is a state of absolute existence, knowledge and bliss [satchitananda]. It is freedom, fullness of peace and bliss. The person who has no personal experience of salvation is like a spoon in the soup. The spoon is inert object and cannot taste the soup.

"If your eyes are sound, your whole body will be full of light", Matt.6:22.

We use light to see our way in darkness. Jesus famously said, 'I am the way, the truth and the light and no man cometh unto the Father but by me', Jn.14:6. The Hindu sages conceived that the Way to truth is not one single path, yet all paths lead to the same destination. The religion is a means of worship unto God. The early

Christians were known as the 'WAY' people. The way is the path to life and it leads us beyond the horizon, yet it begins with a single step. The day's shadows fall across the path, but we stir ourselves and continue forward. We seek help to find the path and grow in spirit but in the end, we must take the path alone. The saint's presence alone transforms the sinner more than his eloquent sermon. Jesus spoke with authority. The disciples heard his voice say follow me, and they followed. His words were not from his mind, but from the Father in heaven. Goodness is not a measure of spiritual transformation. After the death of Jesus Christ, the disciples and other followers of Jesus formed a community called "The Way". St. Paul persecuted The Way to death [Acts. 22:4]. Later, he became an apostle of Jesus Christ.

> "For the gate is narrow and the Way is hard, that leads to Life. And those who find it are few", Luke 13:24.

We transcend desire and attain The Way. Get out of the way to live in The Way. The Heaven and Earth are like weed and wheat. They are infinitely apart. Hold no opinions for or against anything in order to see truth. To set up what you like against what you dislike is the disease of the mind. The Way is the flow of life. It is the force that moves in all things, permeates all things, and governs all things. The Way cannot be manipulated, nor can it be resisted. In the end, it is unknowable. We cannot stop the wind blowing. We yield to divine power like the supple bamboo yields to powerful wind. Accept everything just the way it is and rejoice in life. What happens, happens in life and do not worry for something that you cannot change. A nation that resists change is doomed eventually. If you want inner peace and outer harmony, you have to learn not to push the river. The Kingdom of Heaven is not some kind of perfected world that is ushered in at the end of time. "The Kingdom of God is already here-within you", Mtt.3:2.

"No man cometh unto Father but by me", Jn.14:6.

Jesus is our propitiation and holds the key to kingdom of Heaven which is within us. Enter the Heaven by the narrow gate. The way is hard but it leads to life. Only few choose this way. The gate to enter into this material world is wide and the way is easy but that leads to destruction. Many people choose this easy way. Open the door that is within you, so that you may be a guide to those who wish to follow you. Encourage all those who are ready to follow the Way and receive its blessings. The kingdom is within you and one who knows himself will find it. Jesus is the light and so do I as his child. I am a beacon of light to those who see me. I am a mirror to those who look for me. I am a door to those who knock on me. Follow me and leave the dead to bury the dead. A lamp on the lamp stand alone gives light well. Let people see our good deeds and turn to goodness which is the flow of life. 'It is easier for a camel to pass through the eye of a needle than for a rich man to enter the kingdom of heaven', Matt.19:24. We seek and realize the indwelling kingdom of Heaven though it is hard. Son of man has place to rest his head. We value in kingdom of Heaven those things in life, which are eternal. Everything you say comes from Bliss that is within you. The living God is within you and you are in him. Your thinking and motivation come from Bliss which is already within you. Your life prospers and be service to many. Those who transcend the duality of sorrow and happiness and success and failure surely inherit the king dom of Heaven.

"Ask, and it will be given to you. Seek, and you will find. Knock and the door will be opened to you", Matt.7:7.

Ask, seek and knock: Seek diligently and find the indwelling Lord. The blessed soul is light and rejoice in love, compassion and forgiveness. The duality of light and darkness are comparable to Bliss and sorrow. The unsaved souls ignore the inner Bliss. The inspiration knocks and the door is opened. Lord reveals himself vividly. The thinking ceases and the mind is still. Now you live in kingdom of heaven which is eternal. The world is transcended. The duality of success and failure is transcended. One who finds Lord within sees Lord in all beings. The saint who is in harmony with kingdom of heaven never returns to the material world. God is the seed of this creation and he is the beginning and the end of all. He is our shelter and watches us in silence.

"Flesh and blood have not revealed unto thee but my father who is in heaven", Mt.16:17.

We are conditioned by sin. Salvation transforms material nature into divine nature. It demands faith, which is the belief in the sublime. Men confess their sins on conviction and the conversion or transformation of soul follows. "Repent and be baptized for the remission of sins and you will receive the gift of Holy Spirit",

Acts 2:38. The salvation in essence includes the recognition, elimination of sin and realizes the immanent self. "Om" is symbolic of wisdom in Hinduism. Aim at the Brahman with the wisdom of the bow and the arrow of soul. Realize you are Self, which is the intelligence of the intellect and Lord of all. God is above sorrow and hunger. The Kingdom of Heaven was lost because of original sin and it was regained because of sacrificial death of Jesus Christ. The pure soul, which God created in the beginning, needed no salvation. There is no spiritual life without moral life. Love unites and hatred divides. Love your enemy makes no sense to a sinner.

"Word of God is sharper than any double edged sword", Heb. 4:12.

Religion is philosophy in action. Moral conduct of social acceptance is the reflection of spirit; the spirit remembers the subtle demarcation between sin and righteousness. The source of sin is desire, irrespective whether the desire is good or bad. The light of truth shines forth when the darkness of desire is eliminated. We lived in divine presence in our mother's womb and we all lost his presence after birth because of sin. The kingdom of heaven eliminates duality. "Put off the old man with his deeds and have put on the new man which is renewed in the knowledge after the image of Him where there is neither Greek nor Jew but the Christ is in all" Colossians 9:9. "Any man who believes in Christ is new creation. Behold all things are become new", 2nd Corinth. 5:17. This is self-control through self-realization [Vedic]. "The body is chariot, the intellect is charioteer, and the mind is the reins. Self is the Lord of chariot, the senses are the horses and the objects are the road. The intellect as the charioteer with regulated mind, the senses controlled and the horses tamed takes you into heavenly abode [Vedic]. "The transformed soul loves his neighbor as his self", Rom. 13:8. Good people do good deeds, but the saint does good deeds as worship unto Lord. Surrender to God empowers you that you will see yourself in your neighbor. "Do not grieve the Holy Spirit. Let all malice and bitterness put away from you", Eph.30:31. The sinner thinks that he is the enjoyer, but God is the enjoyer and the creator.

> "Then he took a piece of bread, gave thanks to God, broke it and gave it to them, saying, this is my body given for you. Do this in memory of me", Luke 22:19.

Kuthastha [anvil] is the locus of divine wisdom and it corresponds to the location of the pituitary gland of modern medicine (Vedic). "Sprinkling divine sacred blood that is offered as sacrifice is necessary for the remission of sins" [Vedic]. The inspiration comes from the same source for all religions. The priest shall sprinkle the blood upon the alter of the Lord", Lev. 16:6. All sensual desires are consumed in the fire kindled by wisdom. God accepts all kinds of sacrifices and one who cannot sacrifice is not compatible to live in any world. Life is a movement in transcendence; the transcended soul has even transcended the moral code. Truth realized is superior to truth imparted. Love your enemy and loving your enemy is verily loving yourself. One who hates his neighbor hates himself; and your neighbor is verily yourself. "A person in Christ is a new creature".

Discussion leads to wisdom and the argument is ignorance. Doubts dissolve in wisdom. The revealed scriptures of all religions have one source; all religions flow into one God, like all the rivers flow into one ocean. The truth emerges ultimately from the human consciousness. We cling to oneness of spirit rather than to difference in name and form. Living on surface of life provides you with social comfort and security, but strife begins in life when we become self-conscious of moral sensitivities. The immanent spirit grieves at the falling virtues in human interactions, the mind becomes cloudy and convictions are unsettled. Life becomes precarious with working compromises. We seek a redemptive, divine touch at this juncture. The aspiration for perfection is the mystery, which lurks in the hearts of creation. The working of perfection creates an emptiness in us. The man of will and reason seeks union with God. The impulse to seek God creates agony and fulfillment as well. God in us expresses himself in infinite capacity through self-transcendence. The unity in body, mind and soul is attained through self-realization, which demands intuitive conviction and intellectual analysis of the abstract principle [jnana yoga]. It is to empty the phenomenal content of self and enter into resurrection glory of Christ. Passion dies and the soul rests from earthly encounters. It is the image of God. Self is beyond human comprehension though we know few phenomena of self. The world impedes the intuitive vision of self and we see the celestial glory of self beyond the veil of flesh.

Devotion [bhakti yoga] requires total surrender in mutual trust and love. The devotee is merged with God in both unity and separation. Surrender is an empowerment, which demands faith (Vedic). "The wicked man who worships me with devotion will be attaining salvation", [Gita]. God helps the true seeker to find him. Meekness is the utter prostration of self. The meek inherit the Kingdom of God. The sacrifice of love is simpler than strenuous thinking and tuning of will. "Those who love me shall not perish", [Gita]. Devotion draws the soul closer to God. The truth is above dualism, which demands worship. The Knowledge is not devotion, but it sustains the contemplative process of devotion; devotion or surrender is not detachment from the world. The love of God enters into the world to serve and redeem it. God casts away your sins and transforms your soul in his infinite grace through faith. Obviously, the grace is earned in some and bestowed in some. The path of devotion is like baby clinging to mother ape. The baby is in active participation in the process. The self chooses God and transforms into his image in his grace. God saves some and damns others based on his un-motive choice. Damnation is God's judgment; grace is not selective nor is God partial. Love unfolds self and takes us to higher level of consciousness. We shape God based on our longing. He is eternity for the dying and light for those who are in darkness. The horizon remains at the level of our eyesight and God remains at the level of our consciousness.

> "Keep watch and pray that you will not fall into temptation. The spirit is willing, but the flesh is weak", Matt26 41.

The salvation is attained through conviction and confession of sins. It is not obtained through rituals or mere talking about it. The pure soul is free from sin. The children of God retreat from the world, but they cannot retreat from the action. The saint's action is worship unto Lord. We rather continue to act in service of Lord. The right action is the essence of life. The selfless action is the saint's destiny. An action in the spirit of freedom is the action in the spirit of renunciation. Sage Kapila believed in renunciation of action because we are bound by action and liberated by wisdom. Every desire is an action bound and every action is effect bound. The binding quality of action lies in its motive. Inertia is no action and renunciation is no desire. Renounce the desire without cessation of action. The action in consciousness transcends anger and hatred. The pain inflicted in surgery is ahimsa because it is for healing. Perfection comes through action with detachment. Do not let loose the evil through your egocentric compassion [Gita]. Grow upward from where you stand now and do good without losing your Self Will. Wisdom is not the fruit of action, but it is vice versa. Sacrifice is not self-immolation, but a spontaneous and sacred giving to God. The saint lives in his innermost existence of truth.

Religion is philosophy in action one has understood. What we feel is spirituality, what we believe is theology and what we do is religion. Faith becomes real when it is translated into behavior and demonstrated in action. God is visible not in a church, but in between people. God is vividly visible when the Samaritan reaches the victim. When you reach your neighbor, you are joined in the bonds of holiness. Your faith becomes real when it is translated into action. It is holy to clothe the naked and quench the thirst and hunger of your neighbor. We would rather reach the painful than feeling sorrow for them. We would rather feed the hungry than being thankful to Lord for he gave us our daily bread. Hold the bereaved and dry the tears rather than pity them. I saw God's presence in my missionary days in Nigeria, when the villagers carried the sick by the cot and when the community comes and consoles the bereaving family. The religion is social action. It is comparable to the relationship of wife and husband which is associated with daily strife and love. Faith is in present moment and movement rather than the future imaginations and observations. Christianity is presently diversified and multiplied, but rooted firmly in single faith. The diversification of the church is seemingly in separation from its neighbor, but in reality, all groups are anchored to one substratum that is faith.

"He that planted the ear, shall he not hear?. He that formed the eye, shall he not see?" Ps.94:9.

God knows all. The pure soul is assimilated into divine substance where all levels of consciousness are in harmony with divinity. The transcended soul is free and filled with divine energy and interacts with the world like the lotus in the pond. The purpose of salvation is not to separate Self from self but to transfigure the whole person. The body and soul are a un-reconciled duality. We possess the individuality of body and mind and retain the universality of spirit. The body and mind are not dissolved, but rendered pure and become the divine tools. The personality attains fullness and the divine expression is maximized. The divine soul needs no individuality, but still assumes it by limitation.

Chapter-6

CHRIST CONSCIOUSNESS.

L ord Jesus Christ, was drawn to the teaching of John the Baptist, a Jewish preacher who embodied the messianic and apocalyptic hopes of the time, calling people to repent for the Kingdom of God was at hand. Jesus was the cousin of John the Baptist, and like John, Jesus also called people to repent for the Kingdom of God was at hand. His disciples called people to repent in Jesus' name, he, who was crucified and raised from the dead. John's gospel begins with Jesus as the pre-existent word of God. The world was created through God's word. Jesus was more powerful than death even before his resurrection. He raised Lazarus from the dead. The book of Revelation was written to sustain Christian hope during the persecution. It is filled with symbols, beasts and numerical signs, which are difficult to interpret and understand. For some Christians, it is prophetic book to predict the end of the world and Jesus' second coming. Jesus lived and died, but Jews were still expecting the Messiah then and are still expecting

the Messiah now. It was through the subjective experience of the power of resurrection that the Christians
believed in Jesus as the promised Messiah. The belief
in the resurrection was not a matter of evidence, but it
was a matter of faith. Isaiah's prophecy that, "the calves
and lion cubs will feed together, and little children will
take care of them", Isa.11:6; did not happen with Jesus.
"If someone has been put to death for a crime and the
body is hung on a post, it is not to remain there over-
night. It must be buried the same day, because a dead
body hanging on a post brings God's curse on the land",
Deut.21:22-23. Jews believe in guilt and destiny. The
events of the Bible do point beyond Jesus to a future
Messiah for the Jews. Isaac's sacrifice symbolizes Jesus'
crucifixion to the Christians, but for the Jews, it was
an act of trust and obedience by Abraham to God. The
Persian influence of child sacrifice as trust and obedience to God was spread widely in the region during
Abraham's time.

Abraham believed that God spoke to him. Moses
believed that the God of Abraham wanted him to go
back to Egypt to liberate His people. So did the experience with the risen Lord. The post resurrection period
was filled with controversies and arguments. The
experience of resurrection empowered the believers
by God's spirit that their lives were changed. They
resurrected themselves in their spirit. The history of
Christian movement was conceived as the continua-
tion of the story of Israel because the same Holy Spirit
was at work in both. The Spirit that convicts and transforms people was the driving force behind the proclamation of the gospel. God's appearance in the Bible
is accompanied by wind and fire, so did the apostles

experience the presence of God in wind and fire. The apostles were filled with the Holy Spirit and began to speak, not according to their own designs, but as the Spirit directed them. They spoke in a language they did not know before and the visitors to Jerusalem from all over the Middle East heard them speaking the mighty works of God. "Whoever calls upon the Lord shall be saved" Acts 2:21 was a new tongue. The apostles were enlightened and experienced the risen Lord. The apostles were empowered to go beyond the terms of the covenant at Sinai and extend the saving message of Jesus to everyone. Jesus speaks for all ages.

"In the beginning was the Word", Jn.1:1.

The Word [shabda Brahma/Sanskrit] projected his thoughts, which condensed into electromagnetic images and created this universe of diversity. The human consciousness vibrates and produces images in the dream world. The universe is God's dream world. Jesus is the preexistence principle. Jesus Christ descended as the Son of man that we may ascend as sons and daughters of God. His teachings like "resist not evil" and "love your enemy", are of high moral ground that we can only realize them in the provision of grace. He was his message and his words were his deeds. His ascetic life and self-denial were unparalleled. He lives in our thoughts, shares our pain and removes our suffering.

"If someone takes your shirt, let him have your coat as well", Matt.5:40",

The power in giving destroys the ego of evil spontaneously. You cannot receive unless you give. You cannot breathe in unless you breathe out. "When someone asks you for something, give it to him; when someone wants to barrow something, lend it to him", Matt.5:42. The law of nature is to give. The heart gives out blood it is refilled. Similarly, the air breathed out is replenished spontaneously. God's abundance through rainfall and sunshine awakens the divine abundance within us. The abundance can flow out with a glass of water to the thirsty. Small is beautiful. Do small things in a great way. During my school days, my summer Job required carrying water from the nearby well to a construction site. A glass of water was so precious in that hot, south Indian summer. During my missionary days at Garkida General Hospital in Nigeria, the principal of Waka Secondary School [Malam Gamachi] suddenly visited our home for a glass of cold water from the fridge. A simple smile at a stranger replenishes his heart. The love you showed shall flow back into you in abundance. The abundance or lacking is a state of mind. It is a paradox that, "Much is required from the person to whom much is given; much more is required from the person to whom much more is given", Luke 12:48. More faith receives more grace. Abundance comes to those who have it already. You cannot reap unless you sow One who cannot give is incompatible to live in any world. The abundance is not in possessions, but in contentment. The desire ends, not by keeping your possessions, but by inner renunciation. To have more or less is neither wrong nor right, but the greedy mind is always wrong.

"Then the devil goes out and brings seven other
spirits even worse than itself, and they come and
live there. So when it is all over, that person is in
worse shape than at the beginning", Luke 11:26.

The new believer is vulnerable for the return of the
evil with more vigor. The ego rejoices in an imagined
social superiority and even pretends to be brave though
it is the coward within. It becomes weaker in crisis, but
the rigid ego bounces back even. In the 1970's the for-
eign nationals were teaching in schools and healing the
sick in hospitals of Nigeria. A young woman from India
lost her husband in car accident and she could not be
consoled. "God took away my husband from me", she
cried. She loved her husband very dearly.

In this context Jesus said, "Happy are those who
know they are spiritually poor; the kingdom of heaven
belongs to them", Matt.5:3. Human love is limited
whereas the divine love is unlimited. The human love
needs transcendence to enter into kingdom of heaven.
We love God more than we love our children or parents
to enter into that bliss consciousness. It was humanly
impossible to me bear the sudden loss of David nor it
was possible to love him less than God. In the provision His grace alone I am beginning to bear the pain.
A prisoner revealed his sad story last week that he was
put in prison because he killed a man because the man
had molested his dear little girl. The anger blinded his
intellect fully, which is natural from a human perspective, but the good Lord visited him in the prison. He is
born again and confessed his cruel act in the provision
of grace now.

The ego cannot pretend to be you when you are aware of it. It becomes weaker every time you recognize it. The ego has many faces. The Roman persecution of early Christians and burning Christian saints alive by the medieval church were rigid ego actions. Religiosity is not spirituality, but a divisive force in the spirit world. What humans know is only the relative truth. The absolute truth is the conscious experience of the saints. The essence of the absolute truth is lost when the two rival groups fight and shed blood in the name of God. The blood, which was shed in the name of jihads and crusades, was futile. The ego is also expressed as resentment and grievance. A seemingly quiet person bursts into anger spontaneously; he is preoccupied with the fear of disapproval rather than wanting attention. An humble servant too has one kind of ego. Students seek attention through misbehavior and others through sickness. The ego defends its argument at any cost which is one type of violence. Man is his own worst enemy; his pride goes before his fall. The present technology also enhanced human ego.

"We are a new creation in Christ",
2nd Corinth. 15:17.

The new creation lives in the abundance of love and compassion of the Kingdom of Heaven. The ideal of the universal pure soul is translated into a "new heaven and earth." The new Heaven is the emergence of the transformed state of human consciousness and the new earth is its reflection in the physical form. We live in the beauty and freedom of the present moment like the lilies of the forest and the birds of the sky. We live in this world but are not of this world. The light shines forth from us through love and peace. The rich farmer was preoccupied with future sustenance and ignored the present moment of salvation. "Your Father in Heaven knows that you need all these things. Instead, be concerned above everything else with the kingdom of God and with what he requires of you, and he will provide you with all these other things', Matt.6:32-33. God wants us to live in divine provision like the lilies of the forest and the birds of the sky. Whatever is closest to your heart becomes your conception of God. The meek inherit the Kingdom of God because they are receptive to God's love. The arrogance of the riches resists God's love. The sage eats fruit from the tree, drinks spring water and sleeps on bed of twigs. He is at peace.

> "The time has come, he said, and the Kingdom of God is near! Turn away from your sins and believe in the good news!", Mk.1:15.

God calls us to his salvation individually. Whoever responds to his call becomes his child. Gracious God gave us the choice to choose him. The human instinct is to ignore the indwelling light. "Show us thy mercy, O Lord and grant us thy salvation', Ps.85:7. We cannot embrace the moment of inspiration unless granted by Father. The inspiration descends on those who have capacity to respond. We deny ourselves and become perfect in divine provision, Mt.5:43. Jesus is the son of man and the man becomes the son of God. The human relationships without Jesus are bound to be poor. We live in an environment of love and hate situation. The great men of this world also have poor relationships in life. Human love is conditional, but divine love is unconditional and creates everlasting harmony. God's love transcends the human love and needs no wanting. The conflicts between the spouses and friends arise because of the differences in their individual instincts and behaviors. In Jesus, these differences are transcended and conform to unconditional love of God. The friction is buried and harmony is restored in divine provision. God alone changes human souls. "My commandment is this: love one another, Just as I love you. The greatest love you can have for your friends is to give your life for them", Jn.15:12-13.

"Falling in love" intensifies wanting and for a reason the love marriages fail too often. God's love is behind mother's love. The child who is deprived of a mother's love is anxious. The child's pain is the reflection of the mother's pain. A typical mother is more preoccupied with parental role and control rather than the love and endearment with the child. The child wants none other than mother's love. The children who are deprived of a mother's love express withdrawal symptoms in later life too. When David was one year old, it was my duty to put him to bed. One bed time story was not enough. He wanted to spend in story reading more time. Probably he missed me all day and he listened to stories with attention and excitement. I was tired and wished David would go to sleep earlier. At times I even demanded that he should close eyes and sleep. One day I tapped on his right but delicately, expecting the fear induced might induce sleep in return. David's small hand took my hand gently and put it on his small belly and showed me to tap with love. David taught me about parental love to their child. The child has no idea of our frustration and strife at work place. They want love and quality time with parents. My grandson Armaan Raghav, used to sleep long hours on my pot belly and later he used it as a small play ground. He climbed it and jumped down few times as game. Few times, he sought my refuge when his parents wanted to discipline him. Many times I failed him but few times I was helpful in diffusing tension. He is seven years old now. I visited Armaan for this thanks giving in Lexington. In the morning we were both watching cartoons. 'Tata', (grandpa) "you are my best friend, I love you", Armaan said spontaneously. Then he gave me a big hug. Our children will be more fruitful if we nurture them in love. The happiness is elusive, but the freedom from unhappiness is surely attainable. The unhappiness is not caused by an event but by the recurrent thoughts of it. The suffering is both conscious and unconscious and the conscious suffering destroys the evil. That is what Jesus did on the cross. The consciousness evolves in conscious suffering. The discussion is conscious but the argument is unconscious. "Whoever has come to learn about this world has found only corpse", [Gnostics].

"Do for others what you want them to do for you", Matt.7:12.

It is loving your neighbor as thy self. Your love and goodness returns to you. Others are doing to you the same that you are doing to them and what you react to in others is within you. If someone deprived you of love, give it to him in divine provision. Your love disarms Satan. The life is a conceptualized form. The concepts create separate segments, which are unreal.

The universe is an indivisible whole in which nothing exists in isolation. Every event on earth is controlled by one invisible whole. "If your whole body is full of light, with no part of it in darkness, it will be bright all over, as when a lamp shines on you with its brightness', Luke 11:36. We strive to be perfect as our Father in heaven is perfect. We become whole in unity with Christ. The marriage is a glimpse of wholeness. In unity with Christ, life flows in harmony with the nature. The ordinary life is the content, but not the essence of life. We exercise inner non-resistance to what happens beyond our control.

"My God, why thou have forsaken me?" Matt.27:46

We forsake God rather than he forsakes us. We igore his indwelling presence. The face of Jesus Christ on the Cross is the outer expression of inner reality of mankind. The Cross is the symbol as well the transcendence of our pain. The identification with the pain causes more suffering than the pain itself. Our endemic pain from domestic violence and drug abuse is transcended in the redemptive provision of the Cross alone. The inmates I encounter daily in the prison are tired of their suffering and very receptive to receive the redemptive power. "God dwells in me but I left him and ended in the prison. I left, but God did not and he receives me always when I choose to return", one inmate said. The unconscious couple nourishes hatred, but not love in between. The collective pain through the caste system and slavery continue to haunt the nations. The pain is ultimately your shadow. The pain and the vanity of this world naturally inspire us to seek the redemptive grace. Let the grace be the fuel for the emerging light, which emanates always peace and love. The recognition of pain gives power to choose. The pain cannot pretend to be you anymore when you are aware of its presence. The pain is transmuted into positive energy. We mis-identify with pain and must be watchful of its reentry. Jesus committed himself into the Father's hands and said, "It [pain] is finished", Jn.19:30.

> "For everyone who exalts himself will be hum-bled and he who humbles himself will be exalted", Matt.23:12.

The ego always wants to be higher than some body. It is wisdom that you will strive to be better from where you were a year ago. The meek and humble are ready to sacrifice and be at service to others. They inherit the kingdom of God. All knowing includes the duality of the subject and the object. The human experience includes the sense perceptions, the thoughts and the emotions. What the world thinks of as defeat is vic-tory in the sight of God. Jesus suffered unto death on the Cross, but it is the victory in the sight of God. The nature changes. The expansion in birth and the contrac-tion in death repeats. The universe expanded with the "big bang" and it will contract in the end of age. The heart and lungs expand and contract rhythmically. The ego contracts in crisis and expands in front of the vul-nerable. The inner man expands as the outer man con-tracts. We are formless in sleep and wake up into form. TV time degenerates our mental creative power, but the TV evangelism saves souls. Laughter is healing and the smile is refreshing. You are one with the situation in action in consciousness and the solution comes from the situation itself. Attention is the divine presence. Greatness is in honoring the small things and doing them in a great way.

"Blessed are the meek for they inherit the kingdom of God", Matt.5:3.

Love emanates from the meek and they are receptive to the inspiration. 'I did not come to bring peace, but a sword. I came to set sons against their fathers', Matt.10:34-35. The sword is symbolic of an internal fight between the sin and the virtue within us. For the same reason, 'He sets sons against their fathers'. The peace dawns in our hearts in union with the peace of the Prince. 'Those who should be in the kingdom will be thrown out into darkness, where they will cry and gnash their teeth', Matt.8:12. Jesus made this statement in reference those Jews who rejected the offer to enter into kingdom of heaven. 'I was afraid, so I went off and hid our money in the ground. Look! Here is what belongs to you', Matt.25:25. 'Now take the money from him and give it to the one who has ten thousand coins. For to every person who has something, even more will be given ; but the person who has nothing, even the little that he has will be taken away from him', Matt.25:28-29. How can we escape the penalty for ignoring such an abundant Grace. God's law dictates that the one who has more gets more. The servant here falsely anticipated failure. We are to embrace the grace always. The believers know that the world fails, but not God. The unprofitable servant was thrown out in the darkness;

there he will cry and gnash his teeth., Mt.25:30. We discover God's will and fulfill his will. God forgives us that we may forgive others. One who forgives has experienced the value of forgiveness. The sin, which revisits is indeed seeking healing. It is not an affliction.

"You have been taught 'an eye for an eye' and 'a tooth for a tooth', but I say unto you; do not revenge on someone who wrongs you", Matt.5:38-39. "Love your enemies and pray for those who persecute you", Matt.5:44.

The non-resistance is not non-doing and the non-doing is inner non-resistance. Any doing is non-reactive. Yield to overcome the enemy. "Resist not evil" is not compassionate passivity nor indifference toward the evil. It does not include 'run away' from or 'submit' to evil. Jesus chose to conquer the evil in spirit. Surrender in the power of the spirit is truly a victory. We do not fight nor surrender to the evil. The evil fades away in the presence of courage and love and is emboldened in the presence of fear and vulnerability. In fear, the wolf looks bigger than he is. Fear creates evil and it is the same fear, which compels us to fight against evil. Evil fights you back only when you empower it and entertain it. God is not violent in himself nor is he threatened by any external violence. "Do not resist evil", is forgiveness. Forgiveness is love and an action in consciousness. "Love your enemy", Matt.5:44. Love disarms and transforms your enemy. Evil dissolves and recedes in the presence of non-resistance [either internal or external] and the forgiving grace of God. The grace is the power behind the forgiveness. It is unconditional love from

God. God forgives a sinner when he repents. "Father forgive them", Luke 23:34; Jesus prayed on the cross. He resurrected from the dead because of the power of forgiveness. The sinner has no personal experience of his sins being forgiven and so he cannot forgive. The forgiveness is to overlook or look through. Common man, who lives by his sword, cannot understand the mystic power behind the forgiveness. The society of forgiveness does not negate the social accountability to each other either. Your spirit evolves and reaches perfection every time you forgive. Jesus wants us to forgive infinitely.

Revenge is seeking justification for the hurt received. It is the retaliation against the wrong doer who should be held responsible for his wrongdoing. It bleeds when you prick it. It comes veiled in the garment of justice. The scripture reveals that, "You shall not revenge or grudge", rather "Love one another. As I have loved you, so you must love one another", Matt.13:34. You do not revenge against your own hand, which injured your index finger while peeling an apple because it is a part of your body. We all belong to one body of Christ. The grudge is to remember the previous hurt like "You can take my car keys even though you had an accident last time." If you do not give the car keys at all, it becomes a revenge. A good vengeance is that you should not do what your enemy did to you. If you do what your enemy did, you lower yourself to his level. If you swallow poison, you will be sick, but not others. The vengeful thoughts you harbor empower your enemy and you feel powerless. In revenge, it is good to dig two graves. When someone hurts, he retaliates immediately. It is ego action. The pure soul is ocean of love. The ocean receives all turbulent waters calmly. The pure soul does not hurt nor retaliate; rather it forgives and loves the enemy. The forgiveness radiates positive energy and receives positive vibration from the enemy. This is the life changing power of divine grace. If you hurt someone, confess and clear yourself from the guilt. One who hurts someone is because of his/her behavior and instinct. These bad behaviors (samskars] descend even from the past life (Hinduism). Some one cannot hurt you, because you are not what your enemy thought of you.

In our prayers, we pray for forgiveness of our sins as human beings and hardly remember to forgive our wrongdoers because they are human too. Forgive your divorced husband without further empowering him and cease to define yourself as a victim, which you are not. Define yourself in a new role you deserve to be. Remove him from your heart and liberate yourself. Vengeance is universal and a very destructive instinct. The thirst for vengeance is not for justice, but for power. The metaphysics of revenge is to restore your power, which you lost when you were hurt. You cannot liberate yourself from being a victim as long as you harbor the feeling of being powerless. You are the one holding those thoughts; therefore, you are the one to remove all the thoughts of your victimhood. You live powerless as long as the culprit lives in your thoughts. The only power you have is to evict the offender. Remove that culprit and empower yourself. Holding on to the memory of hurt perpetuates frustration in you. Be not obsessive about what is not possible since we cannot rewrite history. When you lose your integrity, you lose more than you gain. Forgiving is an active deed.

Mandela forgave his oppressors, if not; he should have imprisoned himself with hatred. Jesus forgave his pursuers and Joseph forgave his brothers because they both recognized that forgiveness is superior to hatred. Gandhi and Martin Luther King fought the fire with water letting their righteousness prevail over hatred. Harboring vengeful thoughts pollutes your imagination. Letting it go is the best revenge, whether he deserves your forgiveness or not. Every time you forgive, your spirit grows stronger and forgiveness is the marker in identifying the stronger. It is a favor to yourself. Be kind to yourself and forgive.

In the end, evil is your own shadow. A shadow is an outward expression of the inward mind where evil dwells. Virtue and evil are like light and its shadow; they are two opposite ends of the spirit. Evil is the wound inflicted in separation from God, but is healed in union with God. The shadows are nothing but our sins. Grace descends on the repented soul and washes away the sins, which cast darkness in the present reality. Divine grace takes you beyond the human limitations, which are due to evil. The born again soul has transcended the self-constructed walls of separation and fear. A drop of blood represents the whole blood and the drop that is separated from the whole blood decays and dies. The Wisdom alone reveals God, who is our way and life. Embrace eternity before the death ensues. "Love your enemy", Matt.5:44.

Evil is the primary condition of being human. "Resist not evil" is beyond human expectation, but God can do what flesh and blood cannot do. You can love your enemy in Christ's consciousness. Jesus replaced "An eye for an eye" with "love your enemy."

God exists in many dimensions of our consciousness and his reality varies in each level of existence. The changing perceptions change the many shades of the evil. The enemy from outside mirrors the enemy from inside. The purity of your soul mirrors back to you. Violence escalates when an angry man turns his other cheek, but the enemy is disarmed when the saint turns his cheek. Human nature softens when you turn your other cheek. Turning the other cheek gives us the moral superiority and a demonstration of love and forgiveness to the enemy. The evil cannot face the presence of God for who he is. The evil cannot touch those who are in touch with God. Ignore the evil in the confidence of divine will. Do not resist evil only when you are able to resist. A weakling who does not resist evil because of fear is a coward and he has no part with the Kingdom of God. The new creation restrains its power. Jesus did not annihilate the devil in the wilderness, but his death caused by the devil later became the redemptive power of mankind. Evil is our loveless state and the absence of love is filled with fear and hatred which is evil. Love robs the devil of its place to live. The cosmic war continues between good and evil without a winner or a loser. We live in this world plain like doves and clever and alert like snakes. The snake defends itself well from harm. Jesus does not want us to be trapped or drowned by the world.

He is the light of life, Jn.8:12.

"The light shines but the darkness comprehended it not." Faith in God alone removes the veil of darkness and reveals the light. "In him there is life which is the light of men", Jn.1:4. We become that light in Jesus and he wants us shine before all men through love and service. Our destiny is as equal as to his own. We may know him well that we may experience the full glory of Father in heaven. The darkness of flesh and blood is transformed into divine light through us. The light dispels the darkness of our hearts and shows path into the glory of the unknown. Light sees beyond the darkness and perceives only light in the midst of darkness. This is the self-realization. The relativity disappears in unity with God. Jesus descended as the Son of man that the man could ascend to be the son of God. We become what Jesus is through self-realization. The man belongs to the multifaceted intelligence of the universe. In Jesus Christ, he becomes one with the wholeness of this creation. The body cell reflects the wholeness of the body. The universe thinks through us. "Father revealed his knowledge so that the forgetfulness might be destroyed and that we know Father." Gnostics. The forgetfulness disconnects us from God but the return of the memory in the saving knowledge of light reconnects us with God. The pure consciousness is the light and the love and compassion flow out of pure self unconditionally.

"Thy kingdom come: thy will be done on earth as it is in heaven", Matt.6:10.

Jesus viewed the "kingdom of God" as the world of pure awareness. Christ consciousness that dwells collectively in the transformed souls correlates well with the heaven on earth. The heaven is not construed as structural entity as imagined by many faithful Christians. The transfigured soul lives in heaven on earth. The inner transformation brings God's kingdom into our hearts. Uniformly perfected human experience is compatible with the Kingdom of God. The love replaces an "eye for an eye" in God's kingdom and the people live in the freedom of spirit like the lilies of the forest, which neither toil nor spin. It is total surrender to God both in life and in death and living in the present fullness of grace. It is freedom from the illusive past and the nonexistent future. "For what is life? To me it is Christ", Phil.1:21. The rich man stored all the grain for his future security but he ignored the present fullness of grace. "What profits a man who gains the whole world and loses his soul?" Matt.16:26. Owning the illusive world is not a real gain.

"Seek the kingdom of God first", Matt.6:33.

We have choice to embrace or not to embrace such a great salvation. Both the illusion and the reality are in the same mind. The realized mind reaches the inner silence, "Which is God's enduring treasure that no moth comes near to devour", [Thomas]. The kingdom of God is so precious that a merchant found a precious pearl and bought it for himself by all means. The ashrams and monasteries give small glimpses of God's kingdom. The "Foxes have holes, the birds have nests but son of man has no place to rest his head", Matt.8:20. because men resist receiving the Savior. The poor inherit the Kingdom of God because they are readily receptive to God's love and the humble express their love readily to others. God's grace is always sufficient though our faith is insufficient. The seed which fell in the wasteland [truth not received] did not sprout. The birds [Satan] ate some stray seeds and other seeds sprouted but the weeds [world] crushed them. The farmer came to harvest the crop. The salvation is spontaneous and the spirit grows natural like the crop.

"Abide in me as I abide in you; apart from me you can do nothing", Jn.15:5.

Abiding in Jesus connects us to the cosmic intelligence of Father in Heaven. The divine power flows into every cell of our body and the whole body is filled with God's power. The men who abide in each other are not alone and they live in harmony. One who loves lives in his neighbor. The pure consciousness is participating in the flux of cosmic activity even in this moment. We are manifested God consciousness. The branches, which abide in the vine need pruning to bear much fruit. The pure soul is in conscious alignment with Christ consciousness. We are blinking in and out of the cosmic field but the brain gives the illusion of constancy. We go away as much as we stay here. We have no idea where the universe goes when it blinks. The space within and in between atoms is the un-manifested inner consciousness which is the microcosmic version of the outer space. The moment of stillness between the perception and the conception is the Being of our consciousness that created the universes and directs the inner and the outer purpose of our life. The saint rejoices in the stillness of his consciousness because he abides in God both in life and after death. The restless mind stills itself when connected to the cosmic intelligence of Christ. Little faith leads into shallow spirituality and the divine power turns into a mental concept.

Jesus took a piece of bread, gave a prayer, broke it, and gave it to his disciples. 'Take and eat it', he said; 'this is my body'. Then he took a cup, gave thanks to God, and gave it to them. 'Drink it, all of you, he said; 'this is my blood, which seals God's covenant, my blood poured for many for the forgiveness of sins', Matt.26:26-28.

In the ritual of breaking bread we experience Jesus' flesh and blood through bread and vine. "When we swear by the sanctuary, swear by it and by the one who dwells in it", Mt.25:18. We perceive the invisible essence behind the visible holy objects. In essence, idol worship defiles the basic principle that God is an abstract principle. The pictorial images of God and heaven are mental constructs imprinted in our brains, which vary from religion to religion. In dream and death states, we see our favorite angels and gods. "There are many rooms in my Father's house, and I am going to prepare a place for you", Jn.14:2. 'Many rooms' in Father's house', could refer to many levels of consciousness. The saint sees many rooms in his deep trance and faith solidifies every perception into reality. God reveals his glory in many aspects to many. Heaven or Hell is the level of human consciousness. Hell is the lowest ebb of human nature and an extreme separation from God. It is suffering. We live in constant change and uncertainty in the creation. Man can change from human to divinity. Innocence is not lack of knowledge but being simple and plain in human interactions. The sun rises in the east and the sunset in the west is a relative truth. The prophecies are the inspired revelations but not the predictions.

"'Turn away from your sins', John the Baptist
said, 'because the kingdom of heaven is near!'"
Matt.3.2.

The second coming of Jesus Christ is literal for
many Christians, but Jews are still waiting for Messiah.
Many Christian theologians however, agree with the
conception that Lord Jesus would defeat the anti-Christ
in his second coming through a cosmic warfare and
establish the Kingdom of Heaven forever. His second
coming is intrinsically linked to the universal transformation of human nature. It is the translation of
Jesus' prayer that, "Thy will be done on earth as it is
in heaven", Matt.6:10. It should happen today rather
than tomorrow. Salvation descends spontaneously on
those who recognize its need. Keep awake that the alert
soul may capture the arrival of the master of the house.
The five virgins waited with their lamps burning until
the bridegroom arrived. The burning soul aspires salvation spontaneously. The Kingdom of Heaven is within
you and here. "I thank you because you have shown
to the unlearned what you have hidden from the wise
and learned", Matt.11:25. Children's love is natural
and spontaneous. "Let the children come to me for it is
such as these the kingdom of God belongs", Mk.10:14.
Any other love we acquire in this world needs to be
transcended to enter into Kingdom of God. Love thy
neighbor as thy soul [Gnostics]. The woman caught in
adultery showed much love because her many sins were
forgiven. The great sinners are distinctly enlightened.
The alert intellect [*buddhi*] captures the inspiration to
enter into kingdom of heaven. It also calls forth for
urgency and repentance. "The camel can pass through

the eye of the needle but the rich man cannot enter into Kingdom of heaven", Matt.19:24.

It is not that all rich men go to Hell, nor all the poor go to Heaven. The arrogance of the riches is invulnerable to inspiration. The pride that keeps you away from Jesus keeps you away from your soul too. The Jihads and the crusades were fought in the name of God. Terrorism was neither from Islam nor were the crusades from the Christian faith. Jesus Christ was not a Christian nor was the Prophet Mohammad a Moslem. Prophet Moses fought holy wars in the name of Jehovah and the crusades were fought in the name of Jesus Christ. The victories of Prophet Mohammad were in the name of Allah. This is all richness of ego. God's love and bloodshed of war are incompatible. The misdirected collective consciousness creates greater suffering to mankind. "This is the blood, shed for many", Matt.26:27. Jesus said holding the cup [vine] in his hand. The meek and humble surely inherit the kingdom of God.

"Whoever wants to be the first must be last of all and servant of all", Mk.9:25.

God visits us as a servant. The ego wants first place always too, but it is the last in God's kingdom. Wisdom dictates that we compare ourselves as how much we are better today from yesterday rather than comparing ourselves with others. "Thou should exalt and I should diminish", the Baptist affirmed. Be a servant to become a master. The surrender to God is real victory. God never judges but we do. You are judged the moment you judge others. God judges, but he is not judgmental. Karma demands that you are judged now rather than tomorrow. Jesus promised instant paradise to the thief on the cross. "Take the log out of your own eye first and then take the speck out of your neighbor's eye", Matt.7:13. Hypocrisy is evil.

"You do not know either where I come from or where I am going", Jn.8:21.

Jesus said. Similarly, we do not know where the soul is from or where it goes after disembodiment. The matter is the shadow of the spirit. We live in God more than he lives in us. "Where your treasure is, there your heart is", Matt.6:21. What you value high in your heart, becomes your conception of God. The body consciousness is preoccupied with possessions and survival of life. It is a state of isolation and victimization. God wants our undivided devotion. "You cannot serve God and wealth, nor serve two masters", Matt.6:24. Self-denial demands giving up all possessions. The Pope has no possessions except his passport in Catholic tradition. God is whole, but we divide him. The well-fed West and the ill-fed Africa truly divide the creator. The diabolical terms like inner renunciation and good stewardship of riches provide only temporal comfort to our greedy hearts, but not to hungry children. The early Christians gave away all their possessions. What you give will flow back to you. "A good person brings good things out of a treasure of good things; a bad person brings bad things out of a treasure of bad things", Matt.35. We are expected to serve God with all our heart, with all our mind, with all our soul and with all our strength. We can express Him equally through our physical body as much as we do with mind and soul. God's glory unfolds as our consciousness evolves. The body is God's home, which needs good care. You are transfigured when you surrender your whole body, mind and soul to God. You love yourself when you love your enemy and you kill yourself when you kill your enemy. "Love your enemy and pray for those who persecute you so that you may become the children of Father in heaven", Matt.5:44. No one persecutes you other than yourself in the end.

"All authority in heaven and on earth has been given to Him", Mt.28:18. 'That ye love one another, as I have loved you. Greater love hath no man than this, that a man lay down his life for his friends', Jn.15:12-13. Jesus is our redemptive power through his death and resurrection. We love him more than our mother or father to inherit His kingdom.

We owe our life to God. God loved us when we were yet sinners and for us that we may have eternal life. He gives us unfailing rain and sunshine in abundance. The love is the seed of the spiritual quest, which brings God into our flesh. A mother's love is the greatest on earth, but God's love fills every corner of the universe with the same intensity. What Jesus taught us is from his own transcendental awareness and we learn it well when we become part of Him. His yoke is light. The love of this illusive world is directly connected to karmic bondage. Jesus' words that, "I brought the sword, but not the peace into this world", Matt.34:10. is a symbolic expression of the strife in a new believer. The ego fights with the new master. The two worlds live in harmony when Self [divinity], expresses the Kingdom of Heaven. Jesus is beyond time and we can reach him instantly like the apostle Paul did on his way to Damascus. Jesus visited Paul unasked: God cares

137

his children. Greater love hath no man than this, that a man lay down his life for his friend. He is always with us to the end of ages. The spiritual evolution ends here where we become co-creators and participate in cosmic intelligence of Jesus Christ. The wounds heal and the suffering ends in the fullness of time. The degree of spiritual transformation parallels the degree of spiritual evolution. "Heaven and earth will pass away but his word shall not pass away", Matt.5:18. The Word. is eternal that shall not pass. What is imopossible to man, is possible to God, but it demands great faith. "I assure you that if you have faith as big as a mustard seed, you can say to this hill, 'go from here to there!' and it will go. You could do anything!", Matt.17:20. In Christ we become co creators and we can do what all Jesus did. Christ consciousness means harmony of both the worlds.

"Do unto others as would have them do unto you", Mt.7:12.

Every action has reaction, karma responds with what you deserve. The reaction is spontaneous, but may not manifest immediately at times. The world is the mirror of self. Human relationships are hate and love situations. The human being is a combination of perfection and imperfection. The desire less action, is divine. "The measure you will be, the measure you get", Mt.7:2. Your judgment will revisit you. The evil disrupts harmony of inner and outer dimensions of the self. Faith unites human will with God's will. Jesus exists beyond creation. Suffering comes from evil and the redemption comes from Christ. The man who knows that this life is a dream knows the mystery behind the creation. God is active in his immanent nature and inactive in his true being. Inert self continues to serve ego. Only thing we have to fear is fear itself. If one cannot be generous in difficult times, he cannot be generous in easy times. The habit rules the unreflecting herd.

> "We have divine assurance to receive what we ask, find that we seek and the door opens when we knock", Jn.15:7

God bestows our needs in assurance of his faith; He knows our needs before we ask. The human mind is part of the cosmic mind and prayer innately connects us to God. God answers all our prayers according to his will. "Whatever we ask for in prayer with faith you will receive", Mt.21:22. God becomes whole through our salvation and he needs us as much as we need him. Heaven rejoices when a soul is born again. Jesus said, 'Let the children come to me and do not stop them, because the kingdom of heaven belongs to such as these little ones', Matt.19:14. God's will is that these little ones should not be lost to kingdom of heaven. Hindus and Mormon Christians as well believe in salvation in the next world. The soul continue to evolve through many generations until it becomes perfect like Father in heaven who is perfect. The rebirth ends when the desire is dead. No soul is lost in the end. God's love is an action and an experience, but not mere talk. This is God's creation and my creation as well.

"Your faith has made you well", Mt.9:22.
"Faith is the substance of the things hoped for",
Heb.11:1.

It transforms the human soul and heals the human body. "The faith, the size of a mustard seed can move the mountain", Matt.17:20. It does move the mountain of pain from our heart. A saint is a co-creator and he can do what Christ did. "What is impossible to man is possible with God", Lk. 18:27. Faith eliminates the relativity between God and men. Little faith obstructs miracles from happening, Mt.6:30. We are well clothed in divine glory in faith. Your faith in God is the faith in yourself in the end. A steadfast faith [stitah prajna] liberates grace abundantly. The miracle is the living connection with God and it is the by product of our being in Christ. The miracle happens when the outer world obeys the intention of mind. God is beyond time and space. He is there when a piece of wood split [Gnostics]. God is omniscient. 'Your father already knows what you need before you ask him', Matt.6:8.

"First seek the kingdom of God first and all the things will be given to you as well", Matt.6:33.

The mustard seed is small, but the tree is huge that the birds of the air come and make nests in its branches. The invisible kingdom of God is huge in its physical manifestation. "We live not by bread alone but by every word that comes from mouth of God", Lk.4:4. He is patient with sinners. "If that tree does not bear fruit by next year you can cut", Lk.13:9. "Do not store up riches for your selves here on earth where moths and rust destroy, and robbers break in and steal", Matt.6:19. The worldly riches is not compatible with the heavenly riches, for your heart will be always where your riches are. God's love opposes greed. Jesus came to testify to the truth and those who belong to the truth listens to his voice, Jn.18:37. "It is true that he struck the rock and water flowed out in a torrent", Ps.78:20. The life giving water gushes abundantly through the tap of faith. The more you open the tap, the more water gushes out. It is like spring of water gushing up to eternal life. 'I will get up and go to my father and say, Father I have sinned against you. Iam no longer fit to be called your son', Lk.15:18-19. We do not impose our views on an un receptive soul. The incompatibility of consciousness obstructs the free flow of the truth. A pig naturally underestimates the value of a diamond. Consciousness is shared and a thought triggers a response from the cosmic consciousness. The creation is your friend, but the struggle for existence is continuous. God provides our needs in the inner reality of God's kingdom. Hell or Heaven is in your own level of consciousness. Love and faith are the two creative tools, which can solidify the perception into reality. The God of vengeance in Jehovah became the God of love in Jesus. It is shift in consciousness.

"One who loves his life in this world will surely lose it", Jn.12:25.

To be like Jesus, one should deny his life. The power of repentance releases grace. Repentance is a resolve not to sin anymore and the past sins have dissolved in the power of grace. The soul repents and receives eternal forgiveness. Grace is the unconditional love of God. Forgive yourself and others that you may redeem yourself from all your sins. Forgive those who repent because the spirit evolves each time we repent and forgive. The self is the vehicle for transformation of the heart. The man of wisdom builds his house [self] on the immovable rock of Christ. The Kingdom of God is at hand and it is within and outside of us at the same time. "Whoever drinks from my mouth will become like me" [Gnostics]. "Nothing is covered up that will not be uncovered", Luke 12:1. God is omniscient and it is now that you reveal your secret sins to your grieving soul. You are redeemed the moment you reveal your secrets to your God within. "As long as you do not know yourself, you will live in poverty and you will be that poverty" [Gnostics]. The shepherd is not at rest until he finds his one lost sheep. The flock will be whole again after the one lost sheep is found. "For God loved the world so much that he gave his only son, so that everyone who believes in him have eternal life", Jn.3:16. We ignore such a great salvation, which is an act of love of God. "God's kingdom descended as expected but they did not recognize it" [Gnostics]. Jesus praised the virtuous, but did not condemn the sinner. The sick man alone needs the physician. This is the inspiration for salvation. The burning intention of the soul aspires salvation spontaneously. The moment you grab the moment of his second coming; you are in salvation. You are in salvation the moment you know that you are not in salvation. Keep awake to receive the Master like the five wise virgins who waited with their lamps burning until the bridegroom arrived. God created man in his own image. We are precious in his sight. Even a leaf does not fall on the ground without his permission. Even a sparrow will not fall to the ground unperceived by the Father. Birth and death are mystic phenomena and so does the sound of the wind. We do not know its beginning nor the end. W e are born unasked and we come this way and go another way. The wind and the spirit are within us and around us, but we barely notice them.

"No one after drinking the old wine desires new wine", Lk.5:39.

We feel secured in our old environment, but Jesus did not blend the new with the old and he desired that the salvation by grace should be accepted on its own terms. We are saved by faith, but not by tradition or habit. The grace we receive should grow and the light we receive should glow before all men. He who wants to reach Heaven alone shall never reach there. The servant who abused the Master's grace was "thrown into outer darkness where there is weeping and gnashing of teeth", Matt.8:12. 'But some seeds fell in good soil and the plants bore grain', Matt.13:8. We do not know how the seed sprouts. "The farmer goes in with his sickle to harvest" Mt.4:29. God expects the seed of truth, which is planted in the soil of your heart to grow naturally and spontaneously until the day of the harvest. The dormant spirit wakes up through the perseverance of faith. "Because he is his friend, at least because of his persistence he will get up and give him whatever he needs", Luke 11:8. In the parable of wedding feast, those who were invited refused to attend the wedding feast. The master invited the people from lanes and corners and

143

rejoiced the feast with them. The Jews rejected Jesus as savior.

"Whatever you ask for in prayer with faith you will receive", Mt.21:22.

Prayer [dyana yoga] is an innate communion with God. It is a dynamic principle and an applied consciousness. The prayer from the heart needs no rhetoric. The conscious mind converses with God and brings deeper truth to the surface. Our shared consciousness is connected to one underlying substratum, which is God. In the end, the truth communicates with the truth and God is asking God. The giver and the receiver becomes one ultimately. Jesus is the truth and everyone who belongs to the truth listens to his voice. The prayer, which matches well with God's will, is spontaneously answered. All fulfillment ultimately comes from within self. The perception of approval or disapproval of our prayer by God comes from ego. The prayer from ego is neither received nor answered by God. God gives us anything we ask in his name. "He knows what we need before we ask", Mt.6:8. The universe is with you and you receive all you ask for as co-creator. A continuous prayer removes road blocks and takes you closer to God. Christ controls the cosmic events. All authority is given to him, Mt.28:18. He responds in the context of karma of the person in the past, the present and the future. He is there where two or three are gathered in his name. The thoughts and the emotions are floating everywhere in the cosmic world. The collective prayer offered by the saints generates greater spiritual power.

The faith grows stronger in fellowship. One accord in faith strengthens emotional and spiritual bonding.

"Father who sees in secret will reward you", Mt.6:4.

The outer world is the reflection of the inner world. God knows our inner feelings. Our strife in life is due to mismatch in shared consciousness. Life's struggle is between good and evil. The universe reflects unity in body and spirit. The cults with fixed beliefs are plagued with the shared prejudices. Do not intend to impose your views on others. An un inspired soul has no capacity to respond to gospel. The lost sheep are bound to return to God through self-realization, which is spontaneous like the child's birth. The salvation immediately closes the abyss between the illusion and the reality. The Lord's Prayer addresses all aspects of life. Bread is the basic need for life, but we have it in divine provision. "Man lives not by bread alone but every word that comes out of his mouth", Luke 4:4. The Lord's Prayer is for pure existence, protection from evil and forgiveness for trespasses. Prayer opens the mind, evolves the soul and creates close communion with Lord. The soul in evolution brings inner transformation. The saints' prayer is open-ended and surely is answered. A prayer for material gain ends in futility. Cosmic activity is intrinsically connected to our life's events. The prayer is a circular movement with feedback mechanism. An action has its own reaction. Be alert at all times praying, Lk.21:36. The faith, which is the reality beyond our mind, surely rewards you. The light should glow fully to keep the darkness out. It is innate human instinct to return to

Father's mansion. The life is not in abundance of his possessions, because it is all a dead matter.

> "Take out the log out of your eye and then you clearly see to take the speck out of your neighbor's eye", Lk.6:42.

God hates hypocrisy and it is religious fraud. It is human nature to judge others not knowing that we are judged spontaneously the moment we judge others. This is according to the cause and effect of cosmic activity. Do not judge others and bring judgment on yourself. God Judges us all but he is not judgmental. In the end, judging others is an attempt to excuse yourself from wrong. Do not judge others for what you cannot correct yourself. In judging others, the only persons you are talking about is yourself. The talk reveals more about yourself than the one you are judging. The word "judge not" should not prevent us from being accountable to each other. The salvation to the thief on the cross is an event of an instantaneous judgment.

> "For it is out of the abundance of the heart that the mouth speaks", Matt.12:34.

One's thoughts constitute his personality. The thoughts and instincts [samskars] that we acquire from parents, family and environment are stored and the memory recalls them. The positive personality vibrates positive energy. Your positive vibrations influence others positively. This world gives us the reason to live. We cherish our most needed comfort and security from this world. "Do you believe that I can heal you?.

'Yes sir!' they answered. Then Jesus touched their eyes and said, Let it happen, then, just as you believe!' and their sight was restored', Matt.9:28-30. Faith in Jesus is redemptive. Our faith radiates divine energy to our neighbors and relieves their pain too. "You will see much greater things than this!", Jn.1:50. Jesus could have some glimpse of our modern technology and its wonders. Be aware of who you are and be in touch with God that evil may not touch you. God appears when you seek him and he enters only when you open the door. The sage drinks spring water, eats fruit from the tree and sleeps on the bed of soft leaves [Bhartrihari]. "Jesus came to proclaim release to captives and recovery of sight to the blind", Luke 4:19. "I have not come to do away with the law of Moses and the prophets but to make their teachings come true", Matt.5:17. Jesus ful-filled the law in spirit. He gave us freedom from sin and sight to see into wisdom. He promised us the kingdom of heaven that no one has seen, heard and touched. It has never been conceived by human mind. The symbolism and the literalism oppose each other. Understanding all scriptures from spiritual context avoids confusion and fanatic idealism. Spirituality surpasses religion. Jesus is among us as one who serves, Lk. 22:27. "He is the bread of life", Jn.6:35. "He knows the Father because he is from the Father and the Father alone sent him", Jn.7:29. The direct experience with God excludes faith. In unity there is no second.

"That the person who plants few seeds will have a small crop; the one who plants many seeds will have a large crop", 2nd Corinth. 9:6.

Karma demands a reaction for action: a measure for a measure. It expects us to do to others what as we would have them do to us. Karma responds spontaneously as you deserve. The response is revealed at times in the fullness of time. Good actions give good results and bad actions give bad results. The action after salvation is an evidence of faith and the action before salvation takes you closer to God. The liberated soul is above the rule of karma. Man does good to his family and friends, which is karma bound. The mother's love is karma bound. Karma responds according to your merit, but God does not because of his grace. "Do not judge so that you may not be judged", Matt.7:1. Your harsh judgments flow back to you harshly and your generosity returns to you in many fold. This is the law of nature. The ego judges, but God forgives. We forgive that we will be forgiven. "Be merciful as your Father in heaven is merciful, "Matt.5:7. God convicts every soul and restores our divine status. Christ descended that we may ascend to our divine status. Be aware of the beam in your eye and do not rush to throw the first stone.

In the beginning the Word already existed; the Word was with God, and the Word was God", Jn.1:1.

Jesus ascertained his eternity. He transcended the duality and declared unity with Father. Father in Heaven is well revealed in transcendence of duality. Jesus has seen the Father [Jn.6:46]. "In unity we have direct experience. "His spirit within us is gushing up to eternal life like spring of water", Jn.4:14. We ignore the eternal life and speak only of the ones who are dead.

The world is like a corpse and the dead has no vision. Jesus reveals himself to those who are worthy of his mysteries. In unity Jesus is omnipresent. He is there when you split the wood. He is present in every grain of rice. Our life is empty without Jesus. We came empty and will go empty unless we are born again.

"All who take the sword will die by the sword", Matt.26:52.

The sword is also symbolic of ego. We cannot retaliate even what the ego thinks as a righteous cause. The violence is ego born. Jesus' death is not a tragedy of supreme goodness condemned to die nor a tragic figure fated to shoulder the sin of this world. The crucifixion is the redemptive power. The physical life at its most cruelty can be transcended in Jesus Christ. Own the divine world rather than the illusive one. Jesus recognized this world and paid taxes to Romans though he denied this world. The world is real as we live in it. We live here as the lotus in the pond. We are pilgrims in this world. We rather treasure our possessions in the heaven. We act in divine consciousness and pray for our rulers. The deluded mind mistakes possessions as real and its works are evil. "We have to give up our possessions to become disciple of Jesus Christ", Lk. 14:33. "Blessed are those who have not seen and yet come to believe", Mt.13:12. We experience the same Jesus in our hearts today in faith. Recently I spoke in my brother in law Ernest's funeral service in Chicago. I conveyed the same message to all our relatives and friends that 'Earnest has not died but alive in our hearts'. Me and my wife Joy heal daily ourselves with this conviction

149

that David is alive. God's children are not bygone individuals. Jesus is alive today and we can speak to him and he answers to our prayers. God is visible in Christ consciousness. "The faith releases grace in abundance" and "those who have, more will be given", Mt.13:12. The soul expands in evolution. The life and death are two faces of the spirit, which oppose each other.

"Those who abide in me and I in them bear much fruit", Jn.15:5.

Our ordinary lives live between perfection and imperfection. We grow in spirit and become perfect in divine provision of grace. Jesus exists in everybody in a state of God consciousness. He is there surely where two are three are gathered in his name. The collective consciousness is more powerful. The "Word" is the creator of Heaven and the Earth. His word shall not pass away. He cannot see, but he is behind our sight and he cannot hear, but we hear because of him. "Whoever believes that God is lacking in anything is himself lacking in everything" [Gnostics]. God created man in his own image and he abides in every individual. We hear the voice of the wind but we do not know where from it comes or where it goes. So it is with everyone born of spirit. We comprehend God through wisdom. We should not be swayed by the strength of the tradition, but the new faith should be embraced through subjective experience on its own terms. Whoever hears and does not act on it is like a man who built a house without foundation. He is like a spoon in the soup. The spoon has no taste for the soup but the tongue does.

"Ask, you will receive", Matt.7:7.

Both receiving and giving is fulfilled in self. You receive when your will matches God's will. It is God asking God and God giving God in the end. The creation obeys its creator. The mind is after reward but the saint is after God's will. Human intelligence is part of cosmic intelligence. We realize him within the self and see him through faith. Die like Jesus and resurrect like Jesus. The resurrection is victory over evil. The fuel burns and the car runs and so the divine energy burns, the soul evolves and transforms. God created the evil and transcended it and so we do as co-creators. The world flows out from the self and the same world is the mirror of the self.

"For God so loved the world that he gave his only Son, so that everyone who believes in him may not die but have eternal life", Jn.3:16.

Those who believe in him become his children. We are born of spirit first and then we became flesh later. Christ exists in our consciousness as our Being. We become one with Christ through the self-realization. The forgiveness of self and others creates inner peace which out flows and aligns with the peace in others. The peace is not a state of dullness of mind, but it is a state of inactive consciousness. God's children live in fear because of their unresolved hidden sins. The past guilt casts darkness in the present reality. The guilt that haunts you is not an affliction, but crying for healing and requires your attention. Stand in front of God and repent for all your guilt. The trace of ego keeps the pride and the hypocrisy alive. Self-perceptions change in self-realization. In our salvation, the soul does not change, but our perceptions change. The fixed beliefs dissipate when the self-unfolds and evolves. The inner man grows stronger and the outer man grows weaker as the spirit evolves. A child learns through experience and so does the spirit.

> "One who does not hate his wife and children
> or his own life cannot be disciple of Christ",
> Luke 14:26.

Inspiration descends on those who have capacity to respond. and whoever believes in his name shall be children of God. God does think and act through us. He washed his disciples' feet though he is the Master of his soul. We become the Master through the service alone. Consciousness is our ground state of existence. Christ consciousness is a universal expression where we experience our neighbor's pain directly. Our son David died in car accident in 2004. My heart broke when I heard the news of David's death. The pain of sudden and eternal separation from our son was too much to bear. Jesus tells us that we transcend through divine provision alone. Now, after few years, I am able to bear the pain and David's memory is endearing to me in the living hope in Christ. Salvation is conditioned by the conviction, but grace descends unconditionally. Salvation brings in the spontaneous inner change, but the spirit grows natural as the inner resistance is removed through the power of divine grace. We change when our perceptions change and our perception changes as the level of consciousness changes.

God is translated into physical form through love and service. You are able to love your neighbor only when your body, mind and soul are in harmony in Christ. We live in the independence of spirit like the birds of the sky and the lilies of the forest. The universe acts in the present provision of God. It is not overshadowed by the illusion of the past nor the future. The present moment is unpredictable and spontaneous. We expect the unexpected to emerge. The world lives in the security and the comfort of the known. We own all the worlds by disowning this world. The dead soul does not profit by owning the whole world. The saint rules this world because he refused dominion over it.

'We can do all in Christ', Ph.4:13.

The apostle Peter severed the ear of the servant of the high priest in the garden of Gethsemane. Jesus condemned this egocentric act of St. Peter. Peter became the cornerstone of the eternal because he repented for his sins. Pretentious behavior is self-betrayal. The freedom in Christ consciousness releases us from the illusion. All authority in Heaven and on Earth is given to Jesus in unity with Father. Jesus translated the oneness with the Father into experience, which we witness with others. Jesus is with us in our strife with evil. Our spiritual quest ends here in Jesus. Pruning is necessary for believers to bear much fruit. A drop of blood that is disconnected from the whole blood will soon Perish. " But Jesus was asleep. The disciples went to him and woke him up' Save us, Lord! they said', Matt.8:24-25. Jesus' tired body was asleep but his spirit was not asleep. When the dormant soul is asleep, the sin sneaks into.

Jesus is with us to the end. Ask him, you will receive. The sin builds a wall around the person to keep God outside. The mind is a walled city. The wall that keeps God out locks the self in. One day, the unreal walls built by evil crumble down and the evil sneaks out when the savior within wakes up. Life is more than the mirror reflection of the ego because God is beyond the mind.

"I have come to set a man against his father", Matt.10:35.

This is in reference to internal strife within the new believers. Self-victimization and self-doubt haunt you. Faith is shaken when the unreleased pain overwhelms. Those fluctuations become phantoms in presence of God. The self-created pain is bound to leave you. Release your pain and burn it in the consuming fire of Christ consciousness, and inherit the glory of kingdom of God. The pain that surfaces is rather a message than an affliction. The mind filters lot of information through denial, repression and rejection. Listen to the message and release it in divine provision. Unity is the fate, which releases the fate. Family relationships, which are anchored in Christ, "Will be as full of light"Matt.6:22.

"Nothing is covered up that will not be uncovered", Lk.12:1.

God knows our inner strife and frustration. The human mind has an intrinsic connection with cosmic [God's] mind. The moment you reveal your frustration to indwelling God, you are redeemed of your frustration. Repentance releases infinite grace of forgiveness.

We forgive because God forgives. The forgiving soul evolves and becomes perfect. "Let the children come to me and do not stop them, because the kingdom of heaven belongs to such as these", Matt.19:14. Jesus wanted every soul to be saved. He wants no one to be lost. The flock became whole when the lost one lamb was found. Hinduism believes that the soul continues to evolve through numerous incarnations until it becomes perfect like the Father in Heaven, who is perfect. In the end, no soul is lost. This world is like a corpse and one who believes in this world has no life. But who dies for this world gains eternal life. Death is a transition to eternity like the seed sprouts into a new life. Simeon witnessed the full glory of eternity in baby Jesus. Jesus is our way and life; he not only knows our hearts, but also the mystery behind this creation. The heaven is at hand. Embrace it now and rejoice in the glory of eternity.

"I have not come to bring peace but a sword", Mt.10:34.

The sword symbolizes the ego and consequent spiritual warfare within the new disciple. The ego becomes aggressive and fights back one last time before it recedes. The "double edged sword" [Word of God] alone could regress the aggression of the ego. The Word draws definite line with no compromise between the flesh and spirit. "Agree with one another; live in peace. And the God of love and peace will be with you", 2nd Corinth.13:11. The Jewish nation is plagued with continuous violence. The combination of religion and patriotism has become a lethal element in human history. Hindus worshiped war gods and Jews invoked Jehovah before the battles. Islam fought jihads assumingly in defense of their belief. Jesus intended peace both in individuals as well among the nations. He had no part with the zealots. He asked Peter to put back his sword in its sheath. St. John describes the apocalyptic war between good and evil. Revelation is symbolic expressions and a literal understanding of them is misleading. Amish Christians abstain from violence and they live in social isolation that the world may not tarnish their faith. It is a glimpse of Heaven on Earth. Peace, which surpasses all understanding, is the core of all religions.

Any war is egocentric. It is a clash between two absolutes, which never leaves a breathing space for mercy. We know relative truth and absolute truth is beyond the human mind. The nations fight wars to protect their citizens from fear and injustice. The Christian soldier has to kill his enemy though he loves him at heart. It is his duty . There is no just war in Jesus' view. He believed in action that is born of independence of spirit. God, war, love, and violence are extreme opposites. Jihadists and crusaders fought wars in God's name. War and bloodshed are not spiritual.

"Dont be afraid! Stand your ground, and you will see what the Lord will do to save you today", Exo.14:13.

Living in stillness of peace is a fulfilling experience. The small Jewish nation was fleeing from Pharaoh's Egypt and sandwiched by the red sea in front and mighty army of Pharaoh behind. Moses asked them not to be afraid. God consciousness alone is free from fear and doubt. Jesus calmed the raging storm and the fear departed from the disciples. Jesus is God consciousness and his presence was always an expression of love and peace. Jesus' teachings mirrored our day-to-day plane of existence. The truth is an element of change. Jesus saw the truth in the meek and the powerless. He saw more worth in others than they can see in themselves. Today's winner is tomorrow's loser and today's success is tomorrow's crisis. The winner and the loser are the two sides of the illusion. The crisis of today becomes the peace of tomorrow. The love of today turns into hatred of tomorrow. A new problem arises in the place of the old one resolved. The oppressor and the victim, the wrong doer and the wronged and the weak and the powerful all exist in us. Let us discover the distance between us and our Self. The rule of Self creates all positive energy.

"Jesus is with us to the end of ages", Matt.28:20.

Jesus lives in timelessness, but we live in time. The past and the future blends in the present moment. The present moment is inactive consciousness. The fear from the past memories and the future anticipations haunts the ordinary human lives. The fear persists in the present moment when the past memories and the present experiences mismatch. The past memory overshadows the repressed anger in the present moment. The pain is after all, self–created, but the pain that surfaces is not afflicting, but rather seeking healing which is sought in divine grace. The pain of the memory of David's death ten years ago surfaces, but it is not afflicting in the pro-vision of grace. It is endearing to me rather than the total transcendence and complete loss of the memory.

157

Grace unfolds the truth and heals the wounds. Hope in the future dissolves the fear and the anxiety. Peace is not a passive state, but a dynamic inactive consciousness. Positive energy abounds around you. The soul, which is anchored in Christ, never falls from grace. Christ consciousness is a shared phenomenon and you are not alone if you abide in him. We live in harmony when we abide in each other. We become perfect like the Father in Heaven who is perfect.

> "Those who hate their own life in this world will keep it for life eternal and those who love their own life will lose it", Jn.12:25.

The life is the product of interaction between body and mind. The body nurtures the spirit. We worship God with all our body mind and soul. The world gives us the reason to live but God and the world oppose each other. Jesus revealed the illusive nature of this world and urged us to embrace the Kingdom of God. The truth is the subtle essence but the physicality is the appearance. The level of self-evolution parallels the degree of character. In spiritual transformation, our perceptions change, but God remains the same. Faith fluctuates when the perceptions fluctuate. The enlightened soul is in participation in the flux of cosmic power even at this moment. The innocence is being plain in human interactions. Self-created love is an illusion and God's love fills every corner of the creation with the same intensity.

> "Whichever one of you has committed no sin may throw the first stone at her", Jn.8:7.

Jesus forgave the woman who was caught in adultery and she was freed from public prosecution. She repented and received grace from God. The social condemnation is not compatible with love and forgiveness of Jesus Christ. He wants to seek the solution through independence of the consciousness rather than the law. The change rooted in law is transient. Jesus was behind the despised and the deprived. The Good Samaritan and the Samaritan woman were well credited in God's sight. The spirit transcends the division and gender prejudice. The women's proximity to God is no different from the men's. Jesus came to fulfill the law and he did it in spirit. The moral responsibility of the church is to bring conviction rather than condemnation. We vilify Eve for bringing sin into this world and we idealize Mary for bringing us salvation; both have a supernatural legacy. The women are known for both the sin and the salvation. The eunuch from Ethiopia was baptized by Phillip and became a disciple of Christ. The character and the personality of a person transforms in divine provision. All crises are passing affairs. Heal yourselves from within and transcend the prejudice. Separation becomes unity in Christ consciousness. Do not pretend to be what you are not.

Abortion of Foetus.

"You will know the truth and the truth shall set you free", Jn.8:32.

We know only relative truth. God alone is the absolute truth. The truth in you only gets stronger when you relate it with the truth in your neighbor. The collective consciousness is stronger. In collective entities, there is conformity and mutual assurance. What we think is the absolute truth can be blind truth and the relative truth which we know is not weak either. In the end, the truth alone sets us free. There is no truth in evil.

Fetal abortion issue affects women. All religions and many nations oppose abortion. The nations debate and the families divide on the issue of abortion. Some seek violence to stop abortion. Violence is the self-righteous intolerance, which arises from inner fear. It is ungodly. Rather, seek the remedy in the independence of consciousness in divine provision. The love of God transcends the fear of evil. Tolerance or intolerance to the issue brings no positive change. Hatred between the two mirrors only hatred. The external appearances conflict with the inner feelings. Jesus did not encounter any abortion issue during his earthly ministry. Hinduism disapproves of abortion even for fetal malformations, that the abortion may not interrupt the karmic debt. The female infanticide and the dowry menace are still endemic in India. The abortion of a vulnerable infant is one type of violence. The ahimsa of Hinduism and the love of Jesus Christ are not compatible with abortion. It is traditional for Nigerian women to seek abortion before they travel [hajj] to Mecca. They use toxic herbs for abortion and land in the hospital in a comatose condition. As medical missionary at Garkida mission hospital, I could not reverse those herbal toxic effects. The polygamous society with man's desire for many children usually opposes abortion. The blind belief kills both body and soul. The social status of women should be no different from men. We have two sons, Abner and David. Soon after David's birth by cesarean section we opted for tubal ligation. Joy ended up having ectopic pregnancy and another surgery. After we lost David in 2004, the soul grieved that we should not have opted for tubal ligation. A resident of Garkida in Nigeria, had 5 children. He was a good Christian and worked as building supervisor to our mission station. His wife had tubal ligation by me after that fifth child. The small baby girl died of severe viral lung infection when she was six months old. The rumor in the village was that the baby died of a curse from God because her mother had tubal ligation. The Christian conscience is in constant strife to be sensitive to the needs of the secular society without compromising with the spirit. God forbids church using violence to stop or prevent abortions. The Savior was more into the transformation of souls. The saint has transcended both the birth and the death. Global shift in consciousness is the ideal, Jesus advocated in his earthly ministry.

The waves are the essence of the ocean. We are from God and we will be absorbed into the same source in the end. Life is a blessing and death is a dream. The infinite God is beyond the finite nature of our God and your God. The egocentric master this world. The ego produces success and failure and also pleasure and happiness. Your thoughts become creative and the emotions become positive. The welfare of mankind becomes your goal. The addiction gives initial pleasure and pain in the end. The addicted mind cannot make any choice. You will see the light in the provision of grace the moment you misidentify with the mind of addiction. The born again soul becomes visible in physical world through love and service. Jesus let the devil kill him on the cross. He chose to transform it through grace. His divine power became redemptive power.

"Blessed are the poor", Matt.5:3

This reality contrasts with the world knowledge of the rich are the blessed. The poor in ego are eager to love and serve and they are vulnerable to God's love too. We look poor in our relationship with infinite God. They naturally inherit the kingdom of God. God provides infinite grace in our spiritual poverty. We are human because we are able to love, but not that we are able to think. The arrogance of riches opposes the divine humility. The rich need to squeeze themselves through the eye of a needle to inherit the kingdom of God. The merciful are shown mercy. The outflow of mercy is readily replenished with the inflow of divine grace. The heart, which is stagnant with hatred, has no room for inflow of mercy. The cross we bear precedes the crown we wear.

"Blessed are those who mourn", Matt.5:4

The grieving soul unfolds and yields to divine inspiration. In crisis, the helpless mind craves for God's grace. Healing begins when you mourn for your lost son. The healing begins when you repent and mourn for your sins. Jesus cried on the Cross, for the Father left him alone. He was a wounded healer. He was one with Father when he committed his spirit to the Father. The meek are not week and they inherit the kingdom of God. The saint's hunger is quenched by divine intimacy and the hunger of ordinary men is quenched by food. The saint's thirst is quenched by living water and the hunger in Christ is quenched by his righteousness. "Human beings cannot live on bread alone", Lk.4:4. We live by every Word that comes out of God. The heavenly treasure benefits both here and in heaven. The peacemakers are blessed. They oppose evil and call people for justice. To suffer is not to fail.

"We are the salt of the earth", Matt.5:13

The salt from the Dead Sea evaporates its salty component and loses its salty taste. We are called to make the difference that salt does. Our light should transmit through love and service to the world around. Jesus knows the human potential to become one with God. His word comforts and convicts as well. Grace descends and brings change within you and around you. The pure soul builds up relationships of love and peace. God's perfection is revealed in Jesus Christ [Eph.4:15]. God's love makes you love your enemy. Your love is more empowered than the hatred of your enemy. Harboring a resentment deep within is one kind of violence. God judges more the motif behind the action rather than the action itself.

"If the people in that house welcome you, let your greeting of peace remain; but if they do not welcome you, then take back your greeting", Matt.10:13.

The communication does not flow when there is mismatch in consciousness. Preaching gospel to an un-inspired soul is like throwing diamonds in front of pigs.

One who kills has destroyed his victim's value before he kills him. A carnal look at a woman makes you an adulterer. The emotional depth of your heart is already shared before sharing the physical intimacy. Adultery is seeking intimacy outside marriage. Pornography is one type of adultery. Marrying a divorced woman is adultery. Mutual trust is lost in divorce. The conscious spouse can vibrate positive energy and transform the unconscious spouse in divine provision. It is like forgiving your enemy or neighbor because he/she does not know what they are doing. The prayer offered in a secret place is the measure of depth of your relationship with Jesus. The true prayer has audience of one. The fasting prayer has no worth if the pain is paraded. The ego gives what world wants and it receives what the world gives, but the saint gives what God wants and receives what God gives. Prayer is not to convince God, but to recall his love for us. A weak church in prayer is weak everywhere. The un inspired soul cannot respond to Gospel message and a pig has no value for a diamond. False prophets are known by their fruit.

> Glory of grace. 'When Jesus saw how much faith they had, he said to the paralyzed man, "Courage my son! Your sin are forgiven", Matt.9:2.

Great sinners receive much grace. The woman who washed Jesus' feet showed much love because her many sins were forgiven. We live and survive through grace alone. Abundant grace is ready to descend on those great sinners, if they repent. Judas never repented for betraying Jesus, but Peter repented for his lies and received abundant grace. Jesus chose to build his church on that rock of Peter. St. Paul., who suffered the church also repented and became an apostle of gospel. Grace was extended to those who killed Jesus We love our enemy and pray for those who persecute us. The ideal of the Sermon on the Mount is beyond human reach. We stand before God on the ground as sinners and seek his redemptive grace. In Jesus, there is neither Jew nor Greek, or male or female. He replaced God's exclusive holiness with inclusive grace. A good man and a sinner have no moral difference. We matter to God and one lost sheep is precious to the shepherd. When the lost sheep is found, the flock becomes whole. Jesus was unhappy to die, but endured to the end through grace alone. The bird caged for years is afraid of flying into the freedom of the skies. We do not need to seek Jesus like the wise men from the east because he is indwelling in all of us. He is the source of all healing and power. "But Jesus refused to answer a single word, with the result that the Roman governor, Pilate was greatly surprised", Matt.27:14. Pilate said that he had power to release or crucify Jesus and Jesus reminded Pilate that his power was from God.

"Everyone who asks receives and everyone who searches finds", Mt.7:8.

All healing comes through faith. Faith creates the miracle, but the miracle cannot create the faith. Faith the size of a mustard seed moves the mountain; God creates and dissolves the mountains. The miracle suspends the laws of the nature. It is a supernatural rescue and a living connection with God. Jesus turned water into wine. In nature, the vine absorbs water and turns it into vine in the presence of sunlight. In the last supper, Jesus turned wine into blood and said, "Drink, this is my blood which is shed for many", Lk.22:17. If people believe in miracles, there is no room for faith. Your faith in God is ultimately the faith in yourself. The Self is indwelling God. Man was born blind that God may be glorified through his healing. A sign is a marker for the right direction. The miracle is an early glimpse of restoration. Jesus raised Lazarus from the dead. "If your hand or foot makes you lose your faith, cut it off throw it away!' Matt.18:8. Of course, we fulfill this commandment in spirit. A miracle cannot convict a sinner. Gospel alone convicts a sinner. One who cannot be convicted of Gospel message, cannot be convicted even by a miracle like physical raising of a dead person. Similar message was conveyed to rich man in the hell by Abraham. I know two Hindu converts in my village. They believed in Jesus because their daughter was healed from kidney problem in Jesus name. The other had a son named after Jesus (Jesupadam) who happened to be my school mate in high school. Their belief was limited to rituals and few good deeds. God monitors our lives more intimately than the self, itself. He knows the count of our hair and he knows the fall one single hair.

All healing points to Eden where there was no lame or leper. God's children live in the abundance of their Father. God clothes the grass of the field so well that he would take care of his children much more. The fear of the Lord springs forth the wisdom. The man of wisdom builds his house on the rock.

"Seek the kingdom of God first that all other things will be given", Matt.6:33.

The Kingdom of God is your inner experience of the reality of God. Its fulfillment is in the state of Christ consciousness. Easter is the death and the resurrection of Jesus Christ. It is our death and resurrection, too. We experience the presence of Christ through the resurrection power and it is through faith alone. The Easter experience is the new heaven and the new earth with the resurrected bodies. God did not remove the cup in Gethsemane. Christ, who promised living waters, became thirsty. He became sin for us, but he defeated it on the cross. The moral power has a disarming effect. The thief on the Cross perceived power in the powerless and asked Jesus to remember him in his kingdom. God chose the way of weakness. He chose love, which is a unilateral divine disarmament. Love absorbs evil power, which is the root of suffering. The scars have become life and they remain as memory.

"The gates of hell shall not prevail against the church", Matt.16:18.

The church is nothing, but the Kingdom of Heaven on Earth, which sprouted when Jesus died on the Cross. The Cross is where human perfection is realized in divine provision. It is the transition from pain to healing and death to resurrection. The church in time is also crucified. The disciples received an angelic voice that, "he will return in the same way",Acts 1:11. They experienced the presence of resurrected Jesus in their hearts. We find him always within. God's love is expressed through us. We see Jesus in the poor and the destitute. They too, teach us to love them. However "what we suffer at the present time cannot be compared at all with the glory that is going to be revealed to us", Rom. 8:18. The suffering for a right reason is redemptive. The Kingdom of God is small like a mustard seed, but it spreads and gives love and comfort to the poor and the sick. The farmer sowed the seeds. The birds ate some and the weeds engulfed some. In the end, few seeds bore the fruit. Few of us choose God. God expects good harvest from us and he comes with a sickle to harvest.

"We love one another that all men know that we are his disciples", Jn.13:35.

The new creation denies self and embraces the cross. The inner change brings outer change. The early martyrs fought the sword with the Word. We are still groaning because the confession of every tongue is not completed. "I am the Lord, and I do not change. And so you, the descendents of Jacob, are not yet completely lost...Turn back to me and I will turn to you", Malachi, 3:6-7. Change within brings outer healing. Grace descends on those who are able to receive. Jesus respected the self-respect of the individuals. He revealed himself to the Samaritan woman. He ate with the sinners and the tax collectors. He died for those who opposed him. Jesus transfigured human nature in his second coming. He is no more a baby in the manger in his second coming. The prophets and kings did not see nor did hear his voice, but we see him and hear his voice every day because he lives in us.

"God's kingdom is within every born again soul", Luke 17:21.

The saint rejoices heaven within every second. He is one with God [Brahma purusha]. God [upasya] and the saint [upasaka] become one in the end. We are his kingdom because our righteousness exceeds those of the Pharisees. Jesus saw Heaven as the world of pure awareness. "It is such as these children the kingdom of God belongs",Matt.19:14. "Jehovah lives in the highest heavens and his throne is in the pillar of cloud", Eccl. 24:4. You love yourself when you love your enemy and you kill yourself when you kill your enemy. Christ consciousness is compatible with human nature when it is uniformly perfected. We love our enemies and pray for those who persecute us. We will be merciful because our Father is merciful [Lk.6:36]. God gives sunshine and rainfall to the good and the bad people. The great sinners are distinctly enlightened. "Remain united to me, and I will remain united to you", Jn.14:4. We express his love when we remain united with him. God's love is an action and an experience, but it is not mere talk about it. God becomes whole and his purpose is fulfilled in our salvation. God loves us for his sake too. The murderous cross in the hands Romans is transformed into a redemptive force in the hands of God. The crucifixion is the evidence of extreme cruelty of both God and man. It is the bridge between the death and the life. "We are healed by his wounds", 1st.Pet.2:24.The cross gives us hope where there is no hope. Jesus conquered death by dying. He revealed the Father's full glory that we know how far we fall below the divine standard.

"Let not your hearts be troubled", Jn.14:1.

The mind is delusion. It is entwined with the illusive past and the future, ignoring the present provision where the salvation lies. An emotion is the mind's expression to the body's needs and a thought is the mind's reaction to the body. The brain produces thoughts and the physical body produces emotions. Anger and the fear are the negative emotions with negative energy. Love and peace are positive emotions. The body, thoughts and emotions are interdependent, but any change in one effects a respective change in others. The emotional excesses result when the mind feeds the body with false messages. A seemingly sober person suddenly bursts out with anger because of subconsciously built in anger. In fear, the mind lives in the future, which creates a sense of continuous threat. The unconscious mind wants you somewhere other than where you are now. The future has no real existence. It is the only escape from the unpleasant present. The present has existence, but you have to embrace it to have it. The attention to the future blinds you to the present reality. The unconscious mind fades away when you become conscious of it. Its awareness inspires you to seek God. Offer your ego mind as fuel in the sacrificial flame of Christ consciousness where the mind ends. The consciousness without thought is one with God. The man alone bridges the world with God. The passion for the illusive past and the future dissolves in Christ consciousness. The desire to control others is indeed a weakness, but it disguises as strength. Resentment is the masked resistance to the divine inspiration.

"Husbands love your wives and wives obey your husbands", Eph.5:25.

Obedience is love too. The love born of ego cannot sustain the marriage relationship. The failure of some love marriages is due to ego born love. Do not react to the unconscious behavior that you may not become unconscious too. The world is dear to us and we derive our most needed identity from ego, so we are afraid to lose it. We choose an unhappy, but familiar life. You cannot change yourself or others unless the change comes from a spiritual awakening. The awareness of unconscious behavior is the moment of salvation. Embrace it before it slips. God alone dissolves dishar-mony in marriage in the loving embrace of divine grace. The husband and wife relationship is comparable to the relationship of God and the creation. The disharmony due to a clash of egos dissolves through mutual love and respect. The discussion is wisdom and the argu-ment is ignorance. The ego prevails in argument and disappears in agreement. The argument mirrors each other's pain only. Success and failure are one, but sep-arated by the illusion. Life is like a lake with turbulence on the surface and stillness at the bottom. The world has died in the saint before he dies and he finds neither death nor ego after he dies. His presence absorbs the turmoil of others. The surrender to God is victory and freedom. The spirit unfolds in surrender and becomes a living reality.

"It is God who clothes the wild grass-grass that is here today and gone tomorrow, burned up in the oven. Wont he be all the more sure to clothe you?...So do not start worrying: Your Father in heaven knows that you need all these things", Matt.6:30-31.

The lilies of the forest live today, but not tomorrow. Tomorrow shall take care of itself in divine provision. What I am today is because of what I was yesterday and the present dictates the future. Tomorrow has no independent existence. The illusive past and the future become alive only in the present. The future salvation promised by the cults is to escape the imperfect present. The future is a phantom in the end. The future is in the timeless realm of Jesus Christ. The past ceases to haunt you when you die to every moment in the past and live every moment in the present. Capture the present moment of salvation like the five conscious virgins who had oil [consciousness] and the burning lamps [spirit]. The virgins rejoiced in the arrival of bridegroom and the wedding feast [salvation]. The awakened soul embraces the moment of salvation. God appears directly in crises.

The news I received on Friday the 13[th]of Feb. 2004 at 9 p.m. was extremely painful. David, our second son had died in a car accident and my wife, Joy, was critical. I reached Albany, Ga. and saw David on the mortuary table and Joy in the critical care unit. David was born again when he was eight years old. He studied at Emory and Mercer universities and was living in Atlanta as a website developer. A strong person as body builder, but he is no more now. The eighteen-wheeler truck hit him and his Mercedes Benz car in the front end. Mrs. Carter and her husband, Dr. Carter were at the site of the accident. Later, they told me that David had answered with a smile on his face, "I am David Rayapati from Vidalia". God's presence could not comfort my broken heart. The memories now, after ten years, are more comforting than afflicting in divine provision. The world ends in direct experience with Jesus Christ. The man should not be afraid of asking God for help.

"If your eyes are sound, your whole body will be full oflight", Matt.6:22.

It is the law of nature that whatever is exposed to light itself becomes light. The sin veils the light like the clouds veil the sun light. The darkness of life fades away in the presence of the light. The moment of still-ness between the perception and the conception carries the truth and that is the moment of salvation. The truth emanates from that moment and transforms the son of man into the Son of God. Attention is the focused power of consciousness; it is a state of liberation from the mind. The inner cleaning removes the outer pollution. The ego admires the outer beauty of the flower, but ignores the inner divine glory of it.

"Then it goes and brings along seven other spirits even worse than itself", Mt.12:45.

When the wisdom dawns, the evil becomes aggres-sive. The spirit oscillates in and out as the perceptions of the spirit fluctuate. Today's love will be tomorrow's hatred. The ego rises and falls in our uncertain life. The wisdom blocks the reentry of the evil. The wisdom learns from the mistakes, but the mind repeats the mistakes. The past memories overshadow the present and the lack of true conviction arrests the spiritual growth. The past emotional pain and the present new experiences con-flict often. The solutions descend spontaneously and the moment of change arrives quietly. This is the moment of salvation, which we should embrace. The world is the reflection of the self and the life is an interaction of the body and the mind. The negative energy of flesh and blood becomes a memory by tomorrow in divine provision. The memories are the shadows of the past. We resolve them from within but should not externalize them and blame others. The afflictions, which are haunting, are seeking your help for remedy. The physical body shelters the spirit body. The body, mind and spirit rejoiced in cosmic life in their undifferentiated state prior to their fragmentation. The inner Christ within is the resurrected [causal] body. The causal body grows stronger as the outer body becomes weaker. The human consciousness is in between the manifested and the un-manifested. Christ is at the threshold of the form and the formless. The prosperity is the riches in body mind and soul. The poor man who becomes rich and still feels poor is unconscious. The man who is not contended with what he has now will never be contended with the riches he may have in future.

> "If a man divorces his wife for any cause other than her unfaithfulness, then he is guilty of making her commit adultery. If she marries again and the man who marries her commit adultery also", Mt.5:32.

God holds us responsible for the sins committed by our dear ones. The church conveniently ignores this scripture most of the time. The church is symbolic of the bride and Jesus is symbolic of the bridegroom. The divine whole is realized through marriage, which unfolds the divine purpose of this universe. Marriage ends the duality and gives us a glimpse of bliss in life. It is an unconsciously sought salvation. The strife in marriage relationship brings out pain. Avoiding relationships do not prevent pain either. The human love is one kind of addiction. The addiction is unconscious refusal to face or bear the pain. Any addiction starts with pain and ends with pain. The conscious behavior with love and forgiveness dissolve disharmony in marriage relationship. The divine love is not selective like sun light. It emerges in times of crises that we accept the crisis and open the window of salvation. You are free from pain the moment you recognize the crisis. The communion is the best communication. The burden of pain awakens the spirit and the inner transformation eliminates disharmony in relationships. The awareness of pain creates space for the love to enter. It is the moment of salvation and new birth of consciousness. Accept your spouse as she or he is in the loving embrace of Christ consciousness. A born again wife is a source of enlightenment to her husband. The silence behind the mind controls the noise in the front. The relationships built on the rock of Christ sustain forever. The ego shrinks in the presence of love of Christ. A seventy-eight-year-old prison inmate came into prison in his teen years and still has no parole date in sight. Asked whether he is hostile to society for incarcerating so long; no, he answered. Rather, he is grateful to the society because his enemies could have avenged and killed him long time ago if he were outside. Moreover, he is enlightened man now. He realized light from Lord and knows well what God's will is now. With a delinquent family background, he grew up in the environment of drugs and liquor addiction. He is hoping to go home one day to live for himself and others as well. I assured him that God fulfills a saint's prayers.

"Forgive others, and God will forgive you", Lk.6:37.

Forgive your brother before you worship in the church. Your true Being is revealed in forgiveness and negative energy is depleted. The harmony in relationships is restored. The consciousness bridges the man and God. The awareness that we are all from one consciousness dissolves the notion of "chosen people." You will be unconscious when you react to an unconscious mind. The unconscious mind alone judges others and it is unconscious to be judgmental. No judgment is not meant to be no thought and no thought is not meant to be no dynamic. Love drives away the judgmental behavior. The spirit relives and misidentifies with mind in inspiration. The salvation is through us after all. The wood placed next to fire becomes fire and gospel we preach saves souls. After all, salvation is in the end is through us. A ripple is part of the ocean.

GAY People: "Adulterers and homosexuals...none of those will possess God's kingdom",1st Corinth. 6:9. Gay behavior is one kind of adultery. The perceptions and behaviors transform in the power of confession and forgiveness. The Ethiopian eunuch transcended spiritual and social afflictions through self-realization. He became a new creation in Christ and the new creation alone inherits the kingdom of God. There is always stillness beneath the sorrow. The dormant forces become alive in faith. We are only critical about the homosexuals, but tolerant to the adulterers. We are also well accommodated with the divorcees and the remarried couples in violation of scriptures. All fulfillment is in human consciousness, which is above this world. Jesus forgave the woman caught in adultery because she repented. Yahweh destroyed Sodom and Gomorrah because of adultery in the cities.

"The laws are made for the immoral and the sexual perverts",1st Tim. 1:10. Some civilizations have tolerance for homosexuals. Eunuchs played significant roles in the royal harems of the ancient world. In India, new couples seek blessings from homosexuals that they may not have a homosexual child. For secular society, homosexuality is as valid as the expression of heterosexuality. They argue that the moral rejection of homosexual behavior should not be the basis for the discrimination against a homosexual person. The experience of physical love between two people of the same sex may be engaged and experienced for the sake of art of love, [Kama sutra]. Nations have changed their constitutions to accommodate the demands of gay people whose role has expanded in all spheres of society. "Same sex" marriage is progressive though highly controversial in social and spiritual arenas. It may be that the time has come to resolve gay people's suffering. The idea whose time is come perfectly aligns with divinity and knocks on your door for fulfillment. The power of an idea that is in alignment with spirit finds its fulfillment in the fullness of time. Each one of us is God's unique idea whose time has come. God has purpose in every one of us. A man who is hungry can teach us about love and compassion. Gay people remind us that we need to love them in their strife. We become what we think and we receive what we give. God gives always, but evil neither gives nor receives. As a prison physician, I hear frequently from the homosexual inmates that their behavior is not acquired, but inborn. God created us the way he created other people. God accepts us the way he accepts others. Their demand for medical care to express their inner nature more perfectly is well recognized by the Georgia state government.

The church loves gay people, but not their behavior. I have discussed this at length with a few of the inmate population. The gays are in significant numbers in correctional facilities because they are vulnerable to illicit associations and recreation drugs. They become criminals under a drug influence. Some have even ended up in prisons because they were violent in self-defense against hostile groups in society. Many of them are social and spiritual thinkers. Some believe that they cannot transform themselves in the provision of grace and practice celibacy as the church wanted them to be. God has his provision for them too because they are created by none other than God himself. They reject scriptural texts as flaws of scripture writers. A few other gay inmates confided in me that it is practical for a homosexual to believe in Christ and fulfill the expectations of the church. The majority rules in both the church and society. However, the church should not be critical about gay rights provided by the constitution.

"The lion shall lie down with the Lamb", Isa.11:6.

Kingdom of heaven is one big bliss consciousness. It transcends race and gender differences. The gay community may seek social justice through the Constitution, which oversees the sanity and the security of society. The laws are above prejudice and tailored to the needs of changing times. Compassion is superior to empathy; in compassion, empathy merges in the joy of Being beyond form. The joy from within is uncaused. Wisdom dictates that we all live in harmony on this planet.What you are, rather than what you say, transforms the souls. Success is followed by failure and both the failure and the success end in failure in the end. Accept whatever comes in the way of your destiny. Think of sickness as the rest from the stress. You will be at peace when you accept the annoying noise from the road.

"You will know them by what they do", Mt.7:16.

The strength of one's character depends on the depth of his faith. The false prophet is known by his fruit. The world's perception of you is the reflection of your state of consciousness. Each one of us is unique in his/her reflection and the perception of him/her by the world. The multiplicity of this universe is connected to one underlying oneness. We ignore the surface ripples and embrace the one stillness in the depth of the lake. The stillness comes in when you forgive yourself and others. The weak mind disobeys God. Abraham obeyed God's call and became a blessing to all nations. The internalized pain only expands and the pain you project causes pain in others. Jesus asked us to pray for those who persecute us that we may be the sons and the daughters of the Father in heaven. In the end, those who persecute us are none other than ourselves. Accept the internal when you cannot accept the external. The suffering for higher purpose is redemptive. If that is your crucifixion, it will be your resurrection and ascension.

"Those who remain in me, and I in them will bear much fruit", Jn.15:5.

A drop of blood decays if it does not abide in the whole blood. I am one with Jesus if I abide in him even in this life not after death. The spirit becomes alive in the presence of inspiration, which connects or reconnects us with God. We call upon him any time and abide in him always. He visits his people again and again. The world cannot touch me when I am in touch with him. The evil cannot force us to be what we are intended to be. One sick cell affects the whole body and an individual's actions affect the whole society. The saint reaches others like a seed thrown in the river, which roots and bears fruit elsewhere. He is Self-living from the mind. He has nothing to prove and nothing to attain. He does small things in a great way and he creates uncommon things from common things. He desires conscious death. Aim high and set your goals high in divine provision. Michelangelo found danger in setting lower goals and achieving them in comfort. Not having a goal is feared more than not reaching a goal. Know your goal that you may know when you arrive there. The apostles want us to aspire things in divine provision. We do not rest on yesterday which is no more and we do not worry about tomorrow which is not yet come. What we teach is what we learn and it is good to teach enough that we may learn it all. The teacher appears when the student is ready. Sharing reduces wanting. Nobility is not being better than someone but being better than yourself. The mind fears the unknown. We do not search for God because he indwells in us.

"Up to the present the whole creation and in all its parts groans as if in the pangs of child birth", Rom.8:22.

The suffering you deny expands within and become internalized. The projection of your pain causes pain in others. The death of ego is the end suffering and the ego dies spontaneously with self-realization. Let your ego die before you die. The evil and good live side by side. The duality between the perceived and the perceiver ends in Christ consciousness. Each mind has its own perception of this world. Compassion is superior to empathy. Empathy merges with the joy of being beyond form in compassion. We realize the real through the unreal physical body. The non-violence is non-doing but doing without reactivity. Deal with evil with wisdom and without reactivity. It is an action less activity without inner resistance. The resistance is a weakness. Heaven is collective bliss consciousness. Let the will of God be your resurrection and ascension.

We are all members of one body, Eph.4:25.

We are little images of God. We represent God as a single drop of blood represents the whole blood. Nature changes; ice changes to water. Inner change reconnects us to the Father in heaven. The change in consciousness comes from the change in awareness. We are what we think and we get what we think. The transcended soul is empowered with divine grace. We refuse to live in fear because it is false evidence appearing as real. Our tragedy is our vibration match to fear. The fall from grace only propels you to higher grace. The universe functions through the law of attraction and you attract to what happens to you. The tragedy is the power of an idea whose time has come for fulfillment. What will be, will be. Go there to get here.

"Let everything you do be done in love", 2nd Corinth. 16:14. The action in love is superior to the knowledge about it. One who hears may forget and one who sees shall remember. Love in action makes you happy and benefits others as well. The grace that descends on those who love flows into friends and foes. God never punishes his creation. We disarm ourselves against our enemies because everyone is in pain. The tool we surrender becomes our power tool. We cannot be other than what we are. We are because what God is. We remember the Lord that he may not cease to be part of us. God knows us even before our conception. He knows our ego, which has no memory of its divine nature. Life is understood backwards, but it should be lived forwards. You breathe out before you breathe in. The world and the love in it are illusions. God's love transcends dualities and fills every corner of the universe with the same intensity. We love our enemy because we love God and his creation. The flesh and soul becomes one in a transcended soul. The sin does not leave us at once soon after self-realization; it also sneaks back while the master is asleep. We guard its re-entry through continuous prayer. The love of God is opposed to hatred of ego. The ego creates fear and hatred and lives in denial and repression. It is neither meek nor brave. Above all, it blinds us to God's love. The fear is self-created and we need not externalize it nor blame some body. The fear recedes in the presence of divine grace.

"I can do all things in Christ", Ph.4:13.

The divine intellect [buddhi yukta] takes us into a divine world. Everything that happened; happened before and so happened everywhere. The self-consciousness is connected to cosmic energy field, God and man cannot be separated. The separation is in mind only. A friend shows up soon after you think of him, which is an intuitive power and spirit alignment. We can because we think we can. You will be cured if you think of a cure and you will receive love if you seek love. We subjectively experience psychic awareness and beyond. The events that appear in synchronicity are ignored as superstitions, but they may reveal some message from God. Believe that it is God's message and slow down when a slow driver shows up in front of you. We trust the cosmic synchronicity, which is the intelligence of the universe. Sir Alexander Fleming invented penicillin and it saved the life of Sir Winston Churchill from pneumonia. Sr. Churchill educated Dr. Fleming as a token of gratitude for the help he received from Sr. Fleming in a hunting expedition. Wisdom dictates that we love what we do and we live by what we know rather than what we see.

Life's Purpose.

The purpose of life is to live for true values. It is not a primary motivation nor a secondary rationalization as secular society thinks. It is neither defense mechanism nor a reaction formation. It is not sublimation either. Life's purpose is revealed spontaneously. Self-actualization through self-realization is more enduring.

The expression of God through love and service gives the greatest meaning to life. The empty feeling in life [existential vacuum] frustrates many and it creates depression and drug addictions. The existential vacuum is an evidence of failure to realize the inner fullness within us. Answer your conscience and actualize your inherent dormant potentialities. Suffering for an ideal is redemptive. We suffer for the right cause and transform failure into victory. Unnecessary suffering is masochistic. Hope cannot exist against no hope and the hope anticipated in the midst of hopelessness is tragic optimism. Hope and love cannot be ordered nor pursued because they are unconditional and so is the meaning of life. Transform yourself through self-transcendence to enable yourself to face the tragic optimism. The self-created human misery dissolves in self-transcendence. One who broke his neck is able to find meaning in helping others. His broken neck did not break his life's meaning. The human consciousness may not be the end of cosmic evolution. Suffering shall be rewarded in the other if not in this world. Put your immortal footprint in the sands of time. This temporal life is dynamic with possibilities and potentialities. Your past glory adds up to your life's meaning. The meaning of life is not contingent on the present values alone. Pleasure is attained as a byproduct. You will miss it in hyper intension and get it in paradoxical intension. We are more than psyche; find a reason to be happy and give a reason to laugh. Euthanasia is nihilistic since it disrespects human dignity. We have enough to live but not enough to live for. The hunger blurs all other symptoms.

"Persistent knocking on the door may wake up the friend", Luke.18:14.

The soul, which is dormant, is not sinful because it is still connected to God. Even the greatest sinners have hope because the spirit is still alive in them. Continuous prayer evolves the soul. Jesus did love the sinner and praised the righteous. The dormant soul revives and regenerates with persistence in faith. He descended that we may ascend to divinity. He exalts the humble and humbles the pride. We seek doctor's help when we become sick. The white throne judgment is conceived as subtle event, which occurs within the consciousness rather than a literal moment. The new earth and the new heaven refer to the global transformation of human soul. Jesus died to save all of us but few of us only choose him. The Jewish nation chose not to recognize him as the Savior. It is like, the wedding feast is ready but the invited guests refused to attend the feast. The master eventually called the people from the streets to enjoy the feast. We suffer from alienation from God if we neglect such a great salvation. God wants our undivided love and so we cannot serve God and wealth.

Chapter-7

BUDDHISM

The Self, Atman, of Hinduism is viewed as the non-self in Buddhism. The non-self is temporal and dependent. The concept of non-self rejects the existence of eternal Self. A series of moments constitute a series of processes, which renew themselves incessantly. This phenomenon is viewed falsely as a living being, Buddha affirmed. The suffering, the causation of suffering, the removal of suffering and the attainment of nirvana are the four active principles of Buddhism. Nirvana is a state of perfect freedom of existence. It is independent reality. The desire is transcended and the flesh [subject] and the spirit [object] are in unity. The relative world and the ultimate reality are in harmony and the wholeness is established. The mutable self is absorbed into the immutable spirit and oneness with God is established. The thirst to become ceases and the human consciousness is transformed into God consciousness. Karma ends and the cycle of birth and death ends. Nirvana is beyond all existence and it is an unveiled reality in cosmos. It is sachitananda of Vedanta and the Kingdom of Heaven of Jesus Christ.

Consciousness is conditioned by cosmic activity [karma]. The psycho physicality is conditioned by consciousness: the senses are conditioned by psycho physicality. The receptive faculty is conditioned by senses and the desire is conditioned by receptive faculty. The desire conditions craving and craving conditions coveting. The coveting conditions becoming and becoming conditions birth. The birth conditions aging which is suffering. Eliminate the suffering through wisdom. The existence is illusive, dependent and conditioned. The existence is caused by the dependently coordinated elements that extinct ultimately into the absolute. We compare one with the other in the conception of relativity. The former becomes meaningless without the other. Neither of them real, but both are brought under higher unity of relativity . The real is independent and uncaused and possesses a reality of its own. The reality is unrecognizable from without and unrealizable in concepts. The causation is dependently coordinated. There are eternal and unchanging elements apart from the momentary ones. The truth is both phenomenal and transcendental, which are interdependent. When the phenomenal truth is transcended through wisdom, it becomes transcendental truth. The transcendental truth is manifested through the phenomenal truth. The relative existence becomes the absolute. Every moment of consciousness has thought. The intellect is the product of interaction between the body and the mind. The right insight guided by the mindful intellect brings forth wisdom, which is the insight ability to realize the truth. It is a meditative experience and existential

knowledge. The right insight directs the human free
will in right path.

Karma.

The ignorance [avidya] is intrinsic to karma. The
karma is the product of interaction between the self
and world. Desire blinds the karmic self to its spiritual existence. The world knowledge is the product of
interaction between the body and the mind. The world
process is dominated by non-self. The present status of
consciousness is conditioned by karma, which descends
through mental impressions from the previous life. We
are born different because our karmas in the past life
were different. Karma is sustained through the co-ordi-
nations of combinations of the subtle elements. It pro-
ceeds from cause [hetu prabhava] towards extinction
[nirodha]. The soul is connected to karma through the
moral results of our actions.

Karma holds the five aggregates [physical forms,
perceptions, consciousness, feelings and volitions]
together and gives permanence to human existence.
The universe and human existence are in constant flux
and motion in and out from moment to moment like
the sea waves. It is due to the interplay of the plurality
of the ultimate elements, which are the ultimate real-
ities of the matter, mind and energy. Each element or
each moment is discrete which possesses neither substance nor duration. One moment cannot create, but
leads to another moment. Each moment is self-created,
but coordinated by another moment. The causality
appears between the moments. A thought is evanescent
and consecutive which flashes with a new element in a

new place [kshanikatva]. The human suffering includes both pleasure and pain. The self-effort is ego and lacks conviction and inner change. The cults too, lack conviction and inner change, but the inspiration emerges through the goodness realized through the self effort. The intense quest for liberation is as much as attachment to the desire. Violence is the projection of active unconsciousness. Care for your body, but do not love it. Life after death is speculative for Buddhists. The middle path is between self-indulgence and self-denial. The self, impermanence and suffering are the three markers of existence. The eightfold path [right belief, right speech, right aspiration, right conduct, right means of livelihood, right endeavor, right mindfulness and the meditation] is redemptive of human suffering. The human being is an interwoven field of energy. The body systems are interdependent. The total body is replaced every seven years according to Buddhist belief.

The moment of conception is the first moment of life. The embryo is formed through the coordination of combinations of the elements in space and time far before the formation of the senses. The desire, the intellect and the conscious activities [karma bhava] generate. The causation of suffering like birth, life and death ensue. The child's tender mind grows into maturity. The mental and physical energies grow into full potential through the new forms. The physical and mental changes are born and die every moment. The human being is born and dead every moment. The energy, which is eternal, continues through numerous incarnations. The transmigration of soul is an unbroken series of moments like the flame that appears as one continuous flame but it is not in reality. Several small flames gives the appearance of one continuous flame. The reborn person could be the same person or not but belongs to the same series. The difference between death and birth is the difference in the thought and the moment. The last thought and the last moment conditions the first thought and the first moment of the next life. The present thought and the present moment of life conditions the next thought and the next moment. The body elements are replaced every moment and the matter and the energy interchange continuously. Wisdom is beyond surface illusion and the ego is surface illusion. The ego dissolves when the attachment dissolves in divine provision. The temporal body exists through attachments, which are sense perceptions. Detachment is attained through inner renunciation. Buddhism is spiritual atheism, which avoids the speculation of the unknown and so applies full focus on the liberation effort. This life and the life after death are possible without Atman, the holy spirit of Christian faith.

The body changes constantly and is reinvented consciously or unconsciously. There is skeletal change every moment and every thought creates changes in the brain. The body shelters God. Our purpose is to evolve the universe within and we live for the evolution of consciousness. Thought exits every moment from the consciousness. The good thoughts are desire less. Wisdom descends through mindful meditation [vipasana], which is the sustained concentration of mind in right focus leads to the saving wisdom. Nirvana is independent reality, which is self-existing and needs no causation. Heaven is an inner realm of consciousness. The relative world is made of dependently coordinated combinations of elements. The desire to will and exist remain after death. The greatest force in creation manifests as birth. The child's body and mind grow into maturity and the phenomenon of conscious dying continues. The manifested world is a flow of discrete moments of feelings and ideas.

Great Buddhist teachings.

Wisdom sees reality behind the illusion. It descends on those who overcome their natural resistance to diligent practice. The well-tamed mind alone can receive the wisdom and the mind is tamed through listening to dharma. Those who have not practiced the knowledge of wisdom will only continue to suffer. The wisdom holds the human mind like the carpenter shapes wood. The true monk has a pure and well-controlled mind. The ambitious monk is his own worst enemy. The evil seeds bring forth the harvest of bitter fruits. Wisdom alone knows when to move you forward and when to hold you back. The frail body should be protected against evil by the strong wall of wisdom. The human mind cannot comprehend it. The vagaries of life cannot influence the wisdom. It is like a rock, which cannot be blown away by the wind. The wise possess serenity and are immune to good and evil. They treasure wisdom, but the young in dharma may lose vigilance of it.

Love alone overcomes hate and we should not hate anyone knowing that we are all destined to die. Loving your enemy is to liberate yourself from bondage. An individual of higher consciousness is able to see himself in others. He has infinite compassion for all and treats all equally. You can hurt no one when you see yourself in others. The greatest reward in this world is to take care of others. God appears as sick and destitute and caring the sick is caring for God. Do not wish harm to anyone nor deceive any one. Guard all living beings as a mother guards her child from harm. Spread love throughout the world with a grateful heart. Do good deeds spontaneously, which enhances peace and good-will among the nations. Even if one is firmly attached to the void, if he does not have compassion for others, he will make no progress toward reaching the final goal. Nourish love toward others and your own ill will to others shall diminish. As your compassion improves, your annoyance will diminish. Spread joy and your aversion shall diminish. Your revulsion will diminish when you are considerate to others. Cultivate love and compassion out of the abundance of your heart. Pay attention to what you do or fail to do rather what others do or don't do. It is the wrong path to be ashamed of the things that shouldn't be ashamed of and not ashamed of that which should be ashamed of. It is very difficult to correct those who believe in fanatic ideology because of their pride and hypocrisy. They are ignoring Buddha. He is not a true monk who wears saffron robes, but is filled with desire within. Desire the company of the wise and resist being in the company of fools. The fool who knows that he is a fool is fortunate. A fool who believes that he is wise is a trouble to himself and others.

Buddhist 'Way'.

'Way' is symbolic of divinity. It is mighty and holds all things within it. It is vast and whole like the universe. Seek the Way without through the pure heart. The Way sends all blessings. It holds nothing back from anyone.

Do not lose sight of it for then it might be lost forever. It is like cleaning glass until the dust is removed. Cross the river and leave the raft behind. Seeking within you, you will find stillness and joy where there is no fear or attachment. Practice the Way, seek the truth, and be glad in it. Those who have eyes to see the great Way are blessed. There is no other path to purify the intellect. They are like dry grass that needs protection from the flame of desire. It is hard for those with power and health to follow the Way. The Way annihilates fear and doubt within. To follow the Way is goodness and to conform to it is greatness. Seeking name and fame, while ignoring the Way is pursuing the unreal. The way transcends duality. The cosmic force demands that we evolve in spirit though God does not mandate. God does have direct influence over man's decisions. We are empowered by God in the rhythm and movement of this life. The Way is not in the sky, but in the heart.

The universal mind

The universal mind which is what we revere as God, is beyond thought. It holds all thoughts and actions within itself. It is undisturbed and eternal. The eternal divine mind contains all reality and all truth within itself. It is omnipresent, but it's essential nature is visible through faith. It is without birth and death and beyond all concepts of duality. It's essential nature is pure and free from faults. It is beyond impermanence, distinctions, limitations, desires and aversions. It is unaffected by individuation. Lord Buddha is invisible nor can an audible sound and evil cannot perceive the Blessed One. God is like a vast ocean and the waves on its surface disturb its tranquility but beneath, all is serene and unmoved. He contains all but with no personality. God became an actor playing many parts because of the surface disturbance. "Spirit" pervades all things and causes all things to come into existence. All things are in nirvana and it has been since the beginning. The immovable reality is the cause of movement and this truth is revealed through great insight alone. "Everything manifest or un-manifest, whether thinking or unthinking or beyond thought are from Me so that all beings may reach Nirvana. One intrinsic unity enfolds all manifestations. The intrinsic unity of all things contains all things. All things conform to their own natures. Similar to space which conforms to itself, the Spirit' conforms to itself. The great Buddha is nowhere and no-when. All things exist in relationship to everything else; whether manifest or un-manifest, they come and go in relationship to everything else.

Buddhism views the path of renunciation as to untie the ties that bind. It is necessary to achieve spiritual enlightenment in one's lifetime. It is hard for those who have little value to spiritual pursuits. The false belief that we own family and property leads to only suffering. The bird flies in freedom and is happy; the monk is happy with a single bowl for his daily food. One buries treasure in hope of use in the future. It is better to act with charity and goodness. One who controls himself builds up hidden treasure that no thief can steal. The monk who knows the difference between the path of wealth and the path of freedom renounces worldly desires. One who renounces does no harm to others. Renounce money and gold. Rebirth is a certainty for those who crave sensory pleasures. To be free from old age and rebirth, become an island unto yourself and eliminate all your imperfections. The true freedom comes from renouncing the passions of flesh, which is not possible for a married man. The mind is still imprisoned even with the slightest sexual desire. Celibacy takes you to the greatest virtue. To escape bondage one should renounce the world-no matter how difficult this is.

Ashoka, the great, spread Buddhism throughout the continent of Asia. Sankaracharya of seventh century A.D. revived Hinduism and as a result, Mahayana Buddhism was absorbed into Hinduism. Buddha is worshipped by Hindus as the tenth incarnation of Vishnu.

JAINISM is very much akin to Buddhism. Jiva and ajiva of Jainism are purusha and prakriti of Vedanta. Ajiva is born in lower forms of existence. The infinite jiva becomes finite because of its association with self. The Self is blinded and deluded by self. The karmas, whether good or bad, add burden to Self. The soul is liberated through detachment from karmic bondage. The liberated soul ascends to Heaven where it lives with full consciousness eternally and may join Mahavir and other saints. There is no cosmic soul to merge with in Jainism. Jina is one who transcended the cycle of birth and death. The self-effort and self-reliance are essential elements but a Jain denies inspiration from gods. The renunciation of killing, greed, anger, undue desire and sex are the five great vows, which burn the karma. In Heaven, there are an infinite number of discrete souls, which are not created by God, but eternally existed as individual units. The self is conditioned by time, space and motion. The atomistic approach of Jainism parallels the physicist's view of the matter. Jainism is spiritual atheism. Gods and other jivas need salvation themselves and they likely possess different matter. The Jain scriptures are Agamas.

Prophet Zoroaster viewed that both good and evil emanates from Ahura Mazda. Both evil and good are necessary to life. The man has to turn away from evil and turn to Ahura. Satan is personified evil who turns away men from God. Eternal union with God is through salvation only. Heaven is where there is harmony. There is end time judgment for the sinners and the saints. The virtues like good deed and compassion are important milestones of faith. The cosmos has a beginning and an end. This world is real and is a proving ground. Ahura is personal God and relates to mankind through love and anger. The angels are spiritual intermediaries between man and God. Ahura created the universe and transcended it. He chose to reveal himself to mankind through purity and beauty. The evil is myth of spirit. The man is behind the evil of this world and God is behind the cosmic evil [Maya]. Man has free will to choose. The followers of Zoroaster were persecuted and they scattered themselves into other nations and created Parse communities. The Parse community in India contributed a lot to India's progress in technology and science.

TAOISM.

'Tao' is God consciousness. It is the impersonal force that permeates Heaven and Earth. It is the universal mind and its ways can be known, but not Tao itself. The spiritual path is the flow of life and the way of things for Taoism. We will be happy and successful if we surrender to the ways things are. We succeed in life only when we let Tao flow through us and around us freely. We create trouble for ourselves when we resist the ways of Tao. We should rather be like a bamboo that yields and is supple. The great tree resists the wind and breaks itself. It can neither be manipulated nor resisted. Tao will do what Tao does. It is the force, which moves in all things, permeates all things and governs all things. We cannot make the wind stop blowing. Serenity is achieved when one no longer wishes for "something else." The nation that resists change eventually dooms itself. The un-con-scientious ruler will ruin both the nation and himself. If we want inner peace and outer harmony in society, we have to learn not to push the river.

God's Way.

God's Way is God himself. To live in God's Way, we must get out of the world way. God is beyond human thought and we accept him with humility. The more we simplify ourselves-in alignment with God, the richer our lives will be. God is the way of Heaven and it is complete in itself. It is the Kingdom of God. All blessings come from it and it holds nothing back from anyone. All who seek it could find it. The perfect man is one whose sins are forgiven. He becomes one with the God. God is incomprehensible: he is full and empty at the same time. Find God's true nature with in yourselves through self realization. He reveals himself more vividly to those who have overcome desire. We embrace him through self realization that we may not lose him. He is not hidden from anyone but, people choose to ignore him. He can be recognized without a window. His way is narrow but mighty, but people prefer smaller but wider paths.

The humble sage does not seek to be rewarded by anyone. He finds his reward within himself. Those who say they have found God, have not. That which is eternal cannot be spoken of. When the wise man hears of God, he tries hard to follow it. When the person of passion hears of God, he tries to keep it, but eventually loses it. The ignorant hears of God and laugh at it. Act in harmony with God, and you will become God. Nurture Him within yourself, and you will live a virtuous life. God rewards those who embrace Him. Misfortune waits for those who abandon Him. If you seek God through learning, you will not understand Him. Seek God with a humble heart and find Him. It is good to conform to Divine path. Seeking things of the world will result in disaster. The way of Heaven is to retire from the world. God is empty; but he cannot be filled up. It is like a vast lake that never becomes dry. God can be compared to a raging river that rushes to the sea. One can know the world without ever leaving home.

Metaphysics of Tao.

In essence tao is God consciousness. In the beginning there was only void. Within the void was the One. The One is without form. It has no features, but within it, all things exist. The One came into existence before Heaven and Earth. He is changeless, sacred, silence who is unaffected by actions. One, which never changes. It holds all things in its loving embrace, but asks nothing for itself. He has endless series of names. His nature is beyond human thought and comprehension. He is invisible, omnipresent without beginning nor the end. He created all and all dissolves into him. In the end nothing is lost. He is beyond cause and effect. We cannot hear him with our ears, nor see him with our eyes.

Tao Theology.

All things exist in pairs of opposites, being independent of each other. The origin of all things is revealed within ourselves. Be one with God to be in safe haven. We lose our selves in God similar to fish lose themselves in water. We become eternal in God. The world knowledge comes from within but wisdom comes from knowing oneself. He who knows himself is enlightened and his soul has transcended sorrow. He may wear rags outside but his heart is filled with Gold and silver. Goodness recognizes the Self and amazes at it: The mode of passion hears about self and wonders and mode of dullness ignores the self. The kernel reveals itself when the coconut is broken and the water within emptied. If you seek this material world, you will receive it easily. He who seeks world knowledge accumulates it each day. One who seeks wisdom forgets all that he learns. The pride goes before the fall. The perfect person is one whose vessel is empty: his feet leave no foot prints. The rich and famous are always restless and they have to guard their wealth against theft. The life of a greedy man is miserable. He has all he needs but he wants more. The riches come from giving out of one's abundance to those who are in need. Let no one control yourself that you may not lose your inner self.

I in as fresh as morning breeze, feeling reborn, I wander here and there without a care in the world. Let others chase after wealth. I am content with the gifts provided by Mother Tao. Where passions are established, heavenly things cannot be realized. A wise man does not desire or value things of this world. Physical hunger must be satisfied, but the wise man pays no attention to what his eyes see. If our inner eye were to suddenly open, lust and greed would cease to exist.

Wisdom comes spontaneously to those who seek it. You will find it within you. Wisdom dictates that we live for others and it has no preference to one thing over other. The wise do not seek to be first. There is higher security and self-fulfillment in self-denial. The Wiseman's heart is empty of desires and he loves all equal. Give up pride. To go ahead is to go backward. All things that oppose God's way will soon cease to be. One who knows should remain silent. Love your neighbor as thyself and those who love others as themselves transform the world. Compassion and mercy bring victory and goodness. Heaven belongs to the merciful. True warriors neither carry arms nor get angry. Those who wish to win should not be contentious, that is in harmony with what is natural and pure. Do not turn away those you consider sinful and unworthy. If you have wisdom, you will try to save everyone. If fields did not have weeds, what would farmers do? That way nobody goes to waste. Good works have no tracks behind. Hypocrisy is to claim to be what you are not. It keeps us bound to the chains of illusion. Transcend it through self-awareness and self-transformation. We cannot fix something unless we know it is broken. Being boastful in public lacks sincerity. Such self-conscious acts are not in harmony with Tao and ruin an individual ultimately. The intelligence replaces wisdom and creates hypocrisy.

Boasting and seeking recognition is not of the way of wisdom. The arrogance precedes the failure and the conceited receives no reward. When you lose wisdom, you lose integrity at the same time. Lack of faith on the part of person leads to faithlessness on the part of other.

Death and suffering.

Self creates suffering and death. The Spirit has no suffering. The suffering for a good cause is redemptive. The death of great souls for a good cause is worthy. We cannot avoid suffering or death and we should not try to avoid it either. Learn to endure suffering which teaches, tests and makes you more fruitful. Pleasure and pain go hand in hand on earth. The human instinct is to avoid pain and maximize pleasure, but everything under the sun goes in pairs of opposites, which change from one to the other. The elimination of desire eliminates preference to one thing over other so that good and bad and pleasure and pain are all the same to enlightened mind. The dead body is rigid whereas the living body is flexible; so the rigidity belongs to what is dead. Unite with Tao and become one which is eternity. The body dissolves after death but the One is safe. The death has no power over the eternal spirit. The saint accepts both birth and death equally. The human face is in fear of dying every day. We live on in one form or another after our physical body goes back to the earth from which it came. All things come together in Spirit. The saint had burned all flesh and the Spirit left behind is unharmed by any weapon. Weapons cannot harm him who lives in Tao.

Chapter-8

GOD INCARNATION

"The Word became flesh and dwelt among us",
Jn.1:14. Apostle John said famously.

'Avatarana', is the Sanskrit word for 'God incarnation'. God became flesh and blood and the
human soul is elevated into horizons of divine glory
in God incarnation. His majesty is contracted into the
human frame by his own will and the latent divinity of
man is exalted. The ideal of God incarnation does not
oppose the full physical manifestation of God and the
ascent of man into full divinity. Avatar possesses full
truth of consciousness and avatarana exalts divine glory.
God incarnation belongs to the world of manifestation.
He is expressed in a deeper way and his glory is not
altered in any way in God incarnation. The man who is
God's image is logically transcendental and an eternal
being. He is a combination of divinity and nature. God
is inactive consciousness and man is active unconsciousness. Man is a universal infinite and a universal

particular in subjective form. Every conscious soul is God's descent, but a veiled manifestation. The universe exists in him and he becomes a divine whole through salvation. The inspired intellect alone receives truth and, "Shall make you free", Jn.8:32. "Give your heart to me and I will deliver you from all your impurities", [Gita].

"Whatsoever a man sowed, that he also reap. For he that sowed to his flesh shall of the flesh reap corruption: but he that showed to his spirit shall of the spirit reap life everlasting", Gal.6:7-8.

Hindu sages conceived that the Karma [cosmic activity] is what causes reincarnation. The desire is the root of karma. It is the ever-turning wheel of birth, death and rebirth. Salvation or self realization alone frees us from the wages of karma and ends the rebirth. Hell and Heaven are the negative and the positive realms, which are the products of our karma. They have no location in time and space. In the end, they are mere projections of our own dualistic minds. Jesus, the 'Word' became flesh, died and resurrected. He ascended to glory. His second coming is our living hope. The law of karma is known to Bible prophets and apostles. The karma also responds instantly as such the judgment is also today but not tomorrow.

The doctrine of incarnation is difficult to understand and controversial always.

"I tell you that you will not be released from that prison until you have paid the last farthing", Matt.5:26.

Karma is not superstition, nor pre-destined phenomenon. Whatever you measure out, that you will be returned. Everyone creates their own fate and even life in the womb is affected by the karma from the previous life [Garuda purana]. From the sound, an echo returns. A body creates a shadow, so will misery will come to him who does evil works. The sinner from a previous birth is born into a sinner's womb. Trapped in delusion, they fall ever lower into the realms of existence [Gita]. When a bad person spits at the wise man it is like spitting at the sky. [Buddhism]. Suffering is the end of all those who do evil in this life.

> "Fear those who have the power to kill both body and soul and cast both into the flames of hell", Matt.10:28.

The path of light leads to freedom and the path of evil leads back to this world. If one does not find God in this lifetime, he is doomed to reincarnation. Those who do evil, become evil. Those who do good, become good. What we do in life determines our fate in this life and the next [Gita].

"Seek now the meaning of all things so that your suffering may end. The forgetfulness becomes the body that surrounds the soul. It pretends to be the soul, but it is a false spirit. For with whatever judgment you pronounce, you will be so judged. Those who seek happiness by robbing others of their happiness will find misery after they die. The suffering comes to those who cause suffering. The harm returns to the person who does harm. Become a fortress, both on the outside and within yourself, so that nothing can overcome you. "The pressures in life are like a flowing river. You float away on them from life time to life time", [Dharma pada].

"Father, why you have forsaken me?" Matt.27:46.

"Father into thy hands I commend my soul", Lk.23:46.

Jesus was in a state of anguish and separation from Father when he was on the Cross. With renewed grace, he committed his spirit unto Father. It is the unity with Father which is the redemptive power. 'He gave up the spirit', Matt.23:46. Jesus was aware of his imperfection and cognitive of the Father's Grace. God incarnation is not a bygone personality. The cosmic intelligence of Christ is everywhere and in every one. He speaks to us today as he spoke to Peter and Paul two thousand years ago. The incarnations are immanent in all and transcend over all. They are the objects of our spiritual consciousness and we comprehend them better since we see them more directly. "The worshipper becomes one with God he truly sees", [Brihadaranyaka up]. God is in active observation of our lives. He is with you in your pain and he reaches you willingly. "Purified by the austerity of wisdom, many have attained my status of being", [Gita]. "He is our conscious life and we worship him as life and breath and obtain full life in this world and immortality in heaven", [Kausitaki up]. We admire great souls [mahatma] as avatars.

I visit David every week in cemetery and kneel down on the head end of the marble stone. After a short prayer, I converse with David recalling some of the sweet and bitter memories of our lives together for twenty nine years. I cannot imagine David lying beneath this heavy marble stone. I wish David resurrect physically and speak to me softly as he used to do. I do know that the wish remains as a wish but the time I spend here is healing and restorative. The hope relives that we will see each other face to face one day. Now I see David as one with God. We love God more than our parents or children that we may inherit God's kingdom. We transcend human love to love God.

"Behold the veil of the temple was in twain from top to the bottom", Mt.27:51.

Human suffering is ultimately traced to disharmony between the creative purpose of God and the actual world. It is not limited to man's rebellious mind. The objective and the subjective processes are God's lower and higher natures. The immanence and transcendence of God are compatible to each other, but divine nature and the world appearance contrasts to each other. God descends as Savior when evil threatens human virtues. The Lord, hidden in our hearts, reveals himself in the darkness of midnight. The mirror of understanding, which is cleansed of the dust of desire reflects the light of consciousness well. Self-realization is spontaneous illumination of the self that transforms life. The blind could see and the prison doors were opened. Inspiration opens the eyes blinded by sin. The new birth hears the divine voice, receives divine light and acts in divine will. Human consciousness is uplifted into unborn eternal divinity. It is not the conversion of God into flesh and blood, but the uplifting of the human soul into a divine horizon is the essence of God incarnation.

Every being is an aspirant for perfection. The sorrow disappears in unity with Christ consciousness.

Maya [cosmic delusion] is the power of self-manifestation possessed by God himself. It is the divine energy to create mutable forms, which veils the divinity from us. Maya presents the phenomenal appearances as if they are truthful. In addition, Maya may not mean that the world is illusive nor it is nonexistent. The world is illusive for those who cannot perceive the divine whole in it. The relativity of this world is confirmed by the self-contradictory nature of the process of becoming. The divine Maya fashioned this universe. The divine Maya reflects in Spirit and the natural Maya reflects in ego. Self becomes self when the truth is veiled from human sight. God is enveloped by divine Maya. Maya is logical inconceivability. It bewilders consciousness and the bewildered self loses the sight of its creator. Man is in between divine immutability and human mutability. Life is a combination of freedom and necessity and chance and choice. The reason for the strife between the being and the non being in the process of becoming is only construed, but cannot be explained convincingly.

The Self within us creates a sense of imperfection and vanity of human happiness. The man who is created in God's image is bound to be divine whole again when the Self unfolds self in the process of becoming. The divine immanence evolves and ascends to divine status in man. The transcended soul expresses full potential of divine power. The soul, which is disentangled from social context, stands alone against the might of the evil. The Self lives by the inward rule of truth. The life of social solidarity gives social security at the cost of self-integrity where the true man has not yet emerged. The cults constrict the unfolding of human personality and potential. The pure soul is above the world and the pure nonbeing is below the lowest existence. The freedom of action is intrinsic to transcendence. Self nurtures and guides nature without crushing it. His decisions and thoughts come from the Source. We are no more helpless tools in the hands of nature. The flame of born again souls burns like a lamp in the windless space. Let the creative force rise from the true Self. We become free participants of the world from above into the world below.

"The fear of the Lord is the beginning of wisdom: but fools despise wisdom and instruction", Prov.1:7.

The cosmic process is continuous becoming. The becoming continues as long as the cosmic delusion [original sin] persists. It is not an intellectual error, but a spiritual blindness. Ignorance is false belief in one's self-sufficiency and attributing permanence to it. It is 'avidya' as Hindu sages affirmed. The ignorance of nature of things produces desire. The wisdom illuminates knowledge. Wisdom is not knowledge, but it is not discontinuous with it; wisdom opposes ignorance. The immanent wisdom is not redemptive until it is realized. Ignorance dies like the fire which is deprived of its fuel extinguished when wisdom dawns. The intense collaboration of the subconscious with the conscious is realized only when we return to wisdom. The firm faith is beyond intellectual doubts, which eliminates the obscuring tendencies of the ignorance. We try to reach God through knowledge, emotion and practice which are logically distinguishable, but in practical life they are inseparable [Vedic thought]. They are different aspects of one movement of the soul. The mental traits [gunas]which are goodness passion and dullness.create variety of existence. The passion for divine knowledge inspires intellect which leads to divinity. The self is an undifferentiated matter in the beginning with all its components in sound equilibrium. Self realization restores self its former integrity. We lose self to gain Self, which is the pure inactive principle behind the conscious life. We forget the self when we identify with the universality of spirit.

"know the truth and the truth shall set you free", Jn.8:32.

God is absolute truth and science is partial truth though it prepares the mind for the better. The cosmic process is lower divine nature, which is an order of determinism. There is no radical dualism between nature and supernatural. The evil is a distorted self. The bondage is to identify with nature, which cannot invade you without your approval. The individuals are unique that limits divine intervention in our redemptive process. The ordinary life does not feel laceration of spirit and feel no urge to seek their divine nature. The urge comes to seek God when the discord within is sensed by Self. The redemption from the strife of denial and despair comes through divine grace. The invisible impulse, which lurks at the heart of creation to seek God produces ego that inspires heroic idealism and human fulfillment. God expresses himself in infinite capacity in self-transcendence. God created us all to fulfill his will in our lives. His will is that we overcome the nature and live by his will. One who cannot avail his intelligent will is acting contrary to divine will. The animal lives by instinct, but the humans have to justify their actions. We overcome the determinism through self-realization. The nature becomes the medium of spiritual resurrection through self-realization. The spirit penetrates into nature and realizes it's true relationship with indwelling God. The human frustration and self-accusation are not the errors of moral mind. We seek salvation today rather than tomorrow. Salvation descends when the intellect unites with Self.

"They that plough iniquity and sow wickedness, reap the same", Job 4:8.

Karma, the cosmic action is not a destiny, but a condition. Past karma decides our present condition. The cosmic process imposes on us the birth and death. Hindu sages conceive that the past life karma decides our present life environment. Still, we have the freedom of choice subject to these limitations. Karma responds to our action with reward and judgment. This life environment requires some obligatory activities like saving a drowning cat. The inevitable karma is not binding. Spontaneity is not compulsive: it is full of truth. The children speak spontaneouely and they are divine. Out of the three mental traits, the goodness, which seeks truth, controls the other two, passion and dullness. The goodness is binding too, because the ego operates in good nature also. Through self realization, 'gunas', reach fundamental integration. The transcended soul generates creative activity. Man is movement in the being of God individualized. Every one of us is unique in the sight of God though a single pattern running through us all. Distinctiveness is determined by the content of the mind. The individual intends to transcend until the becoming reaches its end in being. Father in Heaven is perfect.

"The spirit of God was moving upon the surface of waters', Gen.1:2.

The spirit of God was moving upon the surface of waters. God is the eternal "now" seeing the end from the beginning. He is the creative principle who inter-acts with this world of plurality. The cosmic process is God interacting with the world. His creative pur-pose is seemingly to sport in the exercise of his power. His creative principle is the un-manifested potential of the existence. His ideas are materialized through cre-ation. The manifested existence is the reflection of self, which contains past, present and the future in Absolute now. Time and movement are intrinsic to him. Time becomes an appearance in its process of change and it becomes an eternity in its process of transformation. The birth and fulfillment of time is in eternity. The tem-poral movement is connected to inner depth of eternity. 'Narayana', a Snskrit word for God, mean that he floats on the water.

"She brought forth her first born son, and wrapped him in waddling clothes, and laid him in a manger; because there is no room for them in the inn", Lk.2:7. Lord who was hidden in the gloom revealed himself in the thickest of darkness of night to illumine our souls.

The false perception creates a false inference. The causation of weakness by the power of Maya (cosmic delusion) is the mystic phenomenon of this universe. The power of grace, which descended through the crucifixion death of Jesus Christ alone, annihilates the veiling power of Satan. "Whosoever shall not receive the kingdom of God as a little child shall in no wise enter theirin", Lk.18:17. God provides help from above and from within that man may find the truth and ascend to divine status through self-realization. Then the prison doors open and the chains bondage break. Those who seek him diligently find him in their heart. He is at hand. God incarnation is the embodiment of God. One who knows Brahman becomes Brahman. One who dies like Jesus Christ resurrects like Jesus Christ. "The kingdom of heaven is within you", Matt.3:2: is an affirmation that we are one with God. We reveal him through our consciousness, love and beauty.

"He that believeth in me though he is dead, yet he shall live", Jn.11:25.

Avatar (God incarnation) is born of his own free choice unlike the ordinary souls. His birth is not predestined by karma, but he is predestined to save mankind. The ordinary soul reincarnates because of karmic debt. The avatars are co-creators. Jesus lived with full consciousness of his divinity. He healed the sick, raised the dead and walked on the water. He died on the Cross in the fulfillment of his mission. Avatar transforms defeat into victory and tragedy into bliss. He transforms our weakness into our strength. The universe lives in man who believes in cosmic intelligence of Jesus Christ.

He is no more alone or lonely. We love our neighbor with all our heart, soul and might. God who is behind this changing world is changeless. His true nature is identifiable and self-realizable. The mind and intellect change, but the spirit behind them is changeless. There is immutable harmony behind the fluctuations of disharmony in the creation. Have harmony within yourself first and you have harmony with the universe next. The divine spirit within is unaffected by our deeds whether they are good or bad. The emotion is unspiritual and we should not lose our devotion in emotion.

"Before Abraham was, I am", Jn.8:58.

Jesus is one with Father and he knows his crucifixion and death. He knew his past. "In the beginning was the Word and the Word was with God", Jn.1:1. Jesus is not only eternal, he is omniscient as well. Intuition is a spontaneous feeling from the inner voice. It is the direct perception and the truth revealed by Self without the aid of the senses. The friend whom you are thinking about is knocking on the door. It is intuitive power. The ego opposes and the wisdom proposes intuition. The cosmic intelligence of Jesus is in every cell of our body, which is part of cosmic energy. A single sparrow does not fall without the sight of Father. All is connected to cosmic energy. This diverse creation is from one source. A thought is an invisible energy, which is part of cosmic energy. This world is God's dream and the activity on the world stage is his drama. The creation is God's desire less desire and self-realization as well. The world should be our dream and drama too. He created the evil and subjected mankind to strife. We are

213

at times inclined to think that God is playing dice with mankind. This is divine dice ("lela"). We worship Lord with all our strength (energy), soul (divine communication), mind (concentration) and heart. No one is alone nor one cannot own another. Those who worship Atman verily reach me", [Gita]. "He that is least among you all the same shall be great", Lk. 9:48.

"unless you change and become like children, you will never enter the kingdom of heaven", Matt.18:3.

The meek inherit the kingdom of God. Be servant to become a master. The ego is first in this world but it is the last in the kingdom of heaven. The Son of man came to serve but not to be served. He had no place to rest his head and he is knocking on the door of your heart. The waves return to ocean and the men return to God in the end. The waves lose their name and form before they merge with the ocean. God is love and law as well. One sees beauty in a dream and sees duty when he awakes. The saint sees beauty in duty. The snake poison kills everyone except the snake itself. God is not affected by sin. He trenscended it. Man is not a sinner but he is the Son of God. He can return to his Father any time, leaving behind his sin.

In the long history of Hinduism of at least five thousand years, there are ten God incarnations [dasavataras], the last one being Gautama Buddha. The early avatars were represented by fish [matsyavatar] and turtle and later avatar was represented by a combination of man and animal [narasimhavatar]. The recent avatars are represented fully enlightened like Ramavatar and

Krishnavatar. The multiple God incarnations descended from time to time to uphold the truth. "When sin prevails and the righteousness shrinks to its lowest ebb, I body myself to protect the righteousness and to destroy the sin. I come into being every age to restore the righteousness", Gita observed. Hinduism is in anticipation of more avatars. "Though I am unborn of changeless nature, I come into being by my own Maya", Gita concluded. Avatar takes his birth by his own power [atma-mayaya]. We worship him as we worship the Father in Heaven. "In whatever way men worship in the same way I fulfill their desires", Gita observed. God is indivisible, but divided and he is near but far away.

"I have not come on my own but Father sent me", Jn.8:42.

"The Word became a human being and, full of grace and truth. He dwelt among us and we beheld his glory", Jn.1:14. "He gave power to become sons of God to those who believe on his name. They are not born of blood nor the will of the flesh, but of God", Jn.1:13.

We all have received grace for grace through his fullness of grace and truth. Human nature is transformed into divine nature through salvation. The born again soul is one with Jesus Christ. Jesus was with the Father in Heaven before his birth and he returned to the Father after his death and resurrection. Repentance releases the saving grace, which transforms the human nature into divinity. One who knows the mystery behind the divine birth has no rebirth after his disembodiment, Vedanta affirmed. Simeon saw baby Jesus in the temple and said", I have seen thy salvation!", Luke 2:30.

God is not an intellectual abstraction but he is an identifiable and realizable Being. Psalmist experienced the Omni presence of God and said", where shall I go from thy spirit". The evidence of his presence is in human experience of self-realization. He is visible through faith. We express him through love and service. He is free witness of our deeds whether they are good or bad. He is changeless existence behind the changing universe. The man is God descended in a veiled form, but ascends to divinity in union with God. We are one with God when we live in his Kingdom of Heaven. The idea that man is created in God's image negates the idea of the fear of death. He is logically immortal since he is born of eternal cosmic seed. Avatar is a transcendental soul in human embodiment. God is fully revealed and his cosmic nature is confined to a single finite human form in avatarana.

> "This is my body which is given for you: this do in remembrance of me. This cup is the new testament in my blood, which is shed for you", Lk.22:19-20.

We have reverence to the church and the articles of worship in the church. The church is dwelling place of God. God lives in the objects which are considered holy. When we swear by the temple, we swear by it and by the one who dwells in it. We remember and revere Jesus' flesh and blood as bread and wine. The human consciousness is the best of all divine manifestations. The realized soul is God incarnation and visible to human eye directly. God, in his cosmic manifestation experiences both pain and pleasure. The man descended from God realized his soul and ascended in union with God. God is our father and mother. The divine manifestation is an explicit affirmation of un-manifested divinity. The full knowledge of God is manifested in avatar, who is finite form. The purpose of avatarana is to help us and he descends in our need in spite of our free will. Paul on his way to Damascus received divine grace beyond his expectation. In one of our family prayers, I mentioned the traditional fact that God do not intervene in our lives, unasked or unsought. To my surprise, my son Abner who teaches psychiatry in university of Kentucky, said that God comes into our lives unasked also. In life we avoid many a turmoil due to God's grace. God volunteer himself to safeguard us. The vast intelligence hidden in the creation obeys God. The man is bound to perish without God both here and in the next world. He has choice to be or not to be with God. The word "Amen' is full of divine energy. If you say amen without focus and reverence, the power do not enter you. Rather you receive negative energy and express the same in spite of your worship.

"Let there be light: and there was light", Gen.1:3.

God creates finite forms. He creates and dissolves mountains too all the time. Faith heals and moves mountains as well. Little faith does not work. God reveals himself as cosmic vibration [Word]. The subtle sounds, which are born of cosmic vibrations, are audible by the astral ears. The quantum scientist hears them all the time in his lab. The Word is thought. The thought waves dance all the time in human consciousness. God projected diverse thoughts and created this diverse universe. The photons condensed and gave light when God said, "Let there be light", Gen.1:3. God creates finite forms in his infinite dream consciousness. Jesus had two thoughts, one upon the other, when he walked on the water: one for the water and the other to uphold his body on the water. When Lazarus was raised from the dead, Jesus was in Lazarus' body as well in his own body. These miracles are practical enough according to the mystic sages of India. He changed water into wine. God transforms water into wine in the presence of the sun always. The creation obeys its creator. The sages project their conscious intelligence beyond the finite forms and experience the divine infinity. The conscious intelligence descends from cosmic intelligence. The human body is a bundle of energy and every cell of our body has intelligence. The unknown intelligence controls our life. The manifested universe is God's body and the cosmic energy is his astral body. The trinity includes the Father, who is beyond creation, Christ is cosmic intelligence and Word is cosmic vibration.

The spirit dwells in us, 1[st]Corinth.3:16.

Adam and Eve are the primordial man and woman. They became sinners when they yielded to Satan's temptation. Maya is the conscious force that sustains men in delusion. "Satan go behind me", Jesus rebuked, Matt.16:23. The sinner did not create the sin, nor is he happy with his sinful life. He is not in harmony with the world because he is not in harmony within himself. The man walks in his backyard every day not knowing that there is gold underneath. "God loves sinners", Mt.5:44. Jesus, in his second coming, visits the sinner in his consciousness and the sinner becomes a saint. We evangelize to transform souls. The religion is the hive and the nectar is salvation. The parrot caged so long is afraid to leave the cage. Similarly, the soul tends to cling to the familiar environment of the physical body. God's love sustains us but not nutrition and medicare. God's love is behind mother's love. The prosperity is uniform fulfillment of body mind and soul.

> "As many as received him, he gave the power to become children of God... which were born not of blood but of spirit", Jn.1:12.

The resurrection is to relive through conscious self-realization by free will. Jesus transformed death into resurrection. The born again soul resurrects in his true being. The atoms and cells of our body and mind are spiritualized and resurrect into Christ consciousness. The spirit resurrects in spirit body. The seemingly destitute man on this planet becomes a co-creator in the power of resurrection. Salvation dissolves our name and form and unites us with God as the waves lose their identity and merge with the ocean. The response to perception is unique in every individual and, "No man comes to me except the Father who sent me draw him, Jesus affirmed",Jn.6:44. Jesus saw spirit in matter, but we see matter as solid reality. Jesus healed the severed ear of high priest's servant spontaneously through the power of resurrection. We can also resurrect from the consciousness of disease and fear.

219

"The sound eye sight fills your whole body with
light", Mt.6:22.

Our physical body is a bundle of frozen energy and
the unrealized soul that lives in the body is frozen God
consciousness. The living dead are buried under the
soil of sin. "Let the dead bury the dead, Jesus affirmed",
Lk.9:60. Let your ego die before you die. We die daily
that the resurrected Lord may live in us always. The resurrected eye alone sees the resurrected Lord. "Seek the
kingdom of God first and all other are added unto you",
Matt.6:33. We see clear water on the top and the spirit
surfaces in a pure soul. Inner peace comes through the
prosperity which is uniform fulfillment of body mind
and soul. Rejoice in the immutable harmony of this creation through worship of the Father, Son and the Holy
Spirit. "Honor thy father and mother", Exo.20:12. The
mule knows the weight of the box, but not the worth of
the gold in the box.

"Faith is the substance of the things hoped for;
the evidence of the things not seen", Heb.11:1.

Faith is the direct perception of truth without sensory input. The mind of equanimity gives birth to faith
through intuition. The truth is realized through the
intuitive power of perception in the stillness of consciousness. Intuition is a feeling beyond sense perception. Intuition is an inner voice that is revealed by the
Holy Spirit spontaneously without help of the sense
perception. The in folding of intuition reveals faith,
which is the evidence of the things unseen. What you
are thinking about appears in your doorstep, which

is intuitive power. Intuition is nourished by divine wisdom. Reason leads to intuitive faith. The conscience is the intuitive reasoning. The salvation anchored in intuitive faith is unaltered. The miracle is a supernatural event and it occurs through faith. Faith is will power; let God be your will power. Wrong perception begets wrong inference. Religious fanaticism is a blind belief. There is blind belief, but there is no blind faith. Belief is a simple trust in a religion or in an individual. It comes from will and imagination, which are the two powerful forces in creation. Belief born of sentiment or an emotion is transient. It may turn into disbelief or into faith. Waiting to receive the result is uncertainty. It becomes the habit of mind eventually. The belief focused on truth realizes faith.

"Pray to Father in secret. And Father shall reward thee openly", Matt.6:9.

Prayer (dyana yoga) communicates with God only when negative energy is emptied and filled with divine energy from which love and peace flow out abundantly. Your will should match God's will. God flows out freely from a pure soul through love and service. God's love is expressed through us. What we accomplish in the realm of divinity is success. If one is not happy with what he has now, he will never be happy in his future riches. Temporal happiness is delusion. An assumed opinion is persuasion. What I am now is the result of what I was and what I will be is the result of what I am now. The crises bring out hidden powers and the failures can transform into victories. The good vengeance is doing opposite of what your enemy did. God is realized, but not acquired. "If your hand offends you cut it off with the sword of wisdom", Matt.5:30.The bees seek honey and the flies go to filth. "His noise was like the noise of many waters", Ezekiel 43:1.

God is not visible in noisy thunder nor in storm but God is visible in the expression of love and support to our neighbors stricken with storm and thunder.

Our physical body lives in three levels. The physical[stula sarir] and the astral [mental] bodies are like the light and the light bulb. The physical body lives in astral body. The causal body [sukshma sarir] is the resurrected body in spirit. The astral soul evolves in astral planes until it takes its next birth. The physical and astral universes are dissolved into causal body. Causal soul journeys beyond all vibrations. Patanjali, an ancient Indian sage, described seven centers of life [consciousness], which are located in the spine and brain. The consciousness transcends upwards from coccyx to cerebellum and unite with kuthastha, the area of pituitary gland. The aggregate of consciousness [chitta] is the intuitive feeling. The mind [manas] is sense consciousness. The intellect is the discriminative faculty [buddhi]. God projected his consciousness and became immanent in the creation in the form of super consciousness. The mortal consciousness remains in sleep, dream and waking states.

"Him that overcomes will I make a pillar in the temple of my God and he shall go no more out", Rev.3:12.

The breath [prana] is the cosmic vibratory energy, which centers in the medulla. Prana rushes into individuals and causes a restless mind. Pranayama, the breathing exercises, calms restless minds. Karma is law of justice. The yoga sutras include moral conduct [yama], rites [niyama], postures [asanas], breath [pranayama], internalization [pratyahara], meditation [dhyana], concentration [dharna], and super consciousness unite us with God. The Father [beyond and within vibratory manifestation, the Son [God consciousness in creation/vibratory realm of cosmic consciousness], and the Holy Spirit [cosmic creative vibrations]. This trinity corresponds with the trinity of Hinduism; Brahma, Visnu and Siva.

We "take heed that the light within us be not be darkness", Luke 11:34.

Chapter-9

SPACE

Creative God consciousness.

"In the beginning God created the heaven and
the earth. And the earth was without form and
void and the darkness was upon the face of the
deep. And the Spirit of God moved upon the
face of the waters. And God said, let there be
light and there was light", Genesis 1:1-3.

God is "Word" ['shabda Brahma' in Sanskrit] Jn.1:1,
and his Word 'Let there be light", Gen.1:3, created
cosmic vibrations and condensed the photons. God projected his multiple thoughts and created this universe of
multiplicity. The "Word" became flesh and dwelt among
us in Jesus Christ. God consciousness is the eternal
womb of the creation. The Word, subtle cosmic vibrations, which are floating in the vastness of space are
born and die in the silence of God consciousness. The
space is seemingly void, but the invisible electron in

the space create immense energy and activity. The visible is from the invisible. The silence returns when the noise is exhausted. If we view the space as nothing, this universe is created from that nothing and it dissolves into that nothing. Nothing dissolves into nothing and nothing envelops nothing. The infinite space and universe is beyond the comprehension of human mind; but men are inclined to know the mystery behind this universe. Hubble telescope revealed in the early part of 20th century that space contains billions of galaxies and each galaxy contains billions of stars. Many stars have planets around them like the planet earth orbits sun in an outer arm of the spiral "milky way." The universe goes on forever in space. The atoms, which constitute our body, have empty spaces within and in between them. The inconceivable vastness of this universe is within the human consciousness. It is the transcendental reality and internalization of the external space in its true nature. The space between the perception and conception is the moment of bliss. We are in divine bliss in the deep sleep with no thought or emotion. "The essence of all things is nothing", [Buddha]. Our answers are in the skies as the angel spoke, "Ye men of Galilee, why stand ye gazing up into heaven?. This same Jesus, which is taken up from you into heaven, so shall come in like manner as ye have seen him go into heaven", Acts, 1:11. The Hindu sages conceived the universe as God's body as well his self-realization. This world is God's expression.

Matter and energy:

Matter and energy are constantly emerging from and vanishing into the space. The universe can be reduced to nothingness if all the matter is transformed into energy. The matter and the energy are indestructible and they only oscillate into each other at sub atomic level. The sum total of the energy and the matter is constant. The energy in the cosmos creates vibrations but the cosmos does not vibrate. The cosmic field maintains a constant "zero point" which could be the cosmic mind that ancient Indian rishis advocated. The cosmic mind could be the source of everything that could possibly exist rather than what we could observe. The cosmic mind controls the matter, energy and information of the universe with utmost precision through cosmic vibrations. It is like the human mind, controlling our life's activities. The cosmic mind is the switching point between the existence and nothingness. The matter and the energy of quantum physics is the world and God for us.

The mystery behind the creation.

'The wind blows where it listed and thou hear the sound thereof, but cannot tell whence it cometh and wither it goes; so is everyone that is born of the spirit", Jn.3:8.

A thought is a universal vibration. The flap of a butterfly in New Delhi can bring rain in New York. God projected his thoughts and created the worlds on the space screen. He created man In his own image, Gen.1:26, is an affirmation that we can transcend to divinity.

The space screen is like a television screen, and the mechanism of image formation is similar in both the space screen and television screen. The electrons are the source of energy for both. The images on the space screen blink like Christmas lights because the quantum impulses are intermittent. The atoms wink off and return with the same energy. The images come and go like the dust particles in a sunbeam. The earth moves in its orbit and we move in time and space. The space and the dream space are alike where anything can be displayed. The dream is real when it happens and it is unreal when you wake up. The cosmic mind monitors the collision of paired electrons across the cosmos and transfers trillions of bits of information instantly every day with no friction nor medium involved. They are omnipresent and any change in one electron reflects instantly in the other electrons even though it is millions of miles apart. This is "spooky action at a distance", for Einstein, a great physicist of twentieth century. The electrons do not change position in time and space. This is the simple behavior of the matter for a scientist, but it is the root of consciousness, which we revere as God. The spider web reminds us the presence of a spider.

"Truth shall set you free", Jn.8:32.

The mind is beyond body and the spirit is beyond mind. The human consciousness is beyond death. The consciousness is seemingly not the end of the creation. The consciousness is sheltered by brain, but the brain tissue is not the consciousness nor does it have a direct connection with the cosmic mind. It might communicate with the cosmic mind via the signals from the mind. The mind and the brain are distinct at a lower level, but they become one in the cosmic level. The cosmic mind is behind both the mind and brain in our awareness as well unawareness. We think through our cosmic mind and so our thoughts are shared. The cosmic mind could store all the memories such as children with distinct memory could have access to this cosmic source. Brain tissue is transformed into energy after death, which merges with cosmic energy. The energy and information bundled in the mind merges with the cosmic mind. The very consciousness survives death and merges with cosmic mind; so the mind and the cosmic mind are directly connected through the electrons. Thoughts arise and then fall back into these God particles.

Memory.

> "No man knows who the Son is, but the Father, and who the Father is, but the Son, and he to whom the Son will reveal him", Lk.10:22.

Each individual is unique in behavior and memory. The cosmic mind knows all the cosmic events through the cosmic vibrations. God knows the flap of a butterfly and fall of a sparrow. Memory exists in a non-physical form from incarnation to incarnation. We know the anatomical memory center in the brain, but we do not know the physiological basis of memory yet. The memory, which merges with cosmic memory could be reused by the cosmic mind as needed, as conceived by ancient Hindu sages. Men are born different because the combinations of DNA molecules in the cosmos differ. The same pattern of behavior in the twins is believed to be due to the bonding of electrons in the cosmos. The molecules in the memory center are not intelligent and therefore the memory is not consciousness. The information is also not consciousness. The brain filters huge amounts of information and transmits few essential messages. Some information may side track in deficient brains, which explains why some children are brilliant in some areas of knowledge. The photosynthesis is the complex creative activity. The consciousness as well the thought and emotion is energy. The consciousness creates an electromagnetic field around the body, but the electromagnetic energy cannot create the consciousness. Logically, the energy is not consciousness. Oxygen is not consciousness either though it is innately related to the neurons in the brain. The consciousness is connected to cosmic consciousness, which is the root of time and space. The creative leap like death is simply a transit from one consciousness to another (Hindu sages). We do not know where the wind comes from nor where it goes. The DNA molecules could be the ultimate source of life and the consciousness. "I say unto you. Arise and take up thy couch, and go into your house. And immediately he rose up before them and took up that whereupon he lay, and departed to his own house, glorifying God", Lk.5:25-25.

Spirit in Matter.

Jesus saw spirit in matter when he raised Lazarus from the dead. Jesus also healed the severed ear of chief priest's servant. The creative thought of God is restorative and healing always. The spirit and matter are separate in physical dimension, but they merge into one in divine dimension. Human consciousness permeates into cosmic consciousness, which could associate matter with the mind. The matter and energy constantly exchange into each other. The intelligence is neither primitive nor modern. Given equal opportunity, all children achieve equally. The cumulative consciousness from the past life has deeper association with cosmic mind. A dying person is already in touch with the cosmic world. The cosmic soul evolves until such a time that a new personality is born. The soul evolves continuously both in Heaven and on Earth until such a time that the perfect soul merges with the Father in Heaven, who is perfect. The saint lives in Heaven even on Earth and his disembodied soul carries love alone into Heaven. Heaven is bliss consciousness, which is a state of being aware of itself, but not being dead or alive. Bliss consciousness connects us to the universal experience, which is the force of evolution. Cosmic consciousness is above the bliss consciousness. The saints who possess bliss consciousness travel to heavenly places and encounter angels. Death dissolves the consciousness of all objects. What we are afraid of losing is unreal, which implies that the death is unreal. The soul in Heaven is impersonal, but retains earthly memories. Karma hinders continuous evolution of soul. Every insight and every experience is a moment of freedom and a level of energy. The intellect accepts or rejects the experience based on its belief or disbelief. The new belief rings in when the old belief rings out. The end point is also the beginning point. Some of these thoughts are the subjective and intuitive experiences of ancient Hindu sages.

Chapter 10.

QUANTUM SCIENCE AND THE UNIVERSE

Einstein's 'General Theory of Relativity':

> "God is power ful; all must stand in awe of
> him; he keeps his heavenly kingdom in peace",
> Job, 1:1-2.

E instein's general theory of relativity gives us a
glimpse into mysteries of cosmos and God. The
theory abolished the concept of static universe as an
existence in itself or could have been created in its
present form at some time in the past. Einstein over-
threw the concept of 'absolute rest and absolute time'.
He favored ; personal time'. This changed the discussion of origin and fate of the creation also changed our
understanding of time, space, and reality. Everything

was relative in that there was no absolute moral standard. The general theory of relativity agrees with the laws of magnetism and electricity, but disagrees with Newton's laws of gravity. The laws of gravity state that any change in gravitational field in one region of the universe would be felt instantaneously everywhere else in the universe that contradicts with Einstein's belief that nothing travels faster than the light. Light travels at one hundred and eighty thousand miles per second in ether medium in space. The light rays and sound waves travel in ether medium as waves. It takes an infinite amount of energy to accelerate a particle to the speed of light. The particle accelerated increases in its mass and hardly accelerates further. The acceleration and gravitational field can be equivalent if a massive body curves space-time. The sun's mass curves space time and deflects light from stars passing near the sun that produces a slight shift in the apparent position of the star when viewed from the earth [eclipse]. The planets move in straight lines, but appear to be bent by gravitational field. The gravitational forces are an expression of the fact that space-time is curved. The bodies fall together when the matter warps space-time. The theory of curved space-time is the theory of general relativity, which transformed the space and time into active participants in the dynamics of the creation. The theory of special relativity excludes gravity. (read Steve Hawking books on universe and creation for more).

Big Bang:

God hung the stars in the sky-the Dipper, Orion, the Pleiades, and the stars of the south", Job, 9:9.

The universe could have started with the big bang. The universe is still expanding and the distance between any two galaxies is steadily increasing in time. The farther the galaxies are from us, the faster they are moving away from us. The universe might have had a previous contracting phase and the galaxies must have been closer together with a bounce into present expansion. They must have been even one above the other with very large density and temperatures in billions of degrees in order for nuclear reactions to produce the amounts of light elements we observe around us today. The microwave background radiation indicates that the density could be in trillions of tons per cubic inch. The uniformly expanding universe would breakdown if one followed the motions of galaxies back in time [Einstein]. The sideways velocities of galaxies would cause them miss each other. Time has a beginning and that time would come to an end for the massive stars when they reached their end of life and no longer generated enough heat to balance the force of their own gravity, which was trying to make them smaller against their wish [Einstein.]. Einstein thought that such stars, which are less than the twice the mass of the sun would settle down to Become black holes. The black holes are the regions of space time that are so warped that light cannot escape from them. Time would come to an end inside black holes for the stars [Hawking and Penrose]. Quantum science is a journey into unknown space of the invisible particles and shares a sense of mystery of our world. The more accurately one determined a particle's position, the less accurately one could determine its speed and vice versa. Light is both a particle and a wave. This duality of quantum theory is probabilistic and uncertain in nature. It unfolds the universe which exists both inside as well as outside of us.

The radiation from a hot body was explainable if light could be emitted or absorbed only if it came in discrete packets called quanta [Max Planck]. The photo-electric effect is the basis of modern light detectors and television cameras. An object placed over here appeared over there instantly. A stone can be reduced to nothing and solid walls promenaded straight through effortlessly. The experimental cat is half alive and half dead simultaneously. The system cannot be detached from the observer. How the multiple chemical interactions develop into a subjective life and ultimately generate a "person" with a personality, is still a mystic quantum phenomenon. Human consciousness itself should be a quantum phenomenon. We are blind to brain function in its control of vast information networks and human behaviors. "Your joys and your sorrows, your memories and your sense of personal identity and free will are in fact no more than the behavior of a vast assembly of nerve cells and their associated molecules", stated Francis Crick, the co-discoverer of DNA.

Electron: God particle.

> "I talked about things I did not understand, about marvels too great for me to know", Job 42:3.

The electron is very mystic particle, as such it is like 'God particle'. Everything in the universe is from the Electron. It sounds like "in the beginning there was Word, the Word became flesh (Jesus Christ) and nothing was created without the Word", Jn.1:1. The electrons orbit around the central nucleus of the atom like the planets orbit around the sun. Electrons jump from one orbit to another in a mysterious way emitting light with definite colors. The colors correlate with the frequency of the emitted light waves. The light waves are neither particles nor waves: they are both and neither. The electron particle could be a "matter wave" [Schrodinger] and it is a probability wave [Max Born]. Schrodinger's equation was applied to the hydrogen atom and the dance the electron was doing in the atom was observed. The electron waves indeed were ringing in various wave-like patterns much like the ringing patterns of a musical instrument. The matter wave vibrations possess energy and an observable shape. Physicist Schrodinger is the pioneer scientist who worked on Electron particle. The almighty Electron particle was equated to God even like I have written here that, this quantum phenomenon could be Saint John's, "In the beginning there was Word", Jn.1:1. At this point Schrodinger lamented that", had I known that my wave equation would be put to such a use, I should have burned the papers before publishing". Any measurement made on the electron between A and B could disturb any hypothetical path the electron was on because of the existence of the possibilities and probabilities with intrinsic uncertainties [Werner Heisenberg]. The electron orbits around the nucleus like that of a planet going around the star is a meaningless concept if the knowledge of a particular path of an electron is not relevant to determine the atomic behavior [Bohr].

Tunneling.

In tunneling, the impinging electron upon another electron wall has finite probability of passing through the wall. The photon light particles demonstrate this probabilistic behavior. The photons, which emerge from the sun reflect from our face and pass through the glass window. We see our images through the window glass because of a fraction of the photon reflects from the window glass. We cannot predict the photon that reflects or transmits because all photons look identical. However, the probability of reflection or transmission can be computed for a given photon by Schrodinger's equation. The particles exist beyond our observation too. The quantum state changes abruptly and the signals are transmitted simultaneously throughout the universe faster than the speed of light. Determining the properties of an object way over there by measuring the object way over here is spooky action at a distance for Einstein. A definite property cannot exist until a measurement brings it into being [Bohr]. Schrodinger's half-dead and half-alive cat should be in a quantum mixed state. The quantum effects are observable both at micro and macro systems level. The earth spins around the sun at a speed of one thousand miles per hour at the equator though higher speeds were observed in galaxy systems. We do not feel any motion because our surroundings share the same motion of ours. We do not feel any sensation of the motion if the motion is uniform. The most natural state of an object is to be sitting still at rest [Aristotle]. An isolated body in motion will maintain its motion forever [Galileo]. The sun and moon pull on earth's oceans to create the tides. Newton's laws of gravity works across the vast stretches of space and across ninety three million miles between the earth and sun. The planets orbit the sun elliptically both precisely and predictably. Newton's laws of motion cannot explain the higher velocities in reference to quantum particles.

The full knowledge about light, energy and vibration only reveal the full picture of the creation. The light is energy and a wave disturbance. Chemical and the electrical energies can be transformed into light. The sun's light comes from the solar surfaces. The nuclear fusion produces energy, which creates heat. The objects we see reflect light. The longer wavelengths in low temperatures produce the color red. The speed of light is 186, 000 miles per second, whereas the speed of sound is 0.2 miles per second. The light and the speed of light constitute the entire physical universe. The light travels at a higher velocity in straight lines until it meets the surface of a glass of water and refracts. The universe is made up of particles and the light itself is a stream of particles [photons]. The particles carry energy and induce chemical reactions. The light travels through a transparent medium [ether] and fills the whole space. It propagates as circular waves much like the ripples in a pond when a pebble is thrown in it. The water waves and sound waves are produced due to pressure disturbance. This world is filled with water waves, sound waves, and seismic waves. The wave's amplitude determines its energy level. The wave spreading in all directions from a small aperture is known as diffraction. The wave phenomenon is well observed when you see brightly colored striations in a puddle with gasoline spill. The rainbow displays interference of light passing through the tiny droplets of water in the air at different angles.

The light is a wave, which accounts for reflection, refraction, absorption, diffraction and interference [Young].

Atomic vibrations emit light and the frequency of atomic vibrations [one thousand cycles per second] corresponds with the frequency of light waves. The velocity of the light in the vacuum is the same for a candle or the sun. Both visible and invisible light comes from sun, but we do not know how it is generated. We do not know the retinal mechanism of vision, nor the mechanism of absorption of light. The ozone in upper stratosphere filters much of ultraviolet light and the light ultimately touches and interacts with the matter. Salt or a metal gives off characteristic colors in a hot flame. The spectrometer is helpful to reveal wavelengths in regions of prominent colors. The patterns of bright lines from the salts match precisely the patterns of dark lines in the solar spectrum [Fraunhofer lines]. The sun's hot surface emits light of all wavelengths. The light passes through cooler gases of sun's outer atmosphere. Each element, when heated, produces a characteristic set of spectral lines, which were the first clues to the mysterious structures vibrating inside the atom. The earth is composed of hydrogen, helium, lithium, and other. The light from distant stars contains the same elements, which implies that the origin of creation should be common.

An electrically charged particle creates an electric field around it [Michael Faraday]. This electric field acts on any other, which is nearby throughout space. The magnetic force attracts a distant speck of iron within the magnetic field. The electrical, magnetic and the gravitational fields demonstrate the physical visualization of force, which explains how the energy can be transformed. This field effect can explain the action at a distance. The field contains the energy and the momentum. A magnetic field can be generated by passing electric current through a copper wire. This electricity dependent society is built on the law of induction, which gives us full comprehension of electromagnetism. The magnetic or electric field can disturb insubstantial ether medium in the space. The waning magnetic fields create waxing electric fields cyclically. The light is an electromagnetic disturbance [Maxwell]. The light is the product of oscillating electric and magnetic fields propagating through space at a velocity of 186, 000 miles per second. His theory revealed that the electric charges in the atoms are set into vibrations, which radiate the electromagnetic energy and visible light. The atoms are the repositories of the electrical charges. The light waves constitute electric and magnetic forces. They affect green leaves and retina during their travel through space. The electric and the magnetic waves generated in a laboratory by Heinrich Hertz obeyed the laws of reflection, refraction, diffraction and interference.

The "black body radiation" [the glow of toaster wires] emits thermal radiation when heated. The early earth's atmosphere and the mushroom cloud of nuclear explosion are the approximations of the black body emission of thermal radiation. The objects and human beings radiate and absorb energy until thermal dilution is established. The blood flow carries the thermal energy to body surface. The radiation bears the imprint of definite colors of particular atomic transitions. Strontium chloride and barium chloride, which are used in fireworks, produce bright red and green colors as they oxidize. The sun emits light and absorbs light as well because the outer surface of sun is cooler. The toaster wires glow is dull red in quantum description because the light comes in quantum particles but it is blue in classical physics. The shorter wavelengths produce higher frequencies with higher energy [Planck]. Physicists believe that the quanta were pulses of radiation coming from thermally agitated atomic motion in the blackbody walls. The energy of quantum light is directly proportional to its frequency. The electromagnetic radiation emits in lumps. The "quanta" is akin to the concept that the light is particles though it is very likely a wave. The "quanta" model worked both in black body radiation and photoelectric effect, but the wave theory failed in both the cases. The electromagnetic energy propagates as waves throughout the space. Maxwell's theory established direct connection between the light, electricity and magnetism. More frequency gives more brightness of light. Max Planck became a noble laureate in1918 for his discovery, "quantum energy." Einstein became noble laureate in 1905 for his discovery "photoelectric effect." It is a photoelectric effect when you snap a photo with your cell phone, where the light goes in and the electricity comes out.

Electron and Atom.

Electron is a fundamental particle of this creation out of which everything is composed. It knows it all, does it all and all pervading. It is a pinpoint of nature with a mass of $1/2000^{th}$ of an atom. It is electrically charged particle discovered by J. J. Thompson in 1887. Jon Dalton discovered atom in 1803 and Michel Faraday demonstrated the electrical nature of an atom.

The electrons are paired and nowhere yet everywhere at the same time and all the time. They reach from A. to B. instantly with no certainty of path they did take. They are waves with crests and troughs as well as particles. Both the particles and waves demonstrate neither or yet both and all at once. They are above the law of nature. The photon carries a definite amount of energy (Planck's formula) and the photon collides with electron and yield's a recoiling photon and an electron (Crompton's scattering). The light is corpuscles as Newton conceived but these photons could behave like waves in quantum state. Young's double slit experiment favors wave theory of light.

Atom is a tiny solar system with mini planets [electrons] circling around the nucleus in elliptical orbits. The nucleus is one trillionth of atom's volumes. The electrons and nucleus are held together by electromagnetic force. The electrons are interspersed in the empty space of atom and move rapidly around the nucleus. The matter is therefore mostly an empty space . The electrons jump mysteriously from one orbit to another without being in between and produce multiple quantum phenomena. Each orbital has two electrons in different spins and no two electrons can be in the same quantum state simultaneously according to "Pauli's exclusion principle". The electrons hop back and forth from orbit to orbit emitting or absorbing the light. The allowed states of motion that an electron can move in each orbital depends on its own energy level. The electron orbital energy radiates away into electromagnetic waves instantly and the electron spiral down like a wounded bird, crashing into nucleus. The orbits and the atom itself collapse resulting in a dead atom.

The electron in a smaller orbit is closer to the nucleus though the electron could never fall into the nucleus from the orbit [Bohr]. This is the ground state of the lowest energy and the electron cannot go into any state of lower energy level. The electron continues orbiting around the nucleus with no need for more energy. The ground state, which stabilizes the atom, is a feature of quantum systems. The vacuum is the ground state of the universe. The discrete energy levels in an atom contrasts with "intrinsic continuity" [classical view] of nature [Frank Hertz]. Helium is inert chemical because its two electrons are snug well and the Hydrogen atom has one electron in the orbit and welcomes an additional electron only in the opposite spin.

Quantum Particle.vs.Quantum Wave.

Photon is another quantum mystic particle. It is the light particle and "quanta" is the collection of light particles. It is found as particle as well a wave but neither or both at the same time. The accelerated charge must radiate energy in the form of electromagnetic, which is the light [Maxwell]. His light waves are quanta. The particle has definite location in space and time and moves on a trajectory where as the wave is spread all over the space like any other wave function. The string theory is all about particles. The sound wave or an electromagnetic wave gives real numbers at each point of space and time and the quantum wave does not. The electron waves are matter waves and should not differ from water waves or sound waves [Schrodinger]. The electron matter waves looked like a particle on superimposition. Fourier superimposed a large number of waves that their net disturbance could be localized [much like a particle] to a small region of space. The light was known to be a wave until Einstein and Planck discovered "quanta" which also behave like waves. The gravitational waves are composed of gravitons.

Somebody from inside the store can see the reflection of my face outside because of the wave function when the particle transmits or reflects partially. The discrete particles reflect or transmit completely. The matter absorbs photons whole or not at all. Each electron is known to have a quantum wave, which obeys the mathematical behavior of wave function. The waves are small sounds in the end and the particles are the quantum vibrations of a string. The light exists as waves as well the photon particles as tiny lumps [quanta]. The particle has energy and momentum, which can be transferred to another particle through collision. The "quanta" collide with electrons and push them around. Both the position and momentum of a particle cannot be measured simultaneously with definite values [uncertainty principle]. We cannot know the electron's wavelength or its location at the same time. The more we know about the location, the less we know about the momentum. A particle exists in many quantum states and places in time and space but we do not know how they get there. The measurement of a particle disturbs the particle itself that it is forced to go into one of its other possibilities [Paschal Jordan]. The wave function gives the probability of finding a particle in a given place. The particle's each observed possibility has its own probability of being observed in a given quantum state.

The spin, "A" can be determined by measuring the spin "B", though they are far apart in the vast space.

The wave function alone can explain such instantaneous transfer of information across the vast space. There are no observable signals, which can be sent faster than light. The wave function only describes the particles with a set of probabilities [Bohr]. The particles described by the probabilistic wave function correlates well with the spooky action at a distance as well collapse instantly throughout the space without violating the ultimate speed of light [Bell's theorem]. Bell believed that "A" and "B" are not separate existences though they are far apart. Everything in the universe is interconnected [Bell's concept of non-locality]. The propagation of light does not weaken with the increasing distance. A single wave is stretching all over the space with a defined wavelength. What cannot be measured does not exist [Copenhagen interpretation]. The atoms emit the photons and lose mass the exact amount of energy that the photon carries away with it. The light wave has particle properties too [De Broglie]. The electrons could be assigned wave properties if they cannot be considered as particles. The diffractive motion of the electrons as waves in a crystal is the mechanism behind the transistors. Now we can measure the spectral lines as well emission and absorption of the light by an atom. The probabilistic quantum domain is beyond human mind. The disagreement on wave vs. particle concept may be resolved through the probability wave theory and uncertainty relations principle. The photons and electrons in the end are particles and the particle behavior includes probability waves. God may play dice, but man has managed the quantum domain enough to fashion his digital technology.

DNA molecule.

The DNA molecule and the associated chemical reactions could be the basis of our life and self-awareness. We breathe in oxygen and live by oxidation. We know the physical basis of matter and the physiological basis of our daily biological processes. The combination of atoms and the formation of molecules is ultimately a shell filling process. The electron orbiting in the outer orbital of atom joins another electron in the outer orbital of another atom, but the electron in the inner orbital does nothing. Nature draws the things into configurations with minimum energy. The electrons arrange themselves that they occupy the lowest energy state. The exclusion principle takes precedence over the quest for the state of the lowest energy. The electron places itself in the lowest state that it may not impinge on the space of other electron. The two electrons in the same position and spin in the same space get the wave function that equals to zero if swapped. The covalent bond in H has two electrons. The two electrons one from each orbital fills the covalent bond resulting in the combination of two hydrogen atoms. The oxygen attracts two hydrogen electrons to form water, which is an important content of the universe. The atoms are symmetrically merged together and the electrons are cooperatively shared between the two atoms. In ionic bond, the active outer electron as in sodium chloride deserts one atom and joins the other atom. The two atoms are still bonded by their opposite charges. The signals, which are transmitted by the nerve cells to produce thoughts, involve ionic pump where the sodium ion gets into the cells and the potassium ion gets out through the walls of the nerve cells. This mechanism involves hopping of electrons in their orbital of atoms of nerve membrane cells. The delicate balance of these ionic bonds rules our life. Ninety-nine percent of the atom is empty space, but we cannot sink the hand through a table because the electrons in the body cannot penetrate the walls of the atoms. The "Pauli's exclusion principle" prohibits electrons to get too close together. Muon is a charged particle and a heavy photocopy of the electron. It is radioactive particle and disintegrates in two microseconds. Physicists Bohr and Heisenberg hold that the randomness and the indeterminacy described by the uncertainty principle is intrinsic to nature [God]. "My calculation however did not necessarily have anything to do with God", Bell stated to his hosts at Maharishi University in Iowa. The quantum theory gives us insight into cosmology, invisible order of the universe and the operations of human consciousness.

Dirac's sea and quantum energy.

The vacuum in the atom is filled with spin up and spin down electrons with negative energy level [Dirac's idea] which stabilizes the universe from falling into negative energy abyss [Dirac's sea]. Dirac's sea represents infinity of negative energy state. The universe becomes unstable in negative energy state. The positive energy electrons in the atom cannot emit photons [Pauli' exclusion principle]. A gamma ray ejects electron out of its negative energy state into its positive energy state. The collision leaves a hole in the vacuum, which indicates the absence of a negative energy electron. Now the hole left behind by the missing negative energy electron is the positively charged positron particle, which possesses the same as the electron. Every particle has its own anti particle. Electron's anti particle is positron. The positrons are energy particles, which are produced by cosmic rays [Carl Anderson] and they collide with negative energy electrons in the vacuum and produce an electron and a positron. The matter and antimatter collide and produce a positive energy electron, which jumps back into the hole in the vacuum and emits gamma rays. This process is to conserve the energy and momentum.

The nuclear fission of uranium yields abundant energy [nuclear fission]. The lighter nuclei of deuterium combine and form Helium that releases energy in abundance. The sun is another source of energy in abundances which sustains life on earth. The proton is two thousand times heavier than the electron, which forms the nucleus of atom along with neutron. It is an anti-electron and confirms the existence of anti-matter. The particles like quarks, charged leptons, neutrinos Etc. all have anti matter twins. The bosons have positive energy states. The photon is a boson, which is an antiparticle. The early universe had equal abundance of particles and antiparticles, which could annihilate the photons and we would not have existed. Our existence today is because the antimatter does not exist and the how and why is beyond our comprehension. As the universe cooled, most of the matter was annihilated by the antimatter. Now we live in this small visible world left behind.

Gravity and vacuum energy density.

Any object with mass, energy and momentum produces gravity. The vacuum energy density through gravity can crumble down the universe into nothingness though we do not understand the phenomenon yet. The universe maintains its size through its matter content and the vacuum itself is one of the contents of the universe. The vacuum energy density is positive energy state. The bosons and photons in quantum state have positive vacuum energy density but the electrons have vacuum negative energy. The bosons do not belong to Dirac's sea but the positive energies of both the electrons and photons are added to infinite negative Dirac's sea energies. The positive vacuum energy of bosons cancels against the negative Dirac's sea energies of the fermions. The fermions are associated with boson as particle as well anti particle. The cosmic constant is identically zero. The signals cannot travel faster than the speed of light because the sum of all paths for such a signal adds up to zero. This occurs when an association exists between anti matter in the particle and the anti-particle itself. The hologram is the projection of all space onto a space of smaller dimension and the world is like hologram. The "laser" is a flash light that emits photons of light with equal wavelengths. The tunneling microscope has more magnifying power than the electron microscope. We have the nuclear reactors.

Black Hole and Predicting Past and Future.

God knows the future, but man does not. Astrologists historically interpreted events on earth in reference to the motions of planets across the sky. The planets orbit the sun according to Newton's laws. If we know the positions and the velocities of all the particles in the universe at one time, the laws of physics should allow us to predict the state of the universe in the past or in the future [Laplace]. The problem is that a small change in position and velocity of a particle at one place and time can create different behavior instantly or later in a distant place. A voice of a deer in my back yard in Vidalia, Georgia should create a relevant cosmic change in my birthplace in Karavadi, South India. The frequency of events is not repeatable and human behavior is unpredictable from a mathematical model. The scientific determinism that the future somehow is predictable is threatened by the uncertainty principle, which says that we cannot measure accurately both the position and the velocity of a particle at the same time. The most accurately we can measure the position, the less accurately we determine the velocity and vice versa. However, the theory of quantum mechanics incorporated the uncertainty principle and restored the scientific determinism to half of one would expect to predict in the classical Laplace point of view. In quantum mechanics, a particle does not have a well-defined position or velocity, but its state can be represented by a wave function. A wave function is a number at each point of space that gives probability of the particle that is to be found at that position. The rate at which the wave function changes from point to point tells how probable the particle velocities are. Some wave functions are sharply peaked at a particular point in space where there is small amount of uncertainty in the position of the particle. Again, with a large uncertainty in position and a small uncertainty in velocity, the description of a particle by a wave function does not have a well-defined position or velocity. The wave function however can be well defined.

We know the wave function, but the uncertainty principle blinds us from knowing the position and velocity of a particle. Schrödinger's equation gives the rate at which the wave function changes with time. If we know the wave function at one time, we can calculate it at any other time in past or in future. We predict the wave function and we can predict the particle's position or velocity, but not both. Our ability to predict future is half of what it was in the classical Laplace view. Predicting the future times through Schrodinger's equation implicitly assumes that the time runs on smoothly everywhere, forever. Time was assumed absolute, meaning that each event in the history of the universe is labeled by a number called time and that a series of time labels ran smoothly from the infinite past to infinite future. However, Einstein's theory of relativity states that the time was no longer an independent quantity on its own but was just one direction in a four directional continuum called space-time, which cancelled the concept of absolute time in 1905. We can use space-time or an absolute time in Schrodinger's equation to evolve the wave function. The quantum version of determinism is intact even in special theory of relativity.

Black hole.

"Now as he was speaking with me, I was in a deep sleep on my face toward the ground: but he touched me, and set me upright. And he said, behold I will make you know what shall be in the last end of the indignation: for at time appointed the end shall be", Dan.8:18-19.

The more massive stars than the sun possess escape velocity greater than the speed of light. We do not see them because the light they sent out would be dragged back by the gravity of those stars. John Michell called them dark stars. John Archibald Wheeler from Jacksonville, Florida called them black holes. Any planet can become a black hole when all its matter is squeezed into a small sphere. The sun can become a black hole when it is compressed to a size of a couple of football fields. Fortunately, the earth is far from being a black hole. Black holes are not completely black [Dr. Hawking]. The black hole in essence is an unseen compact massive object. The cannon ball that is fired vertically upwards slows its ascent by gravity and it eventually stops moving upward and falls back even [John Michell, 1783]. If the initial upward velocity is greater than the escape velocity, the gravity is strong enough to stop the particle. The light with speed of 300, 000 kilometers per second can get away from earth or sun without much difficulty.

Orion Nebula is a massive star, which forms clouds of gas and this gas contracts under its gravity. The gas heats up eventually and starts a nuclear fusion reaction that converts hydrogen into helium. The helium burns into heavier elements like carbon and oxygen. The heat generated by this process produces pressure that supports the star against its own gravity and stops it from contracting further. A star keeps on burning hydrogen and radiating light into space for hundreds of millions of years. These nuclear reactions do not release much energy so that the stars lose heat and thermal pressure that supports them against gravity. Therefore, the stars get smaller. If they are more than twice the mass of the sun, the pressure will never be sufficient to stop the contraction. They will collapse to zero size and infinite density to form what is called, singularity. The star becomes a black hole and the light cannot get away from the star. A black hole still exerts the same gravitational pull on neighboring objects, as did the body that collapsed. If the sun were a black hole and had managed to become one without losing any of its mass, the planets would be still orbiting.

Objects trap matter and light. Most galaxies might contain humongous black holes that have masses of many billions of times greater than the mass of the sun. They are surrounded by enormous gas clouds and whole star systems, which could fall into them. They create vast amounts of high-energy radiation as they collide. The black hole horizon is a pool of un-shrouded darkness. When the mass of a star is concentrated in a small enough region, the gravitational field at the surface of the star becomes so strong that even light can no longer escape [Karl Schwarzschild]. It is impossible for anything including light to reach a distant observer. When a heavy non-rotating star runs out of nuclear fuel, it will necessarily collapse to a black hole. A black hole with the same mass as the sun would have a radius of two miles.

In theory of general relativity, one can measure time at different rates in different places. Someone outside the black hole cannot observe Schrödinger's wave function inside the black hole. An observer who is sensible not to fall into cannot run the Schrodinger's equation backward and calculate the wave function at early times unless the observer knows that part of the wave function was locked inside black hole. This could be a large amount of information because a black hole of a given mass and rate of rotation can be formed from a large number of different collections of particles. A black hole does not depend on the nature of the body that had collapsed to form it.

The fields cannot be zero even in vacuum state [quantum theory]. The zero vacuum state is in violation of the uncertainty principle, which says that position and velocity of a particle cannot be well defined at the same time. All fields should have certain amount of vacuum fluctuations. It is helpful to think of vacuum fluctuations as a pair of virtual particles that appear together and at some point of space-time move apart and come back together and annihilate each other. One of the particle pair may fall into black hole leaving the other free to escape into infinity. For an observer far from black hole, the escaping particles appear to have been radiated by the black hole. The spectrum of black hole is exactly what we would expect from a hot body with a temperature proportional to the gravitational field on the "horizon" [the boundary of the black hole]. The temperature of a black hole depends therefore on its size. A black hole of few solar masses would have a temperature of about a millionth of a degree above absolute zero and a large black hole would have even lower temperature. Any such quantum radiation from such black holes would be utterly swamped by the 2.7-degree radiation left over from the cosmic background radiation. It is possible to detect the radiation from much smaller and hotter black holes.

Some planets are too distant from us for their light is ever to reach us. The early universe would have expanded too much and too rapidly while that light was travelling toward us. There would be a horizon in the universe like the horizon of a black hole. There should be thermal radiation from this horizon of the universe as there is from a black hole horizon. The spectrum of density fluctuations in thermal radiation should have become frozen in, that we could observe them today as small variations in the temperature of the cosmic background radiation left over from the early universe. The observations of these variations agree with predictions of thermal regulations with remarkable accuracy. The radiation from a black hole will carry away energy, lose mass, and become smaller in the process, in turn, its temperature will rise, and the rate of radiation will increase eventually. The black hole becomes eventually zero mass and may disappear completely at this point. The wave function in the black hole and the information it carries would requires energy to carry it and there is very little energy left in the final stages of a black hole. The information inside the black hole could get out only if it emerged continuously with the radiation rather than waiting for this final stage. According to the picture of one member of a virtual particle pair falling in and the other member escaping, one would not expect the escaping particle to be related to what fell in or to carry information about it. The only answer seems to be that the information in the part of the wave function inside the black hole gets lost. Such loss of information has important implications for scientific determinism. Even if you knew the wave function after the black hole disappeared, you could not run the Schrodinger's equation backward and calculate what the wave function was before the black hole formed. We think we know the past but it is not the case if the information was lost in the black holes. The loss of part of the wave function down the black hole would prevent us from predicting the wave function outside the black hole. The positive energy carried away by thermal radiation from black hole's horizon reduces its mass. This would increase its temperature and the rate of radiation as well, so it loses mass more and more quickly. If the mass becomes extremely small, the black hole may disappear completely.

Energy density.

The horizon area of a black hole could only increase with time but it never shrinks. It shrinks in size with negative energy density on the horizon and warp space-time that make light rays diverge from each other. The evaporation of black holes shows on quantum level that the energy density can sometimes be negative and warp space-time in the direction that would be needed to build a time machine. An advanced civilization could arrange things so that the energy density is sufficiently negative to form a time machine that could be used by space ships. Light rays that just keep going from the black hole horizon and the horizon in a time machine contains closed light rays that keep going around and around. A virtual particle moving on such a closed path would bring its ground state energy back to the same point repeatedly. The horizon of the time machine, the region in which one can travel into the past would have infinite energy density. A person that tried to cross the horizon to get into the time machine would be wiped out by a bolt of radiation, so the future looks bleak for time travel. The energy density of matter depends on the state it is in, so an advanced civilization might be able to make the energy density finite on the boundary of the time machine by freezing out or removing the virtual particles that go round and round in a closed loop. The disturbance we expect that someone crossing the horizon to enter the time machine might set of circulating virtual particles and trigger a bolt of lightning that one might get wiped out by a bolt of radiation when crossing time travel horizon.

In closed loops, the particle goes round and round in time and space and the particles travel back in time even faster than light.

The particle in closed loop histories cannot be observed directly with a particle detector. We only know through their indirect effects, which are measurable experimentally. The electron moving in the closed loops causes small shift in the light given out by hydrogen atoms. Each history will be a curved space-time with matter fields in it. The time travel is indeed taking place in micro level but we do not see it. The closed loop particle histories occur in fixed backgrounds such as flat space and with warping of space-time. A particle moves on closed loop in a given fixed background or that particle stays fixed and the space and time fluctuate around it. Quantum theory may allow time travel on microscopic level. (Feynman sum over histories).

Einstein's universe.

Einstein's universe is different from the universe we live in. The space-time runs static and unchanging from infinite fast to infinite future. The universe is not constricting nor expanding. Einstein's universe is like a cylinder. It is finite in space and constant in time. Because of its finite size, it can rotate at less than the speed of light everywhere. The space directions are finite and close on themselves like the surface of earth, but with one more dimension. Space-time is like a cylinder with long axis being the time direction and the cross section being the three space directions. If you were on the axis, you could remain at the same point of space, just as you do when standing at the center of a children's carousel. If you were not on the axis, you would be moving through space as you rotated about the axis. The further you were from the axis, the faster you would be moving. The points sufficiently far from the axis would have to be rotating faster than light if the universe were infinite in space.

In Einstein's universe, the space directions are finite and there is a critical rate of rotation below which no part of the universe is rotating faster than the light. In flat space, a rigid rotation will move faster than the speed of light far from its axis. Particle histories in a rotating Einstein's universe, when the rotation is slow there are many paths a particle can take using a given amount of energy; thus, the sum over all particle histories in the background gives a large amplitude. The probability of this background gives a large amplitude would be high in the sum over all curved space-time histories that is, it is among the more probable histories. As the rate of rotation of the Einstein's universe approaches the critical value so that its outer edges are moving at a speed approaching the speed of light, there is only one particle path that is classically allowed on the edge, namely one that is moving at the speed of light. This means that the sum over particle histories will be small. Time travel and time loops mathematically equivalent with Einstein's rotating universe as they do with other background that do admit time loops. The other background that is, the universes that are expanding in two space directions. The universes are not expanding in the third place direction, which is periodic that meant if you go a certain distance in this direction you get back where you started. Each time you made a circuit of the third place direction, your space in the first or second direction is increased.

The 'thought experiment' of Einstein, Podolsk and Rosen [1930] reflects that no one is able to send information faster than light. The observer who has measured the spin of one particle knows the direction of the second particle. The thought experiment in reality occurs in black hole radiation. The virtual particle pair has a wave function, which predicts that both particles will have opposite spins. If one particle falls into black hole, it is impossible to predict with certainty the spin of the other remaining particle.

P-branes and brane world.

Cunrun Vafa in 1996 chose to regard a black hole as being made up of a number of building blocks, called p-branes, which move through the three dimensions of space sheets and through the extra seven dimensions, which we do not notice. A black hole can be intersections of p-branes in the extra dimensions of space-time. The information about the internal states of black holes would be stored as waves on the p-branes. A particle falling into a black hole can be thought of as a closed loop of string hitting a p-brane, which excites waves in the p-brane to break of as a closed ring. A number of waves on the p-branes are the same as the amount of information one would expect the black hole to contain. If the waves moving in different directions on the p-branes come together at some point, they can create a peak so great that a bit of the p-brane brakes away and goes off as a particle. Thus, the p-brane can absorb and emit particles like black holes. The mathematical model of black holes, which are made up of p-branes gives results similar to the virtual particle pair picture. In p-brane model, the information that falls into black hole will be stored in wave formation. The p-branes are regarded as sheets in flat space-time and time will smoothly flow forward.

The path of light rays won't be bent and the information in the waves won't be lost. The information eventually will emerge instead from the black hole in the radiation from the p-branes. We can use the Schrodinger equation to calculate what the wave function will be later through p-brane model. Thus, we lose nothing and time will run smoothly on. The virtual particle pair will have a wave function that predicts that the two will definitely have opposite spins. The spin and wave function of outgoing particle can be predicted, but the spin and wave function of the particle that is inside the black hole cannot be measured. It is not possible to predict the spin or wave function of the particle that escapes for this reason. The particle inside the black hole may have different spins and wave functions. It would seem that our power to predict the future would be further reduced. The classical idea of Laplace that one could predict both the positions and velocities of particles had to be modified when the uncertainty principle showed that one could not accurately measure both the positions and the velocities. However, one could still measure the wave function and use Schrodinger's equation to predict what it should be in the future. This would allow one to predict with certainty that the particles have opposite spins. If one particle falls in the black hole, we can make no prediction with certainty about the remaining particle. It means that there is no any measurement outside the black hole that can be predicted with certainty. Our ability to make definite predictions would be reduced to zero. At this point, astrology is no worse at predicting the future than the laws of science. Many theoretical physicists believe that information gets out of black holes as the p-brane model suggests; the information is not lost and the world is safe and predictable. However, Einstein's general theory of relativity concludes that space-time ties itself in a knot and information gets lost in the folds. The theory of everything [M. theory] is a network of different theories. M theory remains incomplete with several jigsaw puzzles left unfilled.

Atom and Brane.

The matter constitutes atoms. The matter is a continuous medium, which possesses viscosity and elasticity. An atom has nucleus, which is made up of protons and neutrons. The protons and neutrons are made up of quarks. A proton has two up quarks with positive electrical charge and one down quark with negative electrical charge. A neutron has two down quarks with negative charge and two up quarks with positive electrical charge. The electrons orbit the nucleus. 'Planck's length' is the smallest length possible, which is useful to probe high-energy smallest particles, which would be inside black holes. It must be a millimeter divided by more than one hundred thousand billion. Space-time is said to have eleven dimensions by probing through high-energy particles and seven of them would be curled up small. One or more extra dimensions might be larger or even infinite, which implies that we lived in a brane world. Four dimensional [brane] surfaces in a higher dimensional face time, matter and electric force would be confined to the brane. Everything that is non-gravitational would behave as if it would in four dimensional surface or brane in a higher dimensional space-time. If we were to live, the atoms should be stable. The electric force between the nucleus and the electrons blocks electrons from falling into nucleus.

Gravity in the form of curved space would permeate the whole bulk of the higher dimensional space-time. Gravity would spread out in extra dimensions. It would fall more rapidly with distance than one would expect. If this rapid fall off of the gravitational force extends to astronomical distances, the planets would be unstable and they would either fall into the sun or escape to the dark and cold of the interstellar space. Those would not happen if the extra dimensions ended on another brane not that far away from the brane on which we live. For distances greater than the separation of the branes, gravity would not be able to spread out, but would effectively be confined to the brane. On the other hand, for the distances less than the separation of the branes, gravity would vary rapidly. The very small gravitational force between heavy objects has been measured accurately in the lab, but the experiments so far would not have detected the effects of branes separated by less than few millimeters. In this brane world, we live on one brane but there would be another shadow brane nearby, because light would be confined to the branes and would not propagate through the space that we could not see the shadow world. However, we could feel the gravitational influence of matter on the shadow brane. In our brane, such gravitational forces would appear to be produced by sources that were truly dark in that the only way we could detect them is through their gravity. In order to explain the rate at which stars orbit the center of our galaxy, it seems there must be more mass than is accounted for by the matter we observe. A second brane near our brane world would prevent gravity from spreading far into the extra dimension and would mean that at the distance greater than the brane separation, gravity would fall off at the rate one would expect for four dimensions. In the brane world, planets may orbit a dark mass on a shadow brane because the gravitational force propagates into the extra dimensions. The cosmological observations strongly suggest that there should be much more matter in our galaxy and other galaxies than we see. It seems stars on the out skirts of spiral galaxies like our own Milky Way orbit far too fast to be held in their orbits by the gravitational attraction of all the stars that we observe. Since the 1970's there is a discrepancy between the observed rotational velocities of stars in the outer regions of spiral galaxies and the orbit velocities that one would expect according to Newton's laws from the distribution of visible stars in the galaxy. The discrepancy indicates that there should be much more matter in the outer parts of the spiral galaxies.

Dark matter.

The dark matter is an ordinary matter which is not readily detectable [perhaps gas clouds] but comprised of protons, neutrons and electrons. The central parts of spiral galaxies consist largely of ordinary stars and their outskirts are demonstrated by dark matter that we cannot see directly. The galaxies are believed to be formed by significant fraction of dark matter. The very light elementary particles like axions or neutrinos could be part or all of dark matter. The dark matter could arise from WIMPS [weakly interacting massive particles]also. We would see a shadow galaxy on a shadow brane because light would not propagate through the extra dimensions, but gravity would, so the rotation of our galaxy would be affected by dark matter. The missing mass could also be an evidence of an existence of a shadow world with matter in it. May it contain shadow human beings?.

Instead of the extra dimensions ending on a second brane, another possibility is that they are infinite but highly curved like a saddle. This kind of curvature would act rather like a second brane; the gravitational influence of an object on the brane would be confined to a small neighborhood of the brane and not spread out to infinity in the extra dimensions. In the shadow brane model, the gravitational field would have the right long distance fall off to explain planetary orbits and lab measurements of the gravitational force, but gravity would vary more rapidly at short distances. Bodies that move under the influence of the gravity will produce gravitational waves, ripples of curvature that travel through space-time at the speed of light. The extra dimensions extended to infinity, but are curved like a saddle. The curvature prevents the gravitational field of matter on the brane from spreading far into the extra dimensions.

The theory of general relativity predicts that heavy bodies moving under the influence of gravity emit gravitational waves. Like the light waves, gravitational waves carry energy away from the objects that emit them. However, the rate of energy loss is extremely low, hence very difficult to observe. For instance, the emission of gravitational waves is causing the earth to slowly spiral in toward the sun but it would take another 10 years [27 zero yrs.]for them to collide. The binary pulsar, a system consisting of two compact neutron stars orbiting each other with a maximum separation of only one solar radius. According to theory of general relativity, the rapid motion means that the orbital period of this system should decrease on a much shorter time scale because of the emission of a strong gravitational wave signal. The change predicted by general relativity is in excellent agreement with careful observations by Hulse and Taylor of the orbital parameters, which indicate that since 1975, the period has shortened more than 10 seconds.

Randall-Sun drum model.

Short wave length gravitational waves can carry energy away from sources on the brane causing apparent violation of the law of conservation of energy. Like the electromagnetic waves of light, gravitational waves should carry energy, a prediction that has been confirmed by observations of the binary pulsar. If we live on a brane in a space-time with extra dimensions, gravitational waves generated by the motion of bodies on the brane would travel off into other dimensions. If there were a second shadow brane, gravitational waves should be reflected back and trapped between the two branes. On the other hand, if there was a single brane and the extra dimensions went on forever as in Sun Drum-Randall model, the gravitational waves could escape altogether and carry away energy from our brane world. This would seem breach the law of conservation of energy. The total amount of energy remains the same but appears to be only our view of what is happening is restricted to the brane. The energy could be the same, but just more spread out.

The gravitational waves produced by two stars orbiting each other would have a wavelength, which would be much longer than the radius of the saddle shaped curvature in the extra dimensions. This would mean that they would tend to be confined to small neighborhood of the brane-like gravitational force and would not spread out much into the extra dimensions or carry away much energy from the brane. On the other hand, gravitational waves that were shorter than the scale on which the extra dimensions are curved would escape easily from the vicinity of the brane. The only source of significant amounts of short gravitational waves is likely to be black holes. A black hole on the brane will extend to a black hole in the extra dimensions. If the black hole is small, it will be almost round that is, it will reach out as far into the extra dimensions as its size on the brane. On the other hand, a large black hole on the brane will extend to black pancake which is confined to a vicinity of the brane and which is much less thick [in the extra dimensions] than it is wide [on the brane].

Black holes emit particles as well radiation of all kinds like hot bodies. They emit gravitational waves also which would not be confined to the brane but would travel in the extra dimensions as well. The particles and radiation like light would be emitted along the brane because matter and non-gravitational forces like electricity would be confined to the brane. If the black hole was large and pancake like, the gravitational waves would stay near the brane. This would mean that the black hole would lose energy and one would expect for black hole in four-dimensional space-time. The black hole would therefore slowly evaporate and shrink in size–until it became smaller than the radius of curvature of the saddle like extra dimensions. The gravitational waves emitted by the black hole would begin to escape freely into the extra dimensions. To some one on the brane, the black hole or the dark state would appear to be emitting dark radiation, radiation that cannot be observed directly on the brane, but whose existence can be inferred from the fact that the black hole was losing mass. A black hole in our world extends into the extra dimensions. If the black hole is small, it will be almost round but a large black hole on the brane would extend to a pancake shaped black hole in the extra dimension. It meant that the final burst of radiation from an evaporating black hole would appear less powerful than it actually was. This could be why we have not observed bursts of gamma rays that can be ascribed to dying black holes though the other more mosaic explanation would be that there are not many black holes with mass low enough to evaporate in the age of the universe thus far.

The radiation from brane world,

Black holes arise from quantum fluctuation of particles. Everything else in the universe will be subject to quantum fluctuations. These can cause branes to appear and disappear spontaneously. The quantum creation of a brane would be a bit like the formation of bubbles of a steam in boiling water. The water consists of billions and billions of H_20 molecules packed together with couplings with nearest neighbors. As the water heats up, the molecules move faster and bounce of each other. Occasionally these collisions will give molecules such high velocities that a group of them will break free of their bonds and form a little bubble of steam surrounded by water. The bubble then will grow or shrink in a random manner with more molecules from the liquid joining the steam or vice versa. Most small bubbles of steam will collapse to liquid again but few will grow to a certain critical stage beyond which the bubbles are almost certain to continue to grow. It is these large expanding bubbles that one observes when water boils.

The behavior of brane world would be similar. The uncertainty principle would allow brane worlds to appear from nothing as bubbles, the brane forming the surface of the bubble and the interior being the higher dimensional face. Very small bubbles would tend to collapse again to nothing, but a bubble that grew by quantum fluctuations beyond a certain critical size would be likely to keep on growing. People such as us living on the brane, the surface of the bubble would think that the universe was expanding. It would be like painting the galaxies on the surface of a balloon and blowing it up. The galaxies would move apart, but no galaxy would be picked out as the center of expansion. Hope that the bubble won't burst.

According to the no boundary proposal, the spontaneous creation of a brane world would have a history in imaginary time that is, it would be a four dimensional sphere like the surface of the earth but with two more dimensions. The important difference is that it was essentially hollow and the four dimensional sphere wouldn't have been the boundary of anything and the other six or seven dimensions of space time that M theory predicts would all be curled up even smaller than the nutshell. On the new brane world picture, the nutshell would be filled; the history in imaginary time of the brane on which we live would be a four dimensional sphere that would be the boundary of a five dimensional bubble with the remaining five or six dimensions curled up very small. This history of the brane in imaginary time would determine its history in real time. In real time, the brane would expand in an accelerated inflationary manner. A perfectly smooth and round nutshell would be the most probable history of the bubble in imaginary time. However, it would correspond to a brane that expanded forever in an inflationary way in real time. Galaxies would not form on such a brane and so intelligent life would not have developed. On the other hand, imaginary time histories that are not perfectly smooth and round would have somewhat lower probabilities but could correspond to real time behavior in which the brane had a phrase of accelerating inflationary expansion at first but then began to slow down. During the decelerating expansion, galaxies could have formed and intelligent life might have developed. According to the anthropoid principle, it is only the slightly hairy nutshells, which will be observed by intelligent beings asking why the origin of the universe was not perfectly smooth.

Holography:

As the brane expanded, the volume of the higher dimensional place inside would increase. Eternally there would be an enormous bubble surrounded by the brane on which we live. In holography, the information about what happens in a region of space-time can be encoded on its boundary. Maybe we think we live in a four dimensional world because we are shadows cast on the brane by what is happening in the interior of the bubble. From a positivist viewpoint, one cannot ask; which is the reality, brane or bubble? What is outside the brane? There are several possibilities. The brane world picture of the origin of the universe differs from that because the slightly flattened four dimensional sphere or nutshell is no longer hollow but is filled by a fifth dimension. Holography encodes the information in a region of space onto a surface one dimension lower. It seems to be a property of gravity as is shown by the fact that the areas of the event horizon measure the number of internal states of a black hole in a brane world model, holography would be a one to one correspondence between states in our four-dimensional world and states in higher dimensions. From a positivist viewpoint, one cannot distinguish which description is more fundamental. There may be nothing outside. Although a bubble of steam has water outside it, this is just an analogy to help us visualize the origin of the universe. One could imagine a mathematical model that was just a brane with a higher dimensional space inside but absolutely nothing outside, not even empty space. One can calculate what the mathematical model predicts without reference to what is outside.

One could have a mathematical model in which the outside of a bubble was glued to the outside of a similar bubble. The model is equally mathematically equivalent to possibility discussed above that there is nothing outside the bubble but the difference is psychological; people feel happier being placed in the center of space time rather than on its edge. The bubble might expand into a space that was not a mirror image of what was inside the bubble. The possibility is different from the two discussed above and is more like the case of boiling water. Other bubbles could form and expand. If they collided and merge with the bubble in which we lived, the results could be catastrophic. It has been suggested that the Big Bang itself may have produced by a collision between branes. They are highly speculative, but they offer new kinds of behavior that can be tested by observation. They could explain why gravity seems to be so week. Gravity might be strong in the fundamental theory, but the spreading of gravitational force in the extra dimensions would mean it would be weak at large distances on the brane on which we live. A consequence of this could be that the 'Planck length', the smallest distance to which we can probe without creating a black hole, would be quite a larger than it would appear from the weakness of gravity on our four dimensional brane. Other observations such as the cosmic microwave background radiation, we may be able to determine whether we live on a brane. If we do, it will presumably be because the anthropoid principle picks out brane models from the vast zoo off universes allowed by M-theory.

Wormhole.

Wormholes are tubes of space time which connect different regions of space and time. You might go through a wormhole to other side of the galaxy and be back for dinner. You can use woemhole and get back before you set out. It is like kissing your mom before you are conceived. If the two ends of the wormhole close together, you could walk through it and come out at the same time. One may think that a bullet fired earler could affect the one who fired it. The space time allows time loops (time like curves that are closed) to return their starting point. Time and space were curved and distorted by matter and energy in the universe. Personal time would always increase in general theory of relativity as it occurred in Newtonian theory. The time increases even in flat space-time of special theory of relativity. Because the space-time is warped so much that one could go off on space ship and come back before you set out. The basis of time travel is Einstein's general theory of relativity. The universe had a well-defined history without uncertainty and quantum fluctuations (general theory of relativity). According to quantum theory, matter behaves with uncertainty and quantum fluctuations. In quantum theory of gravity both matter, time and space are uncertain and fluctuate. The special theory of relativity [wont accept gravity} does not allow time travel nor do the curved space-time. 'Gödel's theorem' discovered a space-time that was a universe full of rotating matter with time loops through every point. Gödel showed that there are problems that cannot be solved by any set of rules or procedures. The twentieth century, particle science is able to tackle some of these problems.

Cosmic strings.

Cosmic strings are objects with length, but a tiny cross section. Two cosmic strings move at high speed past each other. The space-time outside a single cosmic string is flat. It is flat space-time with a wedge cut out, with the sharp end of the wedge at the string. This represents the space-time in which the cosmic string exists. A circle around the apex is shorter than one would expect for a circle of that radius in flat space because of the missing segment. In the case of a cosmic string, the wedge that is removed from flat space-time shortens circles around the string but does not affect time or distances along the string. That is the space-time around a single cosmic string does not contain any time loops, so it is not possible to travel into the past. However, if there is a second cosmic ring that is moving relative to the first, its time direction will be a combination of the time and space directions of the space. This means that the wedge that is cut out for the second string will shorten both distances in space and time intervals as seen by someone moving with the first string. If the cosmic strings are moving at nearly the speed of light relative to each other, the saving of time going around both strings can be so great that one arrives back before the one set out. There are time loops that one can follow to travel into the past.

The cosmic string space-time contains matter that has positive energy density. However, the warping that produces time loops extends all the way out to infinity in space and back to the infinite past in time. Thus, these space times were created with time travel in them. We have no reason to believe that our own universe was created in such a warped fashion and we have no reliable evidence of visitors from the future. There were no time loops in the distant past or more precisely in the past of some surface through space-time. Could some advance civilization build a time machine? No matter how advanced the civilization becomes, it could presumably control only a finite part of the universe. Time travel is possible in a region of space-time in which there are time loops, paths that move at less than the speed of light, but which nevertheless manage to come back to the place and time they started because of the warping of space-time. There were no time loops in the distant past; but there must be a time travel, horizon, the boundary separating the region of time loops from the region without them. 'Time travel horizons' are like black hole horizons. The black hole horizon is formed by light rays that just miss falling into the black hole, a time travel horizon is formed by light rays on the verge of meeting up with themselves. A finitely generated horizon is that is formed by light rays that all emerge from a bounded region. They won't come in from infinity or from a singularity but originate from a finite region containing time loops-the sort of region our advanced civilization is supposed to create.

The cross strings are long heavy objects with a tiny cross section that may have been produced during the early stages of the universe. They were further stretched by the expansion of the universe. A single cosmic string could cross over the entire length of our observable universe. The particle theories suggest that in the hot early stages of the universe matter was in a symmetric phase much like the liquid water; which is symmetrical the same at every point in every direction-rather than like ice crystals which have discrete structure. When the universe cooled, the symmetry of the early phase could have been broken in different ways in distant regions. Consequently, the cosmic matter could have settled into different ground states in those regions. Cosmic rings are the configurations of the matter at the boundaries between these regions. Their formation was therefore an inevitable consequence of the fact that different regions could not agree on their ground states. A finitely generalized horizon will contain a light ray that keeps coming back to the same point repeatedly. The wave crests of a pulse of light will get closer and closer together and the light will get around in shorter and shorter intervals of its time. A particle of light would have a finite history even if went around and around in a finite region and did not hit a curvature singularity. There would be paths moving at less than the speed of light that had only finite duration.

Space-time would have to warp to produce time loops in a finite region. The cosmic strings were infinitely long. To build a finite time machine, you need negative energy. Energy density is always positive in classical theory, so time machines of finite size are ruled out on this level. In the semi classical theory in which one considers matter to behave according to quantum theory but space-time to be well defined and classical. The un-certainty principle of quantum theory means that fields are always fluctuating up and down even in empty space and have an energy density that is infinite.

One has to subtract an infinite quantity to get finite energy density that we observe in the universe. This subtraction can leave the energy density negative at least locally. Even in flat space, one can find quantum states in which the energy density is negative locally although the total energy is positive. These negative values actually can curve space-time to warp in the appropriate way to build a finite time machine. Quantum fluctuations is full of pairs of virtual particles that appears together move apart and then come back together and annihilate each other even in empty space. One member of a virtual particle pair will have positive energy and the other negative energy. When a black hole is present, the negative energy member can escape to infinity where it appears as radiation that carries positive energy away from the black hole. The negative energy particles falling in cause the black hole to lose mass and to evaporate slowly with its horizon shrinking in size. Ordinary matter with positive energy density has attractive gravitational effect and warps space-time to bend light rays toward each other-just as the ball on the rubble sheet, which always makes the smaller ball curve toward it, never away.

Quantum Knowledge and Future Planet Earth.

We have seen an explosion of knowledge and technology in the last two hundred years since ice age ten thousand years ago. The world population doubles every forty years and we are able to feed and protect mankind. There is also a chance that we may annihilate ourselves through nuclear blast. Our physical body is most complex system of all. The life began in the primordial oceans, which covered the earth four billion years ago. Possibly random collisions of atoms built up macro molecules and assemble themselves into structures that are more complex. The source of life DNA emerged half a billion years ago; Francis Crick and James Watson discovered it in 1953. The order in which the four bases [adenine, guanine, thymine and cytosine] occur along the spiral staircase of DNA structure carries the genetic information. The information contained in the sequence of DNA evolves gradually and increases in complexity. Biological evolutions are basically a random walk in the space of all genetic possibilities. We developed written language about six thousand years ago. The information could be passed from one generation to the next without having to wait for the very slow process of random mutations and natural selection to code it into DNA sequence. We are able to dominate the world because we can transmit the data through non-biological means without having to wait for the slow process of biological evolution. We are applying genetic engineering on animals and plants mainly for economic reasons the human genetic engineering is controversial. Creating more evolved human beings may create social and moral issues.

Digital Era and Man's Future.

The human race and its DNA will increase its complexity quite rapidly and we need to prepare ourselves how to deal with it. Human beings are to keep their biological systems to electronic one. The computers have speed, but they are not intelligent. The computers are bound to improve their complexity similar to that of the human brain. The complex chemical molecules operate in human brain and similarly complex electronic circuits may create intelligent computers. The neural implants will offer enhanced memory. Brain size determines the level of human intelligence in general. In the near future, we will be able to grow the babies outside mother's womb and the brain size will increase. The neurotransmitters are responsible for mental activity. We will be quick-witted or very intelligent since any further increase in complexity of the brain will be at the expense of speed. The electronic signals travel at the speed of light. The speed of light is a practical limit on the design of faster computers. The brain has millions of central processing units working together at the same time, which can be parallel for electronic intelligence in future as well.

After the Big Bang, the universe was very hot and optically dense inflationary universe. Matter and energy decoupled. Clusters of matter formed proto galaxies synthesizing heavier nuclei. Three billion years after the Big Bang, the Hubble space telescope recorded galaxies in its deep field exploration. The human race in its present form has been for two million years out of fifteen billion years since the Big Bang. New galaxies like our own with heavier nuclei formed with formation of our solar system with orbiting planets. Three and half billion years ago, life began to appear. Humans appeared .0005 billion years ago. The intelligence is the inevitable consequence of evolution. In the next quarter century computers act in intelligent and conscious ways. The neural implants may dissolve the distance between biological and electronic intelligence. We may even choose to live a virtual existence on the net. The human genome will increase the complexity of human DNA structure. May be after few hundred years the human genetic engineering may replace biological evolution redesigning human race and posing new ethical problems.

Mystic Particle Boson.

The planet earth we are living in is a tiny portion of the enormous universe that we may never see enough of it to figure it all out. The universe can be represented holographically through Dirac's sea. Dirac's equation predicts anti-matter. The universe moves forward in time like a vast wave front of possibilities. The bosons condense into coherent and compact states [Bose-Einstein condensation]. In laser technique, many photons pile up into a state of momentum and move together in the same state of momentum at the same time. In 'super conductors', crystal vibrations bind pair of electrons [quantum sounds]. The electric energy facilitates somehow the coherent motion of many of these bound pairs of electrons sharing exactly the same state of momentum. The 'super fluids' are quantum states of extremely low temperature bosons where the entire liquid condenses into a common state of motion, which is completely frictionless. In Bose-Einstein condensates, the bosons and atoms condense into ultra-compact droplets piling on top of One another in space. The bosons were named after the Indian Physicist, Satyendra Nath Bose, who was a close friend of Einstein.

Angular movement.

The angular momentum is intrinsic to the creation. The indistinguishability of the identical particles is the quantum phenomenon, which has profound consequences to our physical world. The paired electrons in the universe are indistinguishable. The same is true for photons quarks and neutrinos. The boson particles like gravitons have angular momentum with the spin. The mesons [quarks and anti-quarks] have angular momentum. The orbital movement in quantum theory has angular momentum. "No two identical fermions can occupy the same quantum state of the momentum, [Pauli's exclusion principle]. The exclusion property of the fermions accounts for the stability of the matter. The fermions were named after Enrico Fermi. The nucleus is made up of the proton and the neutron, which are made up of the quarks. The two electrons remain in the lowest energy orbital state through the quantum phenomenon that one electron spins up and the other spins down. Any rotating body spins the electron too. We cannot stop the electron spinning though the rotating body stops. A freely travelling particle takes the form of a travelling wave in the space, which can be identified with the wave traces, which includes many troughs [Schrodinger's wave function]. The color of a visible light wave was determined in 19th century through Maxwell's theory of electromagnetism. The longer wavelength produces the red color. The longer wavelengths produce the infrared light, the microwaves and the radio waves. The shorter wavelength produces blue light. The deep violet blue color, the x-rays and the gamma rays are produced by the shorter and shorter wavelengths.

Higgs boson particle.

This world would be a different place without Higgs boson particle. Higgs boson particle vibrates in Higgs boson field and sets up vibrations in matter particles that the Higgs boson particle couples to. The Higgs field is all around us, which is non-zero even in empty space and gives the particle its unique properties. The Higgs boson particle is a vibration in Higgs boson field. The particle decays into two photons and there are no two identical particles in time, place and function. The particles are vibrations in the quantum fields, which rule this universe. The matter particles are discrete vibrations in fermions' field, which is our real world. The Higgs boson particle decays into two photons. The photons are the vibrations in the electromagnetic field. The neutron, which isolates from the nucleus decays in minutes and transforms into a proton. The vibrations in the neutron field transform into proton, electron and antineutrino fields. The cosmos is filled with the fields and one field exerts influence on other fields. In quantum field theory one particles converts into other particles without direct interaction. The concept of virtual particles should be thought of virtual fields. The particles arise from none other than the quantum fields. The matter particles appear and disappear in the nature. If we push the fields away from their preferred quantum state, we give them potential energy. They can vibrate and dissipate energy by transforming into other field. Eventually they settle back to sitting at rest.

Module Fields.

Module fields are the various modes of vibrations of the string. They condense into quantum mix in the vacuum. The module fields vary in space and time and determine the electron mass in any region of the space. Theorist Michael Douglas estimated a number of possible vacuum states that can occur due to various module fields. Nature flips a coin and chooses one of these vacuum states and that becomes our destiny. We live in a large universe with a very small vacuum energy density. The small vacuum energy density drives the universe to expand. The small universe might be dense and too hot. The large universe is unlikely to have enough concentrated matter to clump to make the solar system too cold. The carbon is the essence of life and the nature synthesizes it. Our horizon is the farthest distance that light travelled since the Big Bang, which occurred some thirteen billion light years ago. The awesome universe is beyond our horizon.

Beyond Quantum Science.

The link between the two detectors is a pair of particles like electrons or photons or neutrons etc. They were entangled at birth in the source and that subsequently arrived at the two detectors simultaneously. The radioactive particle decays into a pair of particles: one spins up and the other spins down [Feynman's path integral].

Then there are two paths throughout the space-time to consider. The whole universe is governed by an infinite set of possible paths that govern its evolution in time. The whole universe moves forward in time like a vast wave front of possibilities. The wave regroups and continues onward into future. The quantum uncertainty and quantum entanglement are the parents of quantum cryptography. Quantum physics is the language of nature. Our behavior is the reflection of our belief system. The quantum science gave us the technological wonders of the modern world. The quantum science for all its glitters may not be the whole story [Einstein]. Perhaps the final story is somewhere in the mind of this creation. The quantum phenomena challenge our inadequacy in understanding the nature.

The vast universe is made of quantum particles, which exist in all possible quantum states. Each of the possibilities exists in a different universe. The photon that heads towards a barrier splits the universe into two: one when the photon reflects and the other when the photon penetrates the barrier. The observer also splits into two. There are two universes from a single event. We may be living in an infinite number of universes in any given moment that we are unaware of. The numbers of observers likewise are oblivious to one another. The many universes are actualizing the many paths. Feynman's path integral observes that there are lots of paths that the universe could take representing all possible outcomes. Schrödinger's cat in the box paradox explains how the universe splits into two: one with a dead cat and the other with live cat. The dead cat may not die when someone opens the box. It is due to collapsing the wave function, as per Copenhagen interpretation. Similarly, the effects of spooky action at a distance vanish because there is no collapse of the wave function.

Quantum Future.

The human being can do fast calculations that rivals what a computer can do. The conscious awareness is a coherent sum of many possibilities, which is a quantum phenomenon. We use wave function to store and produce the computational results, which may be distributed beyond our brains. The wave function of human consciousness resides in the mysterious micro tube system in the nerve cells. The human consciousness could be a quantum state since the mind [cosmic mind] appears in quantum science though still we do not have a theory of consciousness. There is the mind [observer] and the system [observed] which is purusha and prakriti of Vedanta. We are yet to know how the human consciousness fits into the physical world, the human body, and the mind. We are yet to know how the brain encodes and processes the huge amount of information. How do these physical and chemical associations develop into a subjective life and generate what it is like to be "you"? Is there an unbreakable quantum code? One world or many worlds? What is the ultimate reality? Does the dice play a role? We seek answers from the stars. Galileo replaced Aristotelian physics then the classical physics of Isaac Newton came into existence. Now we have quantum cryptography and quantum computation through the quantum science. We are confronted with Schrödinger's wave function, Heisenberg's uncertainty relations, and the Copenhagen interpretation. "You, your joys and sorrows, your memories and ambitions, your sense of personal identity and the free will are in fact no more than the behavior of a vast assembly of nerve cells and their associated molecules.", Physicist, Francis Crick writes.

Space and Time.

The events in history take place in the background of time and space. Newton viewed the time as an infinite line independent of the world entity. Both the time and space have their own intrinsic connections. Einstein's general relativity combines time dimension and three space dimensions to form space-time. The path of objects moving through space-time appear bent because their move is affected by the gravitational field. Thus, the general relativity transforms space-time into dynamic participants in what happens and predicts that the universe and time should have a beginning and the end. This was a contrasting belief of other physicists at that time that time should be infinite in both the directions. What happened before the beginning or after the end would not be defined. Einstein thought that a body collapsing under its own gravity, pressure and sideways velocities would prevent all the matter falling together to the same point where the density would be infinite. The expansion of the universe back in time did not all emerge from a point of infinite density [singularity]. The singularity would be a beginning or the end of the universe. The expanding phase of the universe must have been preceded by the contracting phase [matter falls together]. If this were the case, time would continue forever from the infinite past into infinite future. The planets orbit in the gravitational field of a star.

We have nights because the light from distant stars yet to reach us. The existence of stars is not infinite because if the stars existed infinitely, the infinite radiation from the stars would have heated the universe that the whole sky would be as bright as the sun even at night. The universe cannot have existed forever in the state we see today. The stars would have light up a finite time ago [few billion years perhaps]. We do not know why that change occurred. Some of us believe that the creation is only few thousand years old and others believe in the universe as an existence. In 1923, Hubble discovered many other faint galaxies at greater distances that light from them would have taken billions of years to reach us. Obviously, the universe is not few thousand years old [Dr.Hawking].

The galaxies are moving away from each other as the universe is expanding. The ones farther from us are moving away from each other faster. The light analysis from galaxies reveals us whether the galaxies are moving towards us or away from us, but for now, the galaxies are moving toward earth at a specified velocity [Hubble]. The Doppler Effect is the relationship between speed and wavelength. The characteristic lines in the light spectrum would appear in standard position if a galaxy were to remain at a constant distance from earth. The light waves appear elongated, if the galaxy is moving away and they appear compressed if the galaxy is moving toward us. The galaxies moving away from each other must have been closer to each other some billions of years ago.

Maybe the Big Bang itself was the beginning of the universe and time. At the Big Bang, the universe had infinite temperature and density; the temperature would have been in billions of degrees and contain only light elements like photons, protons, neutrons, electrons and neutrinos with their anti-particles. As the universe cooled to about one billion degrees, the protons and neutrons would have begun to combine to form the nuclei of helium and hydrogen. Hundreds of thousands of years later the temperature dropped to few thousand degrees and the light nuclei could capture the electrons to form atoms. The heavy elements like carbon and oxygen from which we are made of formed billions of years later from the burning of helium in the center of stars. The early dense hot state of the universe should still be around today [Gamow], which is the cosmic microwave background radiation [observed in 1965]. Prior to the Big Bang, the universe could have been crunched into a single point of infinite density [Penrose and Hawking]. To comprehend the beginning of the universe seems to be beyond human comprehension. The history of the universe in real time determines its history in imaginary time and vice versa. The universe needs to have no beginning nor end in imaginary time. The general theory of relativity cannot explain the beginning of the universe, because Einstein did not believe in an uncertainty principle on the grounds that God does not play dice. God plays dice surely and the universe is like a big casino. The universe has multiple histories and each one with its probability. The unified theory of Feynman's idea of multiple histories and Einstein's general theory of relativity can predict future, if we know how the histories started. Feynman's path integral was known for particles that travel from one location to another along every possible path through space-time. God place no dice with mankind in the transcendental reality alone.

Light Cone.

The light cone is the paths of the light rays from the distant galaxies through space-time that reach us now. When we look into past down the cone from the vertex, we see galaxies at earlier times and the universe was expanding. Look back further, everything was much closer together and the regions of higher density of matter. A faint background of microwave radiation that propagates to us along the past light cone from earlier time when the universe was denser and hotter than it is now is also observed. Our past light cone must pass through certain amount of matter, which is enough to curve space-time so that light rays in our past light cone are bent back toward each other. The gravity is attractive and the matter always warps space-time so that light rays bend toward each other. The massive objects and the energy within them curve space-time and bend the paths of light rays towards each other. Further back in time, the cross section of our past light cone reaches a maximum size and begins to get smaller again. Our past is pear shaped.

The positive energy density of matter causes the light rays to bend toward each other more strongly. The cross section of the light cone will shrink to zero size in finite time, which should have begun in the Big Bang. [General relativity].

The time had meaning independent of the universe [Kant]. Our past light cone back in time will be bent back by the matter in early universe. The whole universe is contained within a region whose boundary shrinks to zero at the Big Bang [a singularity]. A place where the density of matter would be infinite is singularity. This inconsistency does not matter in most of the universe most of the time because the scale on which space-time is curved is very large and the scale on which quantum effects would be important is very small, but near a singularity; the two scales would be comparable and quantum gravitational effect would be important. Dr. Hawking and Penrose established that the classical region of the space-time is bound to the past and possibly to the future by regions in which quantum gravity is important. The stars collapse under their gravity to form black holes.

Maxwell Field.

The cosmos is filled with fields [Maxwell theory] that transmit dynamic actions of electric and magnetic disturbance from one place to another. They oscillate and move through space. The electromagnetic waves of all frequencies oscillate like pendulum and travel through at the speed of light [Maxwell]. The Maxwell field constitutes different waves and different wavelengths, of electricity, magnetism and light. There is no limit to how short the wavelengths of Maxwell field could be. There are an infinite number of different wavelengths and an infinite amount of ground state energies in any region of space-time . Each wavelength has its own ground state energy. The field in the wave swings from one value to another like pendulum. The ground state of pendulum does not have zero energy as one might expect and will have a probability of being found at a small angle to the vertical. The waves in the Maxwell field won't be exactly zero even in the vacuum state. The higher frequency of the pendulum or wave will have higher energy of the ground state. There is no limit to how short the wavelengths of the Maxwell field can be. The infinite energy density is like matter, a source of gravity. This infinite energy density is a source of gravity and means that there is enough gravitational attraction in the universe to curl space-time into a single point, which obviously has not happened yet. There exists energy density of ground state fluctuations between parallel metal plates [Casimir effect]. The energy density though infinite, is still less than the energy density outside by a finite amount. This difference in energy density gives rise to a force pulling the plates together. The forces are a source of gravity in general relativity just as matter is, so the gravitational effect of this energy difference is significant. Light comes in quanta [Max Planck]. The more accurate one tries to measure the position of a particle accurately, the less accurately he measures its speed and vice versa [Werner Heisenberg]. The Uncertainty principle forbids the precise measurement of both position and velocity at the same time. All particles spin. Einstein cosmological constant was an attempt to have a static model of the universe.

Super symmetry is to say that space-time has extra dimensions [Grossman dimensions] besides the dimensions we experience. Super symmetry is useful to remove the infinities in matter fields in space-time. The fermions with negative ground state energies makeup ordinary matter and the bosons possess positive ground state energies and create the gravitational force between the fermions. Each fermions and boson have a super partner [super gravity theory]. The photon is a boson and a photino is its super partner. The photino becomes a fermions with negative ground state energy with half a spin. The numbers of both the fermions and bosons are equal in the cosmos. The positive ground state energy of bosons is cancelled by the negative ground state energy of fermions, which eliminates infinities.

The String Theory.

The strings are one-dimensional extended objects and one member of a wide class of objects that can be extended in more than one dimension which Paul Townsend called p-branes. The p-branes could be the solutions of the equations of super gravity theories in ten or more dimensions. Six or seven dimensions are curled up so small that we do not notice them. We are aware of the remaining four large and flat dimensions. They move through a background of space-time. The ripples on the strings are interpreted as particles. The super strings were to be the Theory Of Everything [TOE]. The super gravity could be one of the five string theories. We yet to know which of the five string theories described our universe. The oscillating loops in one-dimensional strings that vibrate as an electron and positroncollide and annihilate one another and create a new string with a different vibration pattern. This new string releases energy and divides into two strings, which continue along new trajectories. The electron and positron [anti particle] collide and destroy each other briefly in a burst of energy creating a photon particle, which in turn releases energy producing another electron-positron pair. If those original strings are viewed not as discrete moments, but as uninterrupted history in time, then the resulting strings are seen as a string world sheet. The particle is a single point but one-dimensional strings are not single point particles [string theory]. The strings have ends and the ends may join up themselves in closed loops. Similar to violin strings, the strings similar to violin strings support certain vibration patterns or resonant frequencies, whose wavelengths fit precisely between the two ends. The violin strings give different musical notes with different resonant frequencies. Different oscillations of a string [of string theory] give rise to different masses. The shorter the wavelength of the oscillation on the string; the greater the mass of the particle.

The ground state energies.

Positive ground state energies spin a whole number and fermions have negative ground state energy with half a spin. In the end, both cancel each other that there will be no infinities. We expect infinities in super gravity theory and the super symmetric string theory alone. The low energies are particles with energies of less than billion times those of particles in a TNT explosion. The dualities connect the five string theories as well as eleven dimensional super gravities. The five string theories are different aspects of the same underlying theory. M-theory unites the five string theories within a single theoretical framework. The super strings and super gravity are different expressions of the same underlying theory, but each is useful for calculations in different kinds of situations. The string theories do not have infinities but are good for calculating what happens. Super gravity is useful for describing how the energy of a very large number of particles curves the universe or forms a bound state like a black hole. This is Einstein's theory of curved space-time.

Space-Time.

Einstein combined the real time with the three dimensions of space into four-dimensional space-time. The real time increases along the history of an observer. The space directions can increase or decrease along that history. The time moved from past to future in the real time direction. The real time could increase in any of the three spatial directions. We could reverse direction in space but not in time. The distinction between the real time and the imaginary time is just in our minds. The imaginary time could predict the effects we have already observed as well the effects we have not been able to measure yet. The imaginary time direction is like another space direction, which can increase or decrease. The imaginary time behaves like a fourth spatial direction. It possesses more possibilities than the ordinary real time. The real time has no beginning or an end. The time has shape in this imaginary sense. If the imaginary space-time is a sphere, the imaginary time direction could represent the distance from the South Pole. The circles of latitude become bigger as one moves north corresponding to the universe expanding with imaginary time. The universe reaches maximum size at the equator and contract again with increasing imaginary time to a single point at the North Pole. The universe would have zero size at the poles but the points won't be singularities. The origin of universe in imaginary time can be a regular point in space-time. All the lines of longitude meet at the North and South Poles. Time is standing still at the poles; an increase of imaginary time leaves one on the same spot. Just as going west on the North Pole of the earth still leaves one on the North Pole. The history of the universe begins at the South Pole in imaginary time. What happened before the beginning cannot be answered because such times were not defined anymore.

The information that falls into a black hole may be stored like that on a record and played back as the black hole evaporates. The beginning of the universe in imaginary time can be a regular point of space-time and the same laws can hold at the beginning as in the rest of the universe. All the lines of longitude meet at the North and South Poles where time stands still in the sense that an increase of imaginary time or of degrees of longitude leaves one in the same spot. It is very similar to the way that ordinary time appears to stand still on the horizon of a black hole. The standstill of real and imaginary time [either both standstill or neither does] means that the space-time has temperature. The black hole has temperature and behaves as if it has entropy.

The entropy is a measure of the number of internal states that the black hole could have without looking any different to an outside observer who can only observe its mass, rotation and charge. Thermodynamics is the science of heat and study of entropy. The quantum gravity and thermodynamics are in deep connection.

Holography is the expression of quantum gravity. The information about the quantum states in a region of space-time may be coded on the boundary of the region, which is dimensionless. It is like the way that a hologram carries a three dimensional image on a two dimensional surface. If quantum gravity incorporates the holographic principle, it may mean that we can keep track of what is inside black holes. This is essential if we are able to predict the radiation that comes out of black holes. If we cannot do that, we won't be able to predict the future as fully as we thought. We may like a four-dimensional [three spaces plus one time] surface that is the boundary of a five dimensional region with the remaining dimensions curled up very small. The state of the world in a brane encodes what is happening in the five dimensional regions. The holography is a phenomenon of interference of wave patterns. When a laser is shone through the developed plate, a fully three dimensional image of the original object appears. An observer can move around this holographic, being able to see all the hidden faces that a normal photo could not show. The two dimensional surface of the plate on the left unlike a normal photo has the remarkable property that any tiny fragment of its surface contains all the information needed to reconstruct the whole image.

Chapter-11.

GITA GOSPEL

"You shall know the truth and the truth shall make you free", Jn.8:32.

Gita reminds us of the war within us between right and the wrong. It also inspires the human soul to stand up against evil. The mind unfolds in divine grace in the fight against the life's battles. "God is infinite and the ways to reach him are infinite", [Rig Veda]. He fulfills our desires in the same way we worship him. "Give your heart to me verily you will attain me. (Gita)". "Resist not evil", [ahimsa]. Turning the other cheek", Matt.5:39, is to renounce to resist. It is victory over the evil. It is action in consciousness. There is power in this seemingly submissive act. One who benefits of non-violence is a spiritually strong man who can resist the evil and attain the victory over the evil. We love our enemy in the provision of grace. The virtues like love and sacrifice are practical enough to live by [Aristotle]. Jihads and crusades were fought in God's name though the relationship between God's love and the bloodshed of war is inconceivable. Gita viewed the refusal of Arjuna to fight the war as hypocritical and egocentric. He failed his duty [swadharma] to quell the enemy and reestablish the righteousness in the kingdom. The intellect, which is confused of its duty evolves in divine grace and knows the ultimate truth.

'Eye for an eye', was replaced by, 'love your enemy', Matt.5:4.

Wars are ego bound. The pride of victory haunts the prowess. Religion falsely assures prowess, the paradise [veer swarga] in death and the pleasure on earth in victory. This is inconsistent with the divine nature of love and sacrifice. The inevitability of death and the indestructibility of soul do not justify deliberate killings either. It is not spiritual to create Hell on Earth to gain paradise. Transcend the dualities of pleasure and pain, gain or loss and victory or defeat. The divine soul knows the truth and true victory. God leads you into green pastures if you listen to him with all your body mind and soul. Today I talked to a prisoner as to what had brought him into prison. He was a good man with a good wife and four children, but he was proud and his pride obstructed him from listening to divine voice. Now, his prison life humbled him and, "God's presence is always with me", he asserted. You are liberated in spirit already, but soon the prison shackles also will drop down, I assured him. Gita contends that the multifaceted world problems require a multidimensional approach, which includes emotional and spiritual considerations. The multiple factors unfold and merge into sound judgment in a divine soul, which is an expression of divine will. The individual understands the truth according to his being and he is approached accordingly as a being in the process of formation. Heinous rulers like Nero of the Roman Empire or Hitler in our time were to be stopped from their heinous crimes against humanity even though we love them dearly in Christ. A Christian soldier kills his enemy soldier as his duty though he loves him at his heart. Jewish tradition glorified Jehovah in their war victories and repented for their sins in the defeat. Joshua fought battles in the name of Jehovah for the freedom of the Jewish soul. Jehovah was revealed as pure love in Jesus Christ.

"One who sees me in all things is never separated from me nor I am separated from him", [Gita].

Karma is intertwined with the soul and the unbroken personality of an individual is transmitted through his incarnations. It is bound to the mind and detached from the spirit. The transcended soul is above karma. All karmas are reduced into ashes in the fire of divine grace. The extinction of ego is the self-extinction into God. The ego in a saint is like a marker of a fallen palm leaf. The experience of bliss is like a buzzing bee turning into a sweet humming bee after being filled with nectar. The saint descends from his trance state of mind and deals with the ordinary world without losing touch with the divinity. He always does good and never faces grief. His goodness goes with him into all the worlds. One life is enough to exhaust all karmas and liberate the soul fully. Any karmic debt will be exhausted in next life, which is the hope for a sinner. The virtue in the previous life enhances the evolution of soul in this life. Seems that the disparity of justice has pre existence. Goodness will be rewarded, is not a convincing explanation nor an adequate justification because the cause cannot follow the effect according to the karma concept. The solution to human suffering resolves only when we seek the cause in the continuity of soul into next life. "We all had numerous births in the past and will have in the future also. (Gita)." God is not behind human sorrow.

Isvara is the consciousness of all men. Man is individual consciousness. Maya is the cosmic delusion which creates the multiplicity in the creation. The unity through diversity is the nature of the creation. The transcended soul has an equal eye on all beings. The same rain brings forth the multiplicity of the plant kingdom. God is untouched by the plurality though he is the common cause. Goodness, passion and dullness are the three material modes of nature that men are born with. They also confirm that our present life is nothing but the continuity of our previous life. Our behaviors differ because our karmas in the past life differ. The soul has preexistence and its experience cannot be annihilated. One may be born with all three material modes, but one of them only prevails. The gospel is presented in the level and mode of their understanding. One approaches God according to his own innate nature. Plato graded human beings as spiritual, rational and temperamental. The change in age and gender changes the duty of an individual. Our childhood exists beyond our memory and comprehension. The subjective experience over rules the objectivity. Gita describes three distinct ways to reach God: knowledge, devotion and action. The renunciation is the essence of spiritual life, which is

not a secluded social life, but man performs his duties
in life free from attachment. The deeds of Christian
missionaries are an expression of service to God whose
image we see in the hearts of all men. It is in essence
a karma yoga spiritualized. God created us all equal,
but our expression of him is unequal. Neither equality
nor the universal celibacy is compatible with the creation (Gita).

"God so loved the world that he gave his begotten
son and whosoever believeth in him should not
perish but have everlasting life", Jn.3:16.

Man is born with an instinct to love God. God of
love sent Jesus as our redeemer. The unity in diversity is
the nature of this creation. The human nature is diverse.
Aristotle viewed that self-control; love and courage are
practical enough to live by in daily life. The higher level
of consciousness demonstrates higher level of righteousness. Sins keep you away from the Lord and the
right worship takes you closer to God. "Even one has
beheld, heard and proclaimed it, no one has understood
it", [Katha upanishad]. Man is a compound of a mortal
body and an immortal soul. Preserve the body since
the immortal soul is sheltered in the body. Transcend
the dualities like pleasure and pain (intellectual), gain
or loss (mind level) and victory or defeat (physical)
and attain the salvation, Gita affirmed. He is indeed a
great soul who knows his true end of life and yields to
it. Multiple principles reach a sound judgment in divine
revelation. We seek the God's kingdom first that everything may come together for the good. Life's battles
are the right field to exhaust the sins. An enlightened

soul fights constantly against the forces of darkness of this world in the provision of divine grace. The cloudy mind attracts more evil, but the divine mind sees the right path clearly. Religion consists in living the philosophy one has understood and the action in spirit of yoga is the worship unto the Lord. The Kingdom of Heaven is absolute bliss and one who attains salvation is one with God.

"Flesh and blood have not revealed unto thee but my Father which is in heaven", Mt.16:17.

God is visible through faith alone. We cannot see God through academic knowledge. We trinity body, mind and spirit. The soul is eternal and birth and the death belongs to body and mind. The body is in transition from childhood into old age and the soul leaves the worn out body and enters into a new body. The cycle of birth and death stops when the soul is realized. "Great souls who attained Me do not have birth and death which is the home of sorrow", [Gita]. One who knows this truth cannot slay or be slain. Mankind is conditioned by sin. Salvation is the spontaneous and subjective experience, which transforms the human soul. Inspiration convicts men. God lives in the great sinner like the lotus in the pond. God can be realized in him as gold is recovered from the dirt. God has neither death nor sorrow. [Brihadaranyaka Upanishad]. The moral life is the reflection of the spiritual life. One who knows atman as the life of life knows Brahman. One who has fallen from grace is confused of his true nature only. The light in him is dormant only.

The new creation in Christ "loves its enemy and blesses that curses", Mt.5:43. The man is born with an instinct to know God and the transcended soul alone "loves his neighbor as his self", Matt.5:43. The ideal of oneness eliminates relativity and oneness needs no moral code. Because oneness eliminates conflicts. The scriptures do not make any sense to the sinner. Loving his neighbor is none other than loving himself. One who hates his neighbor verily hates himself. Your neighbor is verily yourself. The waves rise and fall on the ocean surface, but the substratum of the seabed is calm. God is the substratum of all world religions. The baby and the creator lived in oneness in mother's womb. One self-realization to reach one universal God. "If any man be in Christ, he is a new creature; old things are passed away; behold, all things arc become new", 2nd Corith.5:17. In Christ, we put off the old man with his deeds and put on the new man after the image of Christ.